Global Common Good

Prof. Dr. Michael Reder holds the chair in practical philosophy at the Munich School of Philosophy. *Verena Risse* and *Katharina Hirschbrunn* are research associates at the Institute for Social and Development Studies at the Munich School of Philosophy. *Dr. Georg Stoll* is a senior advisor in the Department of Policy and Global Challenges at the German Catholic Bishops' Organization for Development Cooperation MISEREOR.

Michael Reder, Verena Risse, Katharina Hirschbrunn,
Georg Stoll (eds.)

Global Common Good

Intercultural Perspectives on a Just and Ecological
Transformation

Campus Verlag
Frankfurt/New York

Bibliographic Information published by the Deutsche Nationalbibliothek.
The Deutsche Nationalbibliothek lists this publication in the Deutsche Nationalbibliografie;
detailed bibliographic data are available in the Internet at http://dnb.d-nb.de
ISBN 978-3-593-50318-9

All rights reserved. No part of this book may be reproduced or transmitted in any form or by any means, electronic or mechanical, including photocopying, recording, or by any information storage and retrieval system, without permission in writing from the publishers.
Copyright © 2015 Campus Verlag GmbH, Frankfurt-on-Main
Cover design: Campus Verlag, Frankfurt-on-Main
Cover illustration: © Florian Kopp/MISEREOR, Haiti.
Printing office and bookbinder: CPI buchbuecher.de, Birkach
Printed on acid free paper.
Printed in Germany

This book is also available as an E-Book.
www.campus.de
www.press.uchicago.edu

Contents

I. Systematic Introduction

Towards a Just and Ecological Transformation: Methodological
Considerations for an Intercultural Research Project 9
Michael Reder, Verena Risse, Katharina Hirschbrunn, Georg Stoll

II. Perspectives on the Global Common Good from Latin America, Africa, Asia, and Europe

The Peasant Reserve Zones in Colombia as a Contribution
to the Global Common Good 17
Olga Lucía Castillo

Biocivilization for Socio-Environmental Sustainability:
A Brazilian View on the Hard, but Necessary Transition 47
Cândido Grzybowski

The Common Good and Constitutionalism in Zambia 89
Leonard Chiti

The Global Common Good and the Governance of the
Mining Sector in the Democratic Republic of Congo 123
Ferdinand Muhigirwa Rusembuka

Recasting the Development Approach in Indonesia 151
B. Herry-Priyono

Common Good Arrangements in Germany—Ready for Global Challenges? 191
Katharina Hirschbrunn, Georg Stoll, Verena Risse

III. Critical Perspectives on the Intercultural Dialogue Process

Development for the Global Common Good: A Comment 233
Clara Brandi

Development for the Global Common Good: Discussion Points 237
Jan Aart Scholte

IV. Intercultural Reflections on the Global Common Good

Reflections on the Global Common Good:
Systematization of an Intercultural Dialogical Research Process...............243
Olga Lucía Castillo, Leonard Chiti, Cândido Grzybowski et al.

Views from Civil Society Practitioners 261
Georg Stoll

Contributors 269

Index 271

I. Systematic Introduction

Towards a Just and Ecological Transformation: Methodological Considerations for an Intercultural Research Project

Michael Reder, Verena Risse, Katharina Hirschbrunn, and Georg Stoll

1. Starting Point: Global Challenges and the Post-MDG-Agenda

The adoption of the Millennium Development Goals (MDGs) in September 2000 showed the joint commitment of the UN member states to alleviate poverty and inequality around the world. While several improvements can be noted today, new global challenges call for further action and inform the debate about a Post-MDG development agenda.

Two interwoven sets of challenging problems can be discerned: First, increasing social inequality that denies the satisfaction of basic human needs and a life in dignity to a large part of humanity; secondly, increasing environmental degradation resulting from the overuse of natural resources and the planet's depositing capacities. In the light of global challenges such as poverty, hunger and climate change, the contributions of this volume identify concrete ways towards a socially just and sustainable model of civilization.

The cause of the different global problems has generally been seen in a combination of structural determinants, in particular the exploitation of non-renewable resources, economic policies focusing narrowly on growth as well as deficient political institutions at the national and the international level. At the same time, the last few years were marked by the intention to integrate those concerned into the process of designing the relevant development policies. This has led to a focus on the way in which ideas and visions influence development. While alternative notions of social development—like 'bottom-up development' or approaches taking into account the 'limits to growth'—were niche topics of certain social milieus in the past, they have now become part of mainstream debates and of official political agendas. In Europe, this is visible for instance in the work of the Stiglitz-Sen-Fitoussi-Commission in France and the Enquete Commission

"Growth, Prosperity, and Quality of Life" in Germany, which both worked on the question of how to conceptualize welfare without relying on GDP only. In addition, numerous books and conferences deal with new ideas and models for societal prosperity and future development. This trend also shows that development is not a goal that is reserved for the Global South. Rather it is also the societies of the Global North that are defective in various respects and need to undergo processes of transformation.

The central question therefore is whether and in what way these discourses in which the norms and values are articulated can actually change social realities. Societies do not only bring forth a plurality of ideas regarding their own constitution and the norms and values that the legal and political institutions should be based on. At the same time, these ideas translate into social practices in diverse ways and yield different practical results.

2. Methodological perspective: Ethical Reflections on the Basis of Existing Social Values and Practices

Political strategies that are justified by reference to different values are not only accepted because of an abstract normative reason but because they are incorporated into social life and into heterogeneous cultural practices. Ethical reflections should therefore be closely connected to these practices, so that moral principles are related to social reality and can claim universal validity. Of course, there exist several social practices with different embedded moral norms. Therefore, theories in the tradition of Hegel are asking for complementary moral beliefs, because humans are realizing practical coherence between different moral beliefs in their everyday life.

This view is following Axel Honneth in his interpretation of Hegel. Honneth argues that our normative reflections should always be connected to a detailed analysis of society including its different social and normative practices. The aim of a critical analysis of society in the tradition of Hegel's philosophy of rights should be "[to analyze] current institutions and practices according to their normative merit" and to show how "their importance for the social embodiment and realization of socially legitimate values." (Honneth 2010, 711) By doing so, Honneth argues against a clear distinction between facts and values and against a focus on abstract moral principles. Instead he emphasizes the concrete capability to mutual recognition in the Hegelian sphere of *Sittlichkeit*, which is meant to overcome the gap between individual subjective feelings on the one hand and the context of general rights on the other.

Axel Honneth argues that starting ethical reflection from social practices does not imply a necessity to accept all practices. Rather, a critical reconstruction has to analyze and discuss the 'moral' potential of such practices and to ask in what way these practices could be improved in light of the ideas that underlie them. More specifically, an analysis following this model has to focus on what practices can be determined from a view point of a pragmatic approach as theoretically described here. Of course, Honneth focuses on societies within their national borders. Yet it seems likewise possible to expand this focus to the global level and ask which social and normative practices are important in the global sphere of *Sittlichkeit*.

Human rights—understood as a global practice—play an important role as part of a global *Sittlichkeit*. They are accepted because they are incorporated in various global programs and institutions. Global discourses regarding issues such as the Millennium Development Goals or sustainable climate policy are both examples of this. The Universal Declaration of Human Rights from 1948—about which there is a broad consensus within the global community—seeks to provide answers to the multifaceted experience of injustice. From this standpoint, ethical measures are determined with reference to concrete political realities. Ethically speaking, it is about letting all people lead a dignified life. Human rights intend to protect the necessary foundations for such a life.

3. A Dialogue on the Global Common Good: Intercultural perspectives for Transformation

Notwithstanding the importance of human rights and the MDGs, the complexity of the current world order calls for a more-encompassing focus on the common good of all people. Following Honneth's approach, the achievement of the global common good must start by investigating the norms and practices implied at both the national and the global level. This research project therefore deals with alternative practices and values of social development which are currently produced by multiple societal actors and with the actual and potential effects of these ideas on social practice. The intercultural perspective that results from including contributions from different world regions is the specific characteristic of this volume.

In a first step, the different contributions analyze which values and ideas can be found in their region with regard to a socially just and environmentally sustainable society and how they should ideally be implemented in the respective societies. The objective is an inventory of important visions and guiding ideas of societies with regard to their normative self-understanding and their models of development and prosperity. One main focus lies on exploring in what way the common good can serve as a normative guiding principle in the different cultural contexts. The studies assembled in this volume show that the notion of the common good can respond to the (cultural) plurality and heterogeneity of societies. This is reflected in different interpretations of the common good ranging from a stronger focus on human dignity over well-being to an account of biocivilization. Moreover, the studies show through which political institutions and structures normative ideas like the common good are realized. In this context, also ideas regarding global political institutions for securing a global common good are discussed.

In a second step, it is asked how these social values are actually implemented in practice and where discrepancies between normative ambitions and reality exist. In this context, it is being critically discussed in what way traditional development politics really lead to a fair and sustainable development. Especially in the face of current global crises (like, for example the financial crisis, the crisis of nutrition, crises of global resources) the different contributions outline in what way political and economic practices are directed towards a common good and on the other hand unveil discrepancies between the existing practices and the common good. Several lines of conflict can be detected, such as the conflicts between different values within one concept of the common good, the conflicts between the values of different actors within society, or the conflicts between local and global norms and values. Furthermore, there are contradictions between the normative ambitions and the existing institutions or social practices. In particular, several authors find that the dominant development paradigm does not respond to the visions and norms of the local societies, that it conflicts with the rights of indigenous people or peasant communities and that it leads to environmental abuses. Therefore, some papers suggest to give up the notion of development altogether. Other trends that are considered to stand in tension with the achievement of the common good include increased consumption in rising middle classes as well as growing cities that become less manageable. Moreover, in particular the African contributors point to their countries' reliance on the exploitation of resources from which the local population does not benefit. This situation has become known as the 'development paradox'.

The third perspective that the different contributions offer are possible paths to transformation both at the local and the global level. There is agreement among the contributors that democratic structures of different kinds of communities play an important role to deal with current problems. Moreover, several authors stress the importance of human rights and a strong rule of law to achieve the implementation of the common good. Functioning democratic institutions and community organizations also allow reflecting on other pressing questions such as: Which perspectives are there with regard to the possibilities and limits of normative models to influence the actions of individuals, economy and politics? And which political suggestions exist for a global conception of the common good? With this third perspective, the volume is not only criticizing existing systems, but pointing out unrealized potentials for a just and sustainable transformation towards a global common good.

4. Research Project: "Development Serving the Global Common Good"

This volume constitutes one of the outcomes of the research project "Development serving the global common good" launched in 2012. The project brings together positions from different cultures as well as from various academic disciplines, such as philosophy, sociology, political science and economics. The research project was initiated by the Institute for Social and Development Studies which is affiliated as an independent body with the Munich School of Philosophy and by Misereor, the German Catholic Bishops' organization for development cooperation.

The project consists of three entwined parts. In the first part, academics from Africa, Asia, Europe and Latin America reflect on different understandings of the (global) common good in their region, on existent implementations of these norms, on conflicts and on potentials for transformation. This volume presents the results of this intercultural exchange process. In the second part of the project, regional dialogue forums are organized in Africa, Latin America and Asia with the aim to discuss concepts of the common good among representatives of diverse societal groups. Here regional problems and challenges are taken into account without, however, losing sight of the regions' reality as embedded in global economic and political processes. The main results of the regional dialogue forums are summarized at the end of this volume. The third part of the project consists of public relations and advocacy work in Germany and Europe that aims at positioning the results from the project in the political debate and at promoting the transformation towards a socially just and ecologically sustainable model of development.

At the level of scientific research, the aim of the project is to identify visions and norms of social development articulated and endorsed by a plurality of societal actors and to analyze the actual effects of these norms on political institutions, the economy and society. As a normative vision the notion of the global common good is introduced. On this basis, key conflicts that prevent the realization of the common good and potentials for transformation shall be sketched. At the practical-political level, this results in outlining common visions of a (globally) just and sustainable transformation and in building alliances to practically influence social processes in view of a global common good.

This being a dialogical research project, many different voices and views contributed to its richness and diversity. And even if we cannot list all these contributors here, they all deserve our thankfulness. In addition, the editors are especially grateful for the financial support offered by the Franz Xaver Foundation. Special thanks also go to Stephen Henderson, who helped finalize this volume.

Work Cited

Honneth, Axel (2010). "A Theory of Justice as an Analysis of Society. Preliminary Remarks on a Research Program." In Hans-Georg Soeffner (ed.). *Unsichere Zeiten: Herausforderungen gesellschaftlicher Transformationen*, 707–717. Wiesbaden: VS Verlag.

II. Perspectives on the Global Common Good from Latin America, Africa, Asia, and Europe

The Peasant Reserve Zones in Colombia as a Contribution to the Global Common Good

Olga-Lucía Castillo

Introduction

The aim of this text is to contribute to the task of "find[ing] conceptions of the global common good which can cope with the multiple global crises and challenges. In this context, the aim of this study is to identify visions and norms of social development which are currently produced by plural societal actors and to analyze the actual effects of these norms on political institutions, economy, and society, focus[ing] on the analysis of key conflicts and on the description of potentials for transformation."[1]

At the present moment, the Colombian state of affairs offers a number of possible case studies, which seem to include common good propositions with the potential for transformations in the middle of an armed conflict. It is unclear if the amount of such initiatives is fueled by the uncertainties of the armed conflict, or grows in spite of it. Among them we can mention Agrosolidaria ("Building a learning community on Economic Solidarity Circuits in the agricultural sector"); the Association Land and Life—The National Association of Victims for Restitution and Access To Land ("We did not inherit the land from our parents, it was loaned to us by our children"); Peace Communities ("A Humanizing Alternative"); The Cimitarra River Peasant Association ("For the comprehensive defense of Human Rights and the fight for the Land"); the Agricultural Producers Association APAVE; Nasa Project of Indigenous Councils of Northern Cauca ("Territory of the Great People") or the National Association of Peasantry Reserve Zones ("Peasantry Peace is Social Justice") among many others.[2] Through a different kind of social organizations, those experiences

---

1 Kick-Off-Letter of the Intercultural Research Project "Development serving the Global Common Good", October, 29th, 2012.

2 See http://www.agrosolidaria.org/, http://www.associaciontierrayvida.org/; http://www.odpsanjose.org/, ACVC for its Spanish acronym—http://ww.prensarural.org/acvc/,

are not only trying to deal with key conflicts, such as the defense of human rights, the access, distribution and property of the land, and the right to maintain their own way of living, but they also have consolidated consistent proposals for changing social realities. In this case, and from those experiences mentioned, the Peasantry Reserve Zones is the one chosen as a case study.

However, before going into the details of this Colombian case, in the first section of this paper some precisions about the concepts of 'development' and of the 'global common good' are set forth as the conceptual framework of this analysis. In the second part—and in the context of the complex Colombian political armed conflict—the evolution of the Peasantry Reserve Zones is briefly described, as an experience closely linked to the debate of the development model of a country like Colombia. The third and last section of this paper offers, as conclusion, some reflections on the relationship that exists among 'development', common good, and the Peasant Reserve Zones as a practical experience with potentials for transformation.

1. Development and Common Good: A Conceptual Framework

Some precisions about the present debates on the concepts of 'development' and the 'global common good' are briefly set forth in this section as the foundations of the conceptual framework of the analysis offered in this paper.

1.1. Development

While the concept of 'development'—within the economic, political and social context we have today—has been present in the international agenda for the relatively short time of about sixty-five years, it has gained great power in terms of institutional discourses and practices at all levels.

APAVE for its Spanish acronym http://www.apave.org.co/, and http://www.nasaa cin.org/planes-de-vida/plan-de-vida-nasa/213-planes-de-vida respectively.

From a rapid glance at some of the major conceptualizations of 'development' put forward by specialized literature, one can identify some general traits: while the definitions between the nineteen-forties and the nineteen-seventies had an economic bias, concepts developed since then have taken into account a whole array of dimensions of human societies that go far beyond economics. In this effort to integrate different dimensions, alternative development conceptualizations have emphasized and addressed multiple political, social, cultural, environmental and/or ethical issues related to human welfare. Regardless of their theoretical influences, many conceptualizations tend to present some patterns to be followed as universal; however, while undertaking a broader understanding of 'development', these proposals have led to comprehensive and therefore highly complex concepts which become nonviable as they are brought into practice.

These general characteristics in the evolution of the concept of 'development' allow us to distinguish three particular and main conceptual currents of thought: a) the conventional development understanding, strongly biased by the priority of economic growth; b) the wide set of alternative development proposals and practices, trying to integrate into the welfare debate all human concerns that were left out from the conventional (economic) point of view; and c) the post-development insight, which, among other arguments, claims that it is impossible that the conventional and the alternative high levels of 'development' promises can be fulfilled for the majority, so therefore they should be abandoned as the goal that drives human progress. Although these three perspectives have arrived into the development studies scene one after another, it does not mean that in the practice the previous ones have disappeared to give way to the next, but instead they remained all together struggling to gain primacy, depending on the global, regional or local circumstances.

a) Conventional Development

Though since the post-WWII period different development models have been implemented all over the world, at the end of the day all of them have been formed by the same principles of the successful model of society promoted by the Conventional (economic) Development understanding.

Going further back in time, and though the 'development' concept as we know it today was not yet in the daily economic, social, or political agenda, it is possible to trace the industrial revolution as the era that set up a particular dynamic that meant the beginning of an unrelenting and urgent need for the materials that nature offers to humans in order to produce at a higher speed and in higher quantities. The colonization process was key to the industrialization, and through it a few countries appropriated, exploited and plundered nature (including flora, fauna, minerals and people) and also the cultural ways of living of a number of other countries.

The end of World War II marked a milestone into the evolving concept and practice of 'development', not only because the economic and political power had shifted, bringing about major changes in global power relationships, but also because, as stated by post-development scholars, "Harry S. Truman for the first time declared, in his inauguration speech, the Southern hemisphere as 'underdeveloped areas'. The label stuck and subsequently provided the cognitive base for both the arrogant interventionism from the North and pathetic self-pity in the South." (Sachs 1997, 2)

Chasing a higher level of economic growth, which implies further acceleration and increase of the production processes, all countries in the world, to a greater or lesser extent, have gone through the implementation of 'development' models such as the industrialization and imports substitution (inwards economy), welfare state, neo-liberalism (outwards economy) and good governance scheme, to mention the main ones. In spite of the fact that they have been implemented through different processes (and therefore understood as different 'development' models) they are supported by the same conceptual argument. We refer to the trickle down strategy, which states that the profits of the individuals that make up the upper layers of society eventually will reach wider and lower sections, thanks to the virtuous circle of the economy. It consists of the first and wealthier layers of society investing in demanded products and machinery to produce goods that will generate employment, and hence income and therefore 'development'; then this revenue will increase the demand for these or other goods and services promoting their production, which will generate employment, and hence income and therefore 'development'... and so on. However, some of the main criticism towards these arguments came from those scholars who endorsed the dependency theory; they saw in the trickle down a strategy that ended supporting the concentration of wealth and power at the national level in the hands of the country's economic elites, and at the global level in the hands of the industrialized elite countries. They also raised their concerns on the existing power relationships, which lead to a world divided into central and peripheral countries. The dependency theory—that was mainly originated in a core group of the United Nations body named the Economic Commission for Latin America and the Caribbean (ECLAC)—found an auspicious time, given that around the late nineteen-sixties and early nineteen-seventies the disapproval against the narrow view of the conventional economic development also successfully reached the international agendas.

b) Alternative Development

During the late nineteen-sixties and early nineteen-seventies, a number of alternative development proposals were put forward in the 'development' arena, offering new insights based on different theoretical and conceptual commitments. These new concepts, discourses, and practices—all of them excluded from the narrow economic conceptualization of 'development'— purported a shift away from the economic emphasis of conventional development theories.

Among those issues excluded, it is worth mentioning the inequality in access, use, and distribution of multiple resources, veiled by promising national or regional economic growth indicators (Dollar and Kraay 2002; Fernández 2002; and Lübker, Smith and Weeks 2002). Other issues undermined by the econocentric lens belong to the political domain, such as the promotion of democratic pluralism, the rejection of authoritarian regimes, citizen participation, and giving a voice to vulnerable communities (Boff and Betto 1996; Chambers 1994; Blackburn and Holland, 1998 and Blackburn, Chambers and Gaventa 2000). The report on the 'Limits to Growth' was fundamental to spurring discussion and the inclusion of another critical issue, namely the recognition and growing concern about the rapid, and in some cases irreversible, changes to the natural environment (Meadows et al, 1972; Peet and Watts 1996; Adams 2001; Martinez-Alier 2006 and Wilson, Furniss and Kimbowa 2010). A more comprehensive understanding of 'development' and a renewed perception of what 'development' should be and how it could be reached was on the way.

Thus, under the wide blanket category of alternative development, extremely diverse proposals can be found, including explicit anti-capitalist schemes; Buddhist economic approaches; democratization policies; projects that challenge global institutions; alternative practices as basis for local 'development' as well as communitarian initiatives; green pressure groups;

feminist approaches; alternative consumption paths; and cultural criticisms, to name only a few.

However, important criticisms to alternative development have been raised, because: first, a wide variety of concerns have been grouped under this diffuse category; and also because, though it includes a mixture of judicious conceptual proposals on diverse topics, it also involves a range of varied scattered objectives on other issues, and a number of practical implementations of experiences as well, not interconnected at all. Another important critique was that its promoters did not offer a theoretical/conceptual, discursive, and practical body to support and arrange the alternativeness of new ways of achieving 'development'.

Another important critique was whether some of these alternatives were really alternatives after all; this is the case, for instance, with the 'Human Development' model promoted by the United Nations Development Program since 1990. Indeed, several of those 'development' proposals categorized as alternative have been driven by the very same goals as conventional development, only chasing economic growth through different ways (trying to include new agents, attempting to integrate other concerns of human societies, or experimenting with different methodologies); it can be deduced then, that their goal was not to design and implement another kind of 'development', but to further the economic development, though through different paths.

Nevertheless—and despite some valid alternative development proposals which actually challenged the main assumptions of conventional mainstream 'development', offering sufficient elements to consolidate a coherent line of thought—, the most difficult obstacle that alternative Development had to deal with was that those of the structural transformations that were promoted through its concepts, narratives and practices, and which were useful to the conventional development, were co-opted with no intention whatsoever of implementing the structural transformation they were claiming, and thus, alternative development lost its momentum.

There is no shortage of examples of the co-optation process, but because they are closely related to the selected Colombian case, some reflections on sustainable development—as one of the many co-opted alternative development proposals—follow.

The United Nations Conference on the Human Environment in 1972 formalized the promotion of the concept of "sustainable development" as a solution to the presumed environment vs. 'development' dilemma. Promoters of the Sustainable Development concept attempted to integrate in a comprehensive fashion the never-ending dilemma of increasing economic growth (which is fundamental to the 'development' notion) and the need for the conservation of finite elements of nature (which is opposed to economic growth). In others words, the advocacy of sustainable development tried to put together that which was not possible to be integrated, simply because while the natural source for growth is finite, the desire for unrelenting economic growth is infinite. A false dilemma emerges then, because despite the appearance of an irresolvable paradox, the solution had been envisaged even before the spread of the Sustainable Development concept: although Sustainable Development is now part of the mainstream 'development' narratives and is serving all and sundry to green-wash their ever-present agendas of unrelenting economic growth, the sustainability concept in fact emerged as a proposal that questioned the very foundations of how we understand 'development' as the equivalent to economic growth. As Kidd argues, "sustainability emerged as a critical discourse synonymous with the idea of a 'steady-state economy', endorsing a shift from continuous economic growth to low growth or even 'decreasing economic growth' of societies." (Kidd 1992, 15)

What the original notion of "sustainable development" challenged, therefore, was the very understanding of 'development' that human societies should achieve, and by implication, it involved rethinking the way human societies should organize not only their production processes, but also their distribution and consumption patterns (Castillo 2014). "Today the good work done by the social economists needs to be expanded and deepened into a deeply ecological economics (...). Here lies real danger, as our limited knowledge of ecological systems seen through selfish human-centered lenses is the biggest threat to biodiversity and therefore sustainability." (Whelan 2001, 3)

Still, the co-optation process continues; in the case of "Sustainable Development", with the attempt of the mainstream discourses to reply to the increasing criticism on it through what has been presented as green economy or green growth. For example, regarding the topic of climate change, a reflection of a small international organization supporting food systems based on peasant common practices on biodiversity expresses it clearly: "So have we finally succeeded in awakening a consciousness among ordinary citizens, governments and investors? Yes, and at the same time, not at all (...) it is clear that governments and businesses did not recognize this crisis because they somehow finally saw the light, but rather because they succeeded in devising ways to make money from a disaster that affects the very survival of the planet (...) All the big actors of global finance, as well as a growing number of investment funds in climate change (...) have drawn up documents emphasizing big business opportunities that have sprung up from changes in the climate and ecosystems." (GRAIN 2012, 2)

Aware of the important failures in the evolution of the alternative Development current of thought as a way out of the conventional Development mainstream, since the early nineteen-nineties a growing group of scholars and analysts has put forward an "out of the box" way of thinking in terms of 'development'; we refer to it as Post-Development.

c) Post-Development

Due not only to the constant and long lasting failure of the various 'development' models that have been implemented on a large scale during a great part of the last century—a failure that is expressed in the increasingly wider gap between the wealth and poverty of countries, regions, and individuals with high and low levels of 'development'—but also to the progressively clearer evidence that the promise of economic development can only be possible for some countries, regions, or individuals, at the expense of the remaining countries, regions, and individuals, debates on 'development' have reached the point where the question is not on development alternatives, but on alternatives to development; this line of thought is known as post-development.

The rejection of the 'development' notion is not only related to its poor results; another of the main criticisms of post-development is about the imposition of a reductive and singular perspective, with a hegemonic character about the universal goal of human societies: reductionist, because the use of the notion of 'development' as a singular noun (the 'development') and never in plural, implies there is only one singular way of perceiving what the human world should address as its main goal. Also reductionist because the proposals on how to achieve higher levels of wellness promote goals and paths with a strong emphasis on economic growth, even ignoring other dimensions of society. (Escobar 1992, 1995, 2008 and 2010; Georg 1997; Rahnema 1997; Simmons 1997; Rapley 2004; Ziai 2007; Hamid and Arash 2013; Gudynas 2013; Lander 2013; Ulloa 2014; Toledo 2014)

As for the alternative proposals, as it has already been mentioned, some of them at the end of the day also underlined the focus on economic growth, while the others are so attached to the 'development' way of thinking that whatever its name, it is 'development' (the singular noun) plus an adjective, trying to highlight the characteristics that differentiate a particular alternative proposal from the rest of them. That is why there are a high number of types of alternative development proposals, including political 'development', social, environmental, bottom-up, systemic, community, gender-sensitive, humane, participatory, eco-development, ethno-development, rural development and sustainable development, and so on. However, from the post-development perspective, the crisis does not lie in the adjective, whatever it is, but in the noun 'development'.

The attachment to the notion of development with or without an adjective, even if there is enough evidence to demonstrate that it is not able to fulfill its aims and even if there is an increasing number of people around the world perceiving themselves as victims of development, is so powerful and paralyzing that it leads some to assert: "Sachs' metaphor of a crumbling lighthouse could be used by critics of post-development theory to argue that even a crumbling, malfunctioning lighthouse is better than having no guiding light at all!" (Matthews 2004, 373)[3]

Hence, the main criticism to post-development was the lack of specific alternatives it offered: "alternatives to development […] [is] a misnomer because no such alternatives are offered" (Nederveen 2000, 188), despite the fact that its arguments are strong enough to deconstruct the concept of 'development'. A question, then, remains: if 'development' is not it, then what is it?

One answer to this question is the usually local but increasing number of experiences of ways of living that, all over the world, embrace respect of difference, of nature, of spirituality, of solidarity, and that try to behave in such a way that they look to pave the way to a 'good future'.

A complement to this answer is that 'not offering alternatives' has to be understood precisely as one of post-development's greatest strengths (and certainly one of its greatest temptations). If post-development offers the alternative, it will inevitably fall into the logic of deconstructing one way to

---

3 She refers to Sachs' statement: "For almost half a century good neighborliness on the planet was considered in the light of 'development'. Today, the light house shows cracks and it starting to crumble. The idea of development stands like a ruin in the intellectual landscape." (Sachs 1997, 1)

offer another one, the one that it is, the right one, which will reduce its proposal and purpose to change one model for another. In fact, if post-development accepted the claim to have identified a new way to do things, a new model, the new model to advance, it would fall into the very same logic of the 'development' concept as we know it today. And if post-development were able to identify the new model, the next false step would be make it hegemonic in order to spread it, to promote it (or to impose it), to be embraced by the greatest possible number of people, communities, regions, countries, which would be contradicting the very core of its own principles.

To keep within its principles, post-development can only promote the idea (as in fact it has done) of respecting the multiple welfare goals that a variety of different ancient and newer cultures have tried to maintain or to restore, as well as acknowledging new and creative paths. If the post-development approach wishes to remain consistent with its own principles, it cannot support a single way to achieve or search for welfare.

By promoting respect for a diversity of goals and varied ways for achieving welfare, the post-development current of thought is shielded against the need to find the 'true way', becoming by definition inclusive, multiple, and heterogeneous, which is another step away from 'development' as it is currently understood and practiced.

Among the multiple ways to be implemented, post-development has included, then, ancient and creative lifestyles, such as "ways of living" (*modos de vida*), good living, life plans, ways of well-being, and other creative paths of identifying our own goals and our own ways for human societies to prosper as part of the universe.

1.2. The Global Common Good

The evolution of the global common good concept as part of political science, as well its evolution as a main component of the social doctrine of the Catholic Church, are closely related to one another. Those elements of the evolution of the global common good concept that are related to our case study are brought up in this section.

The origins of this concept go back to the ancient Greek civilization and are based in a Platonic dialogue with the Sophists (Plato, The Republic, Book IV). "In this analysis Plato argued that the common good, as the main purpose of the State, transcended the particular goods, while global happiness was to be superior to the happiness of individuals." (Gelardo 2005, 51) Later Aristotle, departing from the fact that the polis is an intrinsic characteristic of human beings, linked the notions of political justice and human good: "To Solon, Pericles, Socrates and Aristotle, equality becomes a synonym of justice, as it is considered a main concern of justice to regulate the distribution of equal or unequal parts […] justice, in a distributive sense, identifies the idea of equality to the fair share." It is thus a 'good' that refers to the whole political realm and was named by the Romans, the citizens' common good (*bonum commune*). "Aristotle completed the Platonic approach by working out one of its key dimensions, the participation mode of the polis members in the common good. It was assumed that a society organized in a state must provide what each of its members needs for their welfare and happiness as citizens. Thus, the good of the whole was not such, if it did not have impact on the happiness of each." (Gelardo 2005, 56—Author's translation)

As expected, during its long journey, the common good has gone through a number of debates, gaining and losing importance and visibility within the international arena. Those of our interest are:

During the middle ages, the Catholic canon established God as the ultimate end of everything, and therefore in comparison with the political sciences' point of view, the end is much further than the polis, reaching instead God Himself. Hence, while for Aristotle's anthropology the identity of a human being was shaped by their status as a member of the polis, for the Catholic theology the identity of human beings and their inviolable rights (human dignity) are shaped by their reflection of man's likeness to the person of Christ. Saint Thomas Aquinas, among other analysts of the common good notion, maintained that natural aims—those that concern the human societies –, spiritual goals, and the supreme end of the subject are not incompatible with the common good of society and, on the contrary, are called to integrate and complement each other.

This and other dogmas of the Catholic Church had strong influence on the Renaissance era and, particularly, on the European jurists that laid the foundations of a political theory of the common good; taking as their starting point the Christian belief of human being, they proposed a conception of society that, following the divine precepts, served to the people in such a way that their theory of the state as ultimate guarantor of the common good turned out into a political theory of the common good.

And in this very brief journey of long jumps from one era to the next one, we have arrived to modernity. In general terms we can say that the virtues of the empirical sciences—characteristics of the modern era—devalued to some extent classical knowledge such as politics, philosophy, religion, and also ethics. Empirical knowledge, being demonstrable, was (is?) considered the socially recognized knowledge and thus, a series of concepts that constitute the domain of the philosophical, the political, religious or ethical, such as truth, justice or good, among many others, became speculative character categories. Concepts as those mentioned came down to the category of notions, to finally end up being opinions and relegated to this point, given that they do not offer means to be verified through facts or any mean valid to the scientific rationality.

"The need to marginalize the ethical and religious representations of the common good to a status of private and relative opinions was defended. The notion of good, therefore, was privatized and relativized (…) in the political realm, the question of the common good was put aside." (Gelardo 2005, 60—Author's translation) Thomas Hobbes offers us a good example of this new condition: "For these words of Good, Evill, and Contemptible, are ever used with relation to the person that useth them: There being nothing simply and absolutely so; nor any common Rule of Good and Evill, to be taken from the nature of the objects themselves." (Hobbes 1909, 45)

About three centuries later, another important contribution to the evolution of the global common good concept was made by the social doctrine of the Catholic Church. In the encyclical of Pope Leo XIII, Rerum Novarum (On the Condition of Labor 1891), his concerns about the social injustices of the working population were evident, and also the concerns about communism as the ideology capable of dealing with the social problems of that time. Revisiting the scholastic and Christian line of thought of the Renaissance era, the proposal of the Church was a model of a society based on social justice and human dignity, derived from the transcendent value of human beings.

Since then, all popes have tried to contribute in this regard, though from very diverse political and theological positions. For example, Pope John Paul II was very cautious and warned against the interpretation of the social doctrine further than theology: "The Church's social doctrine is not a 'third way' between liberal capitalism and Marxist collectivism, nor even a possible alternative to other solutions less radically opposed to one another: rather, it constitutes a category of its own. Nor is it an ideology, but rather the accurate formulation of the results of a careful reflection on the complex realities of human existence, in society and in the international order, in the light of faith and of the Church's tradition [...] It therefore belongs to the field, not of ideology, but of theology and particularly of moral theology." (Pope John Paul II, 1987, 18) However, Stephen Schneck of The Catholic University of America in Washington said, "Pope Francis' point is that governments—unlike free markets—really are moral agents, bear responsibility, and are obligated to work for the common good. Governments have a moral responsibility to regulate market forces for the common good. Many American conservatives are not going to like what the pope has been saying about market forces and government, but Pope Francis is holding fast to traditional church teachings, the provenance of which stretches to Pope Leo XIII's *Rerum Novarum* [1891] and ultimately to the apostles." (Winters 2013, 1)

Without going into additional historical, philosophical and political facts that are important elements on the context of this debate, it suffices to say that some practical consequences of the devaluation of the common good concept are:

- While 'political happiness' that was based in the individual good instead of the collective good gained strength, the modern idea of individual good was associated with material welfare: happiness is no longer, then, a way of being, but the amount of objects one possesses, or the amount or kind of power that might be exerted to have those objects. (MacPherson 1979)
- Politics—being considered constitutive of human beings—and the state as its representation of the common will to coexist are reduced to a body that arbitrates those conflicts generated by individual interests.
- The common good is not the ultimate aim of the state anymore, because the coexistence has come to be the end in itself, though in the very recent times security has been replacing the force that has defined the purpose of the state.
- Since 'good' is considered a relative category, belonging to the private sphere, it is neither possible nor desirable to theorize about it. To the extent that this category is individual, it is also unable to judge what is right or wrong and hence; whereas to classical thinkers justice was one of the fundamental manifestations of goodness, today these notions do not maintain any connection.

- A more evident consequence is that the concept of the common good and its virtues disappeared from the vocabulary of international institutional decision-makers at the global level, as well as from the discourses of politicians in power everywhere.

In order to replace the common good, modern narratives have turned to different expressions such as general interest, public interest, general will, and common interest, among others. However, and as expected, all of them have their own promoters and contradictors. For example, "The common good is no longer the good of the community but the benefit of the individuals who compose it, which are the only real entities; the term that best defines this notion is that of 'general interest'". (Velarde 1997, 20—Author's translation)

Another example is offered by Cochran (1978) who, taking part of the discussion on public interest as related to the concept of common good, has supported Simon (1965), while opposing Held (1971): "Simon rooted his political theory in the concepts of community and common good [...] There are, according to Simon, two types of societies—the community and the partnership—with two (corresponding) kinds of social goods. The common good of a community calls forth a 'common life of desire and action' [Simon 1951]. The good of a partnership does not; the lives of the partners remain private. The common life of desire and action in a community means that 'the most important part of a community takes place in the heart of man.' [Simon 1951, 49] Community is a form of relationship 'characterized by a high degree of personal intimacy, emotional depth, moral commitment, social cohesion, and continuity in time,' to use Nisbet's formulation.' [Nisbet 1966] A partnership, on the other hand, is characterized by ties of mutual self-interest and does not necessarily contain any deep personal commitments. Its good is simply a 'common interest', a sum of private interests which happen to be interdependent." (Cochran 1978, 231)

Among the recent attempts to recover the concept of common good, we have found again the three strands that existed in former times: those that are focused on the view of the political sciences, those that have as a departure point the Catholic Church's idea of the human being, and those that have tried to integrate both. In the latter case, political sciences and the social doctrine of the Catholic Church have kept the same collective principle about the happiness of society being intertwined with the happiness of the individuals, though from obviously different departing points of view.

An additional and interesting trend is the one that has incorporated economics as a fundamental dimension of the common good. "In Economics for the Common Good, Mark Lutz traces the history of social economic thought over the past two hundred years. He sees his work as an 'introduction to economics in terms of human rather than material welfare in the light of community decay and inequality'. Throughout the book Lutz makes the case for a 'broader, more sensitive economic science' that goes beyond the paradigm that produced conventional economics [...] Lutz points out that, following Ruskin, 'Gandhi saw economics as meaningful only if it pursued the right end: an economic system providing the basic necessities while incorporating the social values of human dignity, non-violence and creative labour.'" (Whelan 2001, 1)

After this very brief review of the main currents of 'development' and the history of the common good, evidence suggests that the more we go into the roots of the 'common good', the closer its relationship with 'development' seems to be. Some related points follow, briefly described, given their involvement with our case study:

- There is an undeniable and close relationship between the concept of 'development' and the concept of 'global common good'; one of the elements of this relationship being that their aim is human welfare: happiness, in terms of 'development', and the ultimate end, in terms of the common good.
- In fact, this relationship seems so close that, as has been asserted, the main 'development' goal is the global common good; however, what kind of common good?
- There is an important divergence when the discussion comes to what each of those concepts understands (and promotes) as the ultimate human welfare.
- Even with happiness as the ultimate end which is proposed and pursued for the whole human society, none of those concepts accept that their proposals might be regarded as utopias.
- As pointed out by Cochran (1978), both concepts entail the notion of community in the sense that they involve serving society and not serving individual needs alone. However, as an interesting finding, it seems that—though it corresponds more to the reality of common good con-

cept than to the 'development' history—both concepts have lost this element in recent times, ending up promoting individual interests.
– Lutz's, and other analysts' criticism to the common good concept, is similar to the one that the conventional concept of 'development' has received, in terms of the role that economy has played.
– Whilst conventional development considers that the global common good is achievable only through economic growth, some alternative proposals of 'development' suggest that global common good with 'development' as its goal should integrate additional concerns with economic growth. However, and on the other hand, post-development, which is underlined by the principle of inclusion, purports as its main target multiple and varied options that go back to the very notion of the common good.

2. The Peasant Reserve Zones as a Global Common Good Experience

Here, the evolution of the Peasant Reserve Zones (PRZ) as an experience closely linked to the 'development' model of a country like Colombia—which has had to deal with a very long lasting political and armed conflict—is briefly described, and a short analysis is offered of the complex conflict with which this proposal and practice wants to cope.[4]

Despite some attempts, Colombia never has had a proper agrarian reform: "The land reform, implemented and protected by Act 135 of 1961, far from complying with redistributive purposes, was the product of an exclusive negotiation between political sectors of the ruling classes, through the party system and absolute [...] exclusion of new social forces as the peasantry" (García 1973, 51). Some of the main social and political problems in Colombia at present, such as the origin of guerrilla groups, the longest armed conflict in Latin-America, the growing of illegal crops and drugs dealings, and the political violence, are derived from this fact.

The historic origins of the Colombian struggle for the land, including the PRZ initiative, can be traced back to the Spanish colonial times in Colombia, when most of the poor people liberated from the Spaniards—

---

[4] Based mostly in Ferro & Tobón (2012) and Fajardo (2012).

though still subjugated by the Spanish colonial agrarian system, the *hacienda*—established themselves in settlements inhabited by indigenous people, *mestizos* (indigenous and white), *cimarrones* (rebel African slaves), and poor whites. These settlements followed the example of the peasant communities that, even in the late XIX and early XX centuries, were settled in the lands outside the large colonial estates. (Herrera 2002—Author's translation)

The *hacienda* was a form of economic organization typical of the Spanish colonial system and, in Latin America, it was formed by large estates that were self-sufficient and produced very little for exporting. Huge tracts of land were granted by the Spanish crown, mostly to minor nobles, which included the power over life and death of all the people living in those domains (especially indigenous people), constituting symbols of social status. It is noteworthy that the Society of Jesus also made up part of the *hacendados* (landowners), as proprietors and administrators of vast amounts of natural resources (and "human resources") until their expulsion from the country, in 1767.

"[T]he land policies of the Colombian state had been oscillating from favoring the large property [...] to stimulating the medium property, to driving towards the formation of peasant settlements." (Fajardo 2012, 57—Author's translation) However, the peasants began to demand their right to property titles on the unoccupied land over which they had been working, while the landowners had the intention to appropriate it. The clashes between the landowners and the autonomous communities of peasants, *mestizos*, *cimarrones*, and poor whites not only spread, but were increasingly frequent and violent. Through Decree 1110, in 1928 the Colombian state established agricultural colonies that guaranteed land to the peasants, while at the same time set up the legal foundation for the peasant settlements.

Tensions around the modernization of Colombian society and economy led to a deep political crisis in the late nineteen-forties, which drove to a long armed conflict that still lasts. The way to repress social movements, both urban and rural, when the Conservative party was in power, was through persecutions, torture, illegal detentions, selective and collective killings, and all kind of abuses from the national army, which gave origin to the first guerrilla groups in Colombia. In their attempt to stop the progress of the political violence, and implement a plan of colonization of idle land, the Liberal government that was in power between 1958 and 1962 reached an agreement with Liberal guerrilla groups and when they handed over their weapons, the government granted them titled lands, while also guaranteeing them health and education. However, after a few years, those lands ended up in the hands of businessmen and traders. These are key players of the cycle in which, after peasants improve their land and make it acquire greater value, businessmen and traders come into the scene, buying the land as an investment, concentrating again the land property, and displacing rural inhabitants. These displaced peasants, then, went into new vacant territories, thus expanding the agricultural frontier, and starting the cycle all over again.

In order to prevent this from happening again, the peasants of the Ariari region[5] implemented what they first called "peasant reservations". Trying to focus on how to stop this new process of land concentration at the hands of entrepreneurs and traders, peasants decided that the size of the piece of land that each family owned could not exceed 50 hectares. (Molano 2010 Author's translation)

Since then, in the middle of serious struggles for the right over the land, rural populations in Colombia—including indigenous, afro-Colombian and peasants –, have had to face exclusion, dispossession, exploitation, and a long history of violence from all sides in conflict, depending on the resource that is at stake. However, they have also put forward a number of initiatives as they persist on defending their right to settle down in their own land, and to work and live in peace.

As part of those initiatives, the peasants formally presented their proposal of the PRZ only in the early nineteen-nineties, as part of the process to issue a new law of agrarian reform. However, "the aim of this National Agrarian Reform System promoted by the government was to endorse the neo-liberal precepts as following the recommendations of International Financial Institutions for including the land into the markets dynamic of defining its price based on the logic of the supply and demand" (Ferro and Tobón, 2012).

The legal origins of the PRZ are in "law 160 of 1994, which established the National Agrarian Reform System and, in the 'colonization chapter', briefly expressed: 'colonization areas and those predominantly unoccupied are Peasant Reserve Zones', and pointed out that the then Institute of Agrarian Reform (INCORA) would establish standards and conditions for

---

[5] The region is located in the Southeast of the country and part of the Amazon forest.

the allocation of land in those zones. Later, given the demands of social mobilizations, regulative norms were established, opening the possibility that not only were they declared over public and unoccupied areas, but in other zones in accordance with social needs." (Fajardo 2012, 56—Author's translation)

As if the conflict over the agrarian reforms and property of the land was not complex enough, during 1996 there were huge public demonstrations by the peasants who ended up being involved in the growing of illicit crops; these demonstrations were against the appalling violence they suffered, fueled by the drug trafficking. The peasants welcomed instead the substitution of the illegal crops for legal ones through the PRZ scheme. The first accusation this movement received was that it was led by guerrillas looking for the destabilization of the government at that time, and as usually happens with resistance movements, they were stigmatized as rebels.

However, the strength of the movement was enough to, in junction with other events, get further acknowledgment of the PRZ from the government in the form of new laws and decrees. For example, through the Decree No. 1777 it was declared that, "Peasant Reserve Zones are intended to promote and stabilize the peasant economy, overcoming the causes of social conflicts that affect them, and in general, will create the conditions to achieve peace and social justice in those respective areas." (Colombian Presidency 1996, first article—Author's translation)

The last two decades of armed conflict only exacerbated the problem. During the eight years of the administration of President Uribe, he discredited the PRZ scheme, suspended those that already existed, and stopped the establishment of new ones. An agrarian counter-reform took place, through the violent mass eviction of rural inhabitants, in which the participation of the national army has been demonstrated, and also that of the regional (political and economical) elites, which supported paramilitary forces. According to the Monitoring Committee on Public Policy on Forced Displacement activities during 2009, that is why Colombia had a humanitarian crisis and millions of forced displaced people, coerced to abandon 6.65 million hectares of land of the total 38 that form the country. During this dark time, it was considered that we did not have displaced people because we had an armed conflict, but that we had an armed conflict in order to have displaced people (to pave the way for the arrival of national and transnational agribusiness).

And still there is one more fact: the growing agro-fuel market has come to encourage land-grabbing, consistent with the massive buying and renting of land in other countries by transnational corporations and governments, which are destined to hold mega-crops, mega-dams, or mining activities: "In 2010, the World Bank [2010] reported that 47 million hectares were leased or sold off worldwide in 2009 alone while the Global Land Project [Friis and Reenberg 2010] calculated that 63 million hectares changed hands in just 27 countries of Africa". (GRAIN 2011, 1)

In the middle of this desolate landscape, what are the PRZ? "Peasant Reserve Zones, PRZ, are a way to implement government policy over the public lands of the Colombian state, with the objective of controlling inadequate expansion of the agricultural frontier; preventing and correcting the phenomena of inequitable land concentration or uneconomic ownership fragmentation; creating suitable conditions for the consolidation and sustainable development of the economy of peasants and colonizers with low resources; and regulating the occupation and use of public lands, giving preference in the allocation to peasants or poor settlers. In short, this legal scheme is intended to prevent further concentration of land, to defend the peasants' economy, to socially, productively, and environmentally regulate the territory, and to overcome the causes of social conflicts faced by the peasants in the settlement territories." (Ferro and Tobón 2012, 81—Author's translation)

Indeed, to create a PRZ, peasants should organize and design a 'development' plan which will set out how to meet their basic needs, all within the norm that there is a determined amount of land for each family, which avoids the main problem: land concentration. The state has to give them the support they need to have good living conditions: infrastructure, health, sanitation, energy. (Revista Semana 2010—Author's translation)

In principle, the recognition, strengthening and creation of the PRZ is vindicating the traditional ways of the peasants to build sociality and territoriality through solidarity in work, community spirit, and their particular family lifestyle (including its social, emotional and economic dimensions); it is also vindicating the desire of being autonomous.[6] (Ferro and Tobón 2012)

---

[6] If in this paper I have not referred to farmers but to peasants, it's because in the so-named "third world" context, there are significant differences between those two types of rural inhabitants.

For peasants, afro-descendants, and indigenous communities, inclusion is another key issue, not only in terms of their own claims to "mainstream society", but also as one of their practices, which recognizes the knowledge of others, while at the same time demanding respect for their own ancestral knowledge.

In 1998 the first PRZ (El Pato-Balsillas)[7] was officially established and five more have been established since 2000 in different regions of the country. A series of events have, surprisingly, driven the PRZ scheme to be on top of the present governmental agenda as part of a national controversy.

To finish this brief description, it must be emphasized that, even knowing that in some cases some contradictions and conflicts have emerged within the very same groups promoting these initiatives when proposals as the PRZ are brought into practice, this does not mean that they cease to be valuable and viable.

3. How Do 'Development', Common Good, and The Peasant Reserve Zones Relate?

In this section, some reflections are presented about the relationship that exists between 'development', common good, and the Peasant Reserve Zones as a practical experience with potential for transformation.

World history has shown that the problem of land ownership was always present in the process of formation of all nation-states, and that this is a structural issue. It has also shown that some countries resolved (or overcame) this problem through their industrialization processes, in which rural areas were depopulated to provide labor. This radically changed not only their demographic structures, but also their idiosyncrasies, culture, and many other elements of their daily lifestyles. Most of these territories are presently known as the 'developed' countries.

But the question over land ownership, whether it is considered resolved or not, remains as valid today as in the early days. In this context we should not forget that absolutely all commodities—not just for industriali-

---

7 El Pato is the name of the specific region in which the PRZ was settled, while Balsillas is the name of the hacienda over which it was established.

zation, but for people to work in it—inevitably require the elements that nature provides: land, water, minerals, and so on.

In this regard, Colombia, as a particular case, is characterized for having two types of land property: large estates and smallholdings. This also creates a combination of two production systems: those of the huge agricultural businesses (for example, palm oil and other agro-fuels), and traditional forms of production, characteristic of the peasant economy. Both have been in dispute since the Spanish colonial times.

During the late nineteen-sixties, Colombia began following the models of industrialization and imports substitution (the inwards economy already mentioned), dedicated especially to textiles, pharmaceuticals, leather products, and processed foods. One of the possible outcomes of this model was a change in the demographic structure, since rural populations needed to move to the cities to provide the necessary workforce for these processes. The implementation of this 'development' model was unsuccessful because of factors such as a lack of technology, lack of appropriate equipment, need for trained people, among others. However, the demographics changed because the political conflict displaced people from their lands, increasing poverty levels in the cities, while the land problem has remained as crucial as usual.

When this industrialization model failed in the early nineteen-nineties, what followed was a process of opening up the economy under the rules of the neo-liberal 'development' model (the outwards economy, already mentioned as well). This model, whose main characteristic is to go into open competition as part of the global market, has only widened the gap between "winners" and "losers", given its logic to determine the processes of production and prices based solely on the laws of supply and demand.

As a consequence of this complex historical process, the once promising industrialization phase failed. In this case, this led to what is known as the re-primarization of the economy, meaning that our economy depends again on raw materials, commodities, and no elaborated products. As it is well known, it also means that Colombia fell again into the vicious circle in which its raw materials come back into the country as imported manufactured or industrial products from industrialized countries. This is only one of the expressions of the unequal global power relationships that 'developed' countries exert over 'developing' countries. And how is 'development' related to the common good?

In the literature, one finds a variety of common good concepts, and some of them are related to 'development' goals. For example, one of the concepts proposed by the Catholic Church asserts: "The common good is the primary focus of all social and economic life. By common good we understand 'the set of social life conditions that make possible, for the associations and also for each of their members, the complete and easiest fulfillment of integrated development itself'." (Compendium of the Social Doctrine of the Catholic Church 2004, quoted by Bustince 2012, 5—Author's translation)[8]

The Human Development Report "Deepening Democracy in a Fragmented World" (2002), produced by the United Nations Human Development Program, argues that: "For politics and political institutions to promote human development and safeguard the freedom and dignity of all people, democracy must widen and deepen." (UNDP 2002, 1)

A concept that comes from the perspective of political science states: "Working for the common good means respecting the dignity, the integral human promotion and their fundamental rights. This is the task of all citizens. The common good is the reason for the political and economic authority, if it wants to be human. The government's task is rightly harmonizing the various autonomous or regional interests. The common good is the aim of all economic and political leaders in a just and humanized society." (Bustince 2012, 6—Author's translation)

Whether those concepts have as a starting point the Catholic Church, political science, or political institutions, most of them agree on the importance of values such as dignity, justice or human rights.

For the sake of discussion, some elements of the literature review seem to put forward a relationship between 'development' and common good that could be simplified as if the first tried to express pragmatically what the second wants to reach as an ultimate end for all human beings.

One of the most pressing worries in terms of the global crisis posed by the current model of 'development' is related to the deterioration of the environment, expressed mainly through large extractive practices where productivity is the vision that is encouraged against the caring of nature. The challenge in this regard is, then, to reformulate the cognitive domain under which the idea of 'development' is conceived, an issue that involves

---

8 Compendium of the Social Doctrine of the Catholic Church was prepared by the Pontifical Council "Justice and Peace" (2004).

emerging alternative wisdoms, as represented by peasants and other rural communities.

Another topic for deeper discussion is to rethink that, although both 'development' and the common good are defined as universal, there are significant arguments that would demonstrate that 'development' is not universal but hegemonic. This is not the case for the common good, because although there are significant differences between the proposals from the Catholic point of view and the secular approaches from political science, in terms of its global extent, they have not shown elements of coercion or imposition.

To the extent that common good implies inclusion, the experience of the PRZ again is consistent with it: not only because this is a proposal that might be replicated and multiplied globally, but also because advocating respect for difference calls for "a world in where all worlds fit".

To summarize the main arguments of this debate—all related to the global 'development' model and the options that a country as Colombia has in this regard—and to conclude these reflections on the relationship between 'development' and common good and how they are expressed in the Peasant Reserve Zones as a practical experience, nothing better than some excerpts from the words that Francisco de Roux, S.J. pronounced during the talks "to end of the conflict, and achieve a stable and lasting peace in Colombia", that currently are taking place in Havana (Cuba):

"What is at the core of this participatory dialogue is the discussion on the DEVELOPMENT MODEL, because the model we have had so far has produced inequality, is at the heart of the conflict, is involved with the savage migration of forced displacement, and has not achieved the expected growth of the rural areas. In fact, what Colombia is doing is discussing the model, although it is said that one cannot argue about it, that it is not negotiable. [...] Let's have a look at the ethical challenge that is at the core of these conversations. I will not speak of religious ethics. I'm going to talk about the ethics that still remain, when in Colombia the political theories, ideologies, philosophical explanations and public morals are no longer useful, and all that remains is human dignity.

Dignity is the profound experience that we all have, that matters to us as individuals, as families, as people. Dignity is what we have seen in women and men in the rural areas, who have not allowed others to displace them, who have not allowed other to attack their councils, or to be kidnapped. Dignity is what we have seen in those who stood up unarmed against those with power and guns, defending something they could not give up because then they would not have had value as human beings. You feel it and know it. We do not owe human dignity to anyone. It is not owed to the State, or the Army, or the FARC or the ELN[9]. We do not owe our dignity to any politician, or any employer that gives us a job. Dignity is equal in each and all, it is absolute to everyone; we have it simply because we are human beings [...] What we do with the regional development is to establish and improve the conditions for ethnic groups, peasant communities and rural villages, and businesses working with solidarity, to express, celebrate, share, protect, and live their dignity [...] This is the way we understood many of the proposals that have been heard in these halls during these three days. I will express, then, my feelings on some of them: Peasant Reserve Zones, because these communities can be protected from the voracity of the market that monopolizes the land in large estates and expels the inhabitants from the land; there, food is produced efficiently with the least human and ecological cost, and with quality; there, the organization for peasants to exert their rights is present; there, they cultivate a sense of responsibility to the environment [...].

Some people fear that peasant reserve areas are an instrument for the arrival of the guerrillas at the end of the conflict. I wonder, what could be better than, once the armed conflict ends, having areas of food production and protection of forests and rivers, where ex-combatants can make a reality of what they dreamed as social justice and participation?" (De Roux 2012, 1—Emphasis in the original; author's translation)

Going back to the outline of the intercultural research project, and as an invitation to further debates to our readers, some conclusions are offered in the form of a dialogue:

"While alternative notions of social development—like 'bottom-up development' or taking into account the 'limits to growth'—were niche topics of certain societal milieus in the past, they have now become part of mainstream debates and official political agendas." This is only further evidence of how alternative development proposals have turned into mainstream development; or in the mocking words of Nederveen (1998), mainstream alternative development (MAD).

"The central question is in which way such discourses or models (can) actually change social realities." Right now those discourses and models cannot change social realities in any way. They would have been able to do so, if the movements that supported them had clear goals and had been able to fight and resist the process of co-optation when those proposals were raised; now, however, they have lost their momentum.

---

9 Revolutionary Armed Forces of Colombia (FARC by its Spanish Acronym) and National Liberation Army (ELN by its Spanish Acronym) are the guerrilla groups currently active.

"Societies do not only bring forth a plurality of ideas regarding their own constitution and the norms and values that they should be based on. At the same time, these ideas translate into social practices in diverse ways and yield different practical results." Societies, indeed, have promoted a variety of valuable and original ideas, but they have not been translated into structural changes; only their discourses have been co-opted by the conventional development, which has remained unchanged in practical terms.

"Which models and ideas can be found with regard to a socially just and environmentally sustainable society, and how are they ideally to be implemented in the respective societies? What are the visions and ideas that express normative orientations for living together in society? Which societal level do they refer to (individual, family, community, nation etc.)?"

A practice, such as the one promoted by the PRZ, includes most of the elements that interest us, and its logic, intrinsic sense and dynamic might go much further than the rural areas in third world countries, reaching the global level.

Ethics are a fundamental issue that has been scarcely mentioned in the discussions about 'development', and to some extent we have the same situation in the debates about common good. It is essential to approach it in further discussions.

In finishing this paper I want to return to the range of alternatives to development noted when starting it; knowing that these are just a small sample of the many and varied alternatives that surely exist at the global level, they are also evidence of the dissent with the failed 'development model', and also of the creativity and capacity of human societies to recognize our mistakes. Now it only remains that people and groups that are in the current power centers understand that these skills are essential to human survival.

Works Cited

Adams, William (2001). *Green Development: Environment and Sustainability in the Third World.* London: Routledge.

Blackburn, James, and Jeremy Holland (1998). *Who changes? Institutionalizing Participation in Development.* London: Intermediate Technology Publications.

Blackburn, James, Robert Chambers, and John Gaventa (2000). "Mainstreaming Participation." In Development, Operations Evaluation Department (OED)

World Bank, *Working Paper Series* No. 10, Summer. http://lnweb90. worldbank.org/oed/oeddoclib.nsf/a7a8a58cc87a6e2885256f1900755ae2/1d8e c8bb36c8c76e85256977007257c1/$FILE/Mnstream.pdf (27.01.2011).
Boff, Leonardo and Betto Frei (1996). Mística y Espiritualidad. Madrid: Trotta.
Bustince, Lázaro (2012). *Humanizar la política y la economía, en favor del bien común, según los principios de una ética global—Análisis y propuestas desde una perspectiva africana.* Head of Madrid: Fundación Sur. http://www.africafundacion.org/IMG/pdf/Bustince__Humanizar_la_politica.pdf (13.07.2013).
Castillo, Olga-Lucía (2014). Sustainability vs. Development? Mining and Natural Resources Governance in Colombia. In Nem Singh, Jewellord and Bourgouin, France (eds.) *Resource Governance and Developmental States in the Global South: Critical International Political Economy Perspectives*, 149–171. Palgrave, McMillan: London.
Chambers, Robert (1994). Participatory Rural Appraisal (PRA): Analysis of Experience. *World Development*, 22(9), 1253–1268.
Cochran, Clarke (1978). Yves R. Simon and 'The Common Good': A Note on the Concept. *Ethics*, 88(3), 229–239.
Colombian Presidency (1996). Decree No. 1777 by which is regulated partially the Chapter XIII of Act 160 of 1994, regarding Peasant Reserve Zones. http://restituciondetierras.gov.co/media/descargas/pdf_tomo1/doc56.pdf (15.07.2013).
De Roux, Francisco (2012). "Closing Words". presented at Foro de Desarrollo Integral Agrario Regional—Palabras Finales, 19th December, in Bogotá, Colombia. http://mundoroto.wordpress.com/?s=De+Roux (15.07.2013).
Dollar, David, and Aart Kraay (2002). Growth is Good for the Poor. *Journal of Economic Growth*, 7 (3) 195–225.
Escobar, Arturo (2010). Latin America at a Crossroads: Alternative Modernizations, Postliberalism, or Postdevelopment? *Cultural Studies*, 24(1), 1–65.
Escobar, Arturo (1992). Imagining a Post-Development Era? Critical Thought, Development and Social Movements. *Social Text 31/32 Third World and Post-Colonial Issues*, 20–56.
Escobar, Arturo (1995). *Encountering Development: The Making and Unmaking of the Third World.* Princeton: Princeton University Press.
Escobar, Arturo (2008). *Territories of Difference—Place, movements, life, redes.* Durham: Duke University Press.
Fajardo, Darío (2012). Experiencias y Perspectivas de las Zonas de Reserva Campesina. In Juan Ferro and Gabriel Tobón (eds.) *Autonomías Territoriales: Experiencias y Desafíos*, 55–70. Observatory of Ethnic Territories, Javeriana University, Bogotá: Javegraf.
Fernández, Ana (2002). "Distribución, Crecimiento y Desarrollo: Principales Aportes Teóricos que explican su Interrelación. Buenos Aires: Asociación Argentina de Economía Política." http://www.aaep.org.ar/anales/works/works 2002/fernandez.pdf (27.01.2011).

Ferro, Juan, and Gabriel Tobón (2012). Las Zonas de Reserva Campesinas y la naciente Autonomía Regional. In Juan Ferro and Gabriel Tobón (eds.) Autonomías Territoriales: Experiencias y Desafíos, 81–104. Observatory of Ethnic Territories, Javeriana University, Bogotá: Javegraf.

Friis, Cecilie and Anette Reenberg (2010). "Land grab in Africa: Emerging land system drivers in a teleconnected world." The Global Land Project Report No. 1, Denmark, August. http://farmlandgrab.org/post/view/14816 (31.07.2013).

García, Antonio (1973). *Reforma Agraria y Dominación Social en América Latina*. Buenos Aires: Ediciones SIAP.

Gelardo, Teresa (2005). "La Política y el Bien Común. Navarra: Instituto Martín de Azpilcueta." http://dspace.unav.es/dspace/bitstream/10171/18793/1/La%20pol%C3%ADtica%20y%20el%20bien%20com%C3%BAn.pdf (15.04.2014).

Georg, Susan (1997). How the Poor developed the Rich. In In Majid, Rahnema and Victoria Bawtree (eds.). *The Post-Development Reader*. London: Zed Books.

GRAIN (2011). "It's time to outlaw Land Grabbing, not to make it 'responsible'!" http://www.grain.org/article/entries/4227-it-s-time-to-outlaw-land-grabbing-not-to-make-it-responsible (26.06.2013).

GRAIN (2012). "Behind the Green Economy: profiting from environmental and climate crisis." http://www.grain.org/es/article/entries/4571-behind-the-green-economy-profiting-from-environmental-and-climate-crisis (26.06.2013).

Gudynas, Eduardo (2013). Transiciones hacia un nuevo Regionalismo Autónomo. In Lang, Miriam, López, Claudia y Santillana, Alejandra (eds.*) Alternativas al Capitalismo-Colonialismo del Siglo XXI*, 129–160. Quito: Ediciones Abya Yala.

Hamid, Ahmadi and Bidollahkhani Arash (2013). The Post-Development Interest and Critical Representations of Development Debate - A Democratic Approach. *Journal of Iranian Social Development Studies*, 5(3) 47–63.

Held, Virginia (1971). Public Interest and Individual Interest. New York: Basic Books.

Herrera, Marta (2002). *Ordenar para Controlar - Ordenamiento espacial y control político en las llanuras del Caribe y en los Andes centrales neogranadinos (Siglo XVIII)*. Bogotá: Instituto Colombiano de Antropología e Historia (ICAHN).

Hobbes, Thomas (1909). *Leviathan*. Oxford: Clarendon Press (reprinted from the edition of 1651). http://files.libertyfund.org/files/869/Hobbes_0161_EBk_v6.0.pdf (26.06.2013).

John Paul II (1987). "Solicitudo Rei Socialis on Social Concern." Encyclical Letter, December 30th. http://www.vatican.va/holy_father/john_paul_ii/encyclicals/documents/hf_jp-ii_enc_30121987_sollicitudo-rei-socialis_sp.html (25.06.2013).

Kidd, Charles (1992). The Evolution of Sustainability. *Journal of Agricultural and Environmental Ethics*, 5 (1), 1–26.

Lander, Edgardo (2013). Crisis Civilizatoria, Límites del Planeta, Asaltos a la Democracia y Pueblos en Resistencia. In Lang, Miriam, López, Claudia y

Santillana, Alejandra (eds.) *Alternativas al Capitalismo-Colonialismo del Siglo XXI*, 27–62. Quito: Ediciones Abya Yala.

Lübker, Malte, Graham Smith, and John Weeks (2002). Growth and the Poor: a comment on Dollar and Kraay. *Journal of International Development*, 14, 555–571.

Lutz, Mark (1999). *Economics for the Common Good: Two Centuries of Social Economic Thought in the Humanistic Tradition*. London: Routledge.

MacPherson, Crawford B. (1979). *La Teoría Política del Individualismo Posesivo—De Hobbes a Locke*. Barcelona: Fontanella.

Martínez-Alier, Joan (2006). *El Ecologismo de los Pobres: Conflictos Ambientales y Lenguajes de Valoración*. Antrzyt: Icaria.

Matthews, Sally (2004). Post-development Theory and the Questions of Alternative: a view from Africa. *Third World Quarterly*, 25 (2), 373–384.

Meadows, Donella, Dennis Meadows, and Jorgen Randers (1972). *The Limits of Growth: A Report for the Club of Rome's Project on the Predicament of Mankind*. New York: Universe Books.

Molano, Alfredo (2010). "Zonas de Reserva Campesina." Speech presented at the First National Summit of Peasant Reserve Zones, August 29–31 2010, in Barracabermeja, Colombia. http://www.youtube.com/watch?v=Waa6c Ehh99o (10.07.2013).

Nederveen, Jan (1998). My paradigm or yours? *Development and Change*, 29, 343–373.

Nederveen, Jan (2000). After Post-development. *Third World Quarterly*, 21 (2), 175–191.

Nisbet, Robert (1966). *The Sociological Tradition*. New York: Basic Books.

Peet, Richard, and Michael Watts (1996). *Liberation Ecologies: Environment, Development, Social Movements*. Routledge: London.

Plato (2003). *La República*, book IV, 8th edition, translated by José Tomás y García, 137–176. Bogotá: Editorial Panamericana.

Pontifical Council 'Justice and Peace' (2004). *Compendio de la Doctrina Social de la Iglesia, 2nd April, Ciudad del Vaticano*. http://www.vatican.va/roman_curia/pontifical_councils/justpeace/documents/rc_pc_justpeace_doc_200605 26_compendio-dott-soc_sp.html (25.06.2013).

Rahnema, Majid (1997). Towards Post-Development: Searching for Signposts, a new Language and a new Paradigm. In Majid, Rahnema and Victoria Bawtree (eds.). *The Post-Development Reader*. London: Zed Books.

Rapley, John (2004). Development Studies and the Post-Development Critique. *Progress in Development Studies*, 4(4), 350–354.

Revista Semana (2010). "Zonas de Reserva Campesina: otra fórmula para restituir tierras." *Revista Semana*, 29th September 2010. http://www.semana.com/nacio n/articulo/zonas-reserva-campesina-otra-formula-para-restituirtierras/122641-3 (17.06.2013).

Sachs, Wolfgang (1997). *The Development Dictionary—A Guide to Knowledge as Power*, 6th edition. London: Zed Books.

Simmons, Pam (1997). Women in 'Development': A Threat to Liberation. In Rahnema Majid and Victoria Bawtree (eds.). *The Post-Development Reader*. London: Zed Books.

Simon, Yves (1951). *Philosophy of Democratic Government*. Chicago: University of Chicago Press.

Simon, Yves (1965). *The Tradition of Natural Law*. New York: Fordham University Press.

Toledo, Víctor (2014). Latinoamérica como Laboratorio Socioambiental: Pueblos Indígenas, Memoria Biocultural y Cambio Civilizatoria. In Eschenhaguen, María y Maldonado, Carlos (eds.). *Un Viaje por las Alternativas al Desarrollo: Perspectivas y propuestas Teóricas*, 143–162. Bogotá: Editorial Universidad del Rosario.

Ulloa, Astrid (2014). Conocimientos, Naturalezas y Territorios. Repensando las Alternativas al Desarrollo y partir de Prácticas y Estrategias de los Pueblos Indígenas en Colombia. In María Eschenhaguen and Carlos Maldonado (eds.). *Un Viaje por las Alternativas al Desarrollo: Perspectivas y propuestas Teóricas*, 119-142. Bogotá: Editorial Universidad del Rosario.

UNDP (2002). *Human Development Report Deepening Democracy in a Fragmented World*. New York: Oxford University Press. http://hdr.undp.org/en/reports/global/hdr2002/ (26.07.2013).

Velarde, Caridad (1997). Liberalismo y Liberalismos. *Cuadernos de Anuario Filosóficos*, No. 40, Navarra: University of Navarra.

Whelan, Ben (2001). *From individualistic to social economics—A book review on Lutz, Mark (1999) Economics for the Common Good. Feasta Review Series, No. 1*. London: Routledge.

Wilson, Gordon, Pamela Furniss, and Richard Kimbowa (2010). *Environment, Development, and Sustainability: Perspectives and Cases from around the World*. New York: Oxford University Press.

Winters, Michael (2013). Pope Francis spotlights social teaching with blunt calls for ethical economy. National Catholic Reporter. http://www.ncronline.org/ (05.07.2013).

World Bank (2010). "New World Bank report sees growing global demand for farmland." http://farmlandgrab.org/post/view/15309 (31.07.2013).

Ziai, Aram (2007). *Exploring Post-Development—Theory and practice, problems and Perspectives*. New York: Routledge.

Biocivilization for Socio-Environmental Sustainability: The Hard but Necessary Transition

Cândido Grzybowski

Introduction

This analysis responds to an invitation to participate in the intercultural research project named "Development for the Global Common Good". As a contribution to this joint project, I have decided to review my research and reflections of the last five years, based on studies and debates that took place at Ibase, Rio de Janeiro, having Brazil as the main reference, and the World Social Forum as an inspiration. Further research was not possible. However, while compiling and synthesizing partial analysis, something integrative and qualitatively new came up, something that points towards a direction of investigation and, above all, of proposals to build "other worlds". However I would like to clarify that this analysis does not hold the intention to be a representation of the complex reality of Brazil, a country-continent. I stand for my point of view regarding it, but other analyses, with other approaches, can be made.

The paper will be structured as follows. In part one, I briefly characterize the civilization crisis based on the capitalist development as a society model and project. Then, in part two of my reflection, based on my definition of biocivilization as an inspiring direction and an alternative path, I point out the philosophical, ethical and political basis of the relations we need to strategically strengthen within societies. At last, in part three, taking "emerging" country Brazil as an emblematic case, I analyze the political and economic difficulties of abandoning the current developmentalism.

1. Systemic Crisis Context

I believe it is now all too common to speak of a crisis that incorporates and combines several crises such as: global economic-financial, of global governance, of social welfare state in developed economies, food crisis, environmental crisis, crisis of principles and perspectives. Looking from the perspective of the rising planetary citizenship, we are facing a deep systemic and paradigmatic crisis of the industrial, productivist and consumerist capitalism, generator of wealth as well as destruction, concentrator and yet excluder, all on a global scale. However the crisis will not necessarily generate alternatives, it might be the sign of the aggravation of the same situation, or even something worse.

As elements of the systemic crisis, I point out the global logic of private businesses that are unaware of national borders and do not respect the diversity and specificity of territories as expressions of natural and human-made conditions. The consequences that such an exploitation and domination logic causes immediately acquire a planetary dimension. Life is now globalized, and so is citizenship. Against global companies and their businesses, which make the state subservient to their own interests, a citizenship rises that refuses the privatization and commercialization of virtually everything. "Our planet is not for sale" perfectly synthesizes the aforementioned refusal in the context of the crisis (Grzybowski 2009).

It is essential to keep in mind the individualist, competitive and speculative character deeply ingrained in our societies, their economies and public authority structures. The financial capital circulating the globe is ten times the world's Gross Domestic Product. All humankind depends upon the unregulated wills of the few "owners" of this capital, and on their moods and bets. We live in a global "casino".

A new form of colonialism and usurpation of the planet's resources arises through the commodification of all things. Lands and natural resources are covered by an extraction-based logic. Geo-engineering allows to access previously inaccessible natural resources. Genetic engineering, mostly with its transgenic seeds, imposes one same production and consumption pattern upon the whole world. This context facilitates financial speculation, where food safety itself depends on business in future markets. The crisis reveals how deeply each local production is connected to the global moods.

It is worth reminding how unequal the world has become. The issue of social justice is globalized. Nowadays, migrants from all corners of the globe are counted in millions. In general, they are the biggest and more evident expression of the inequality and injustice that rule the world: inequality in terms of life conditions, unequal rights, with growing racism, xenophobia, and intolerance.

The issue of environmental destruction represents the other side of globalization. Given the natural interdependence of ecological systems, the threat to their integrity and their ability to regenerate inevitably gain a planetary dimension. Globalization does not respect natural limitations.

Since this is a systemic crisis, it is essential to behold its political dimension. There is a crisis of politics for its privatization or control of large capital. The evaluation of governments and their management abilities by private financial conglomerates is in the very core of the political crisis. National states lose the ability to govern and fund public policies that are crucial for citizenship in their territories. Democracy itself is cloistered and loses substance due to the prominence of the "private over public" logic.

Finance dominates politics, even if resorting to it for help. From 2008 until today, what the states have mostly done was save banks that had made a bet on speculation, preventing their bankruptcy from dragging the whole system down. Billions and billions have been spent, and the most remarkable result was the transference of the banks' problems to the states themselves, or better saying, to the citizens that support them.

In fact, we are now living the consequences of the dictatorship of financial markets, which submit everything to their own rules, their dirty casino game that circumvents any political regulation. We are the ones who pay, with our taxes and with our devastated citizenship rights—rights we earned thanks to our struggle and the struggle of generations before us.

Neoliberal globalization has produced an interdependent world, at least at the level of human conscience—this is the good side of it. But it was not capable of breeding a new form of interdependent power, from local to worldwide. We have a long way to go before generating a new commitment "order" among all the involved, an essential condition for change. We need another world, a world of equality in diversity, of well-being in complete and utter respect for the integrity of life and of the planet itself. Humankind faces the challenge of making fundamental choices. The chosen option may mean walking towards the irreversible in terms of the destruction of life and of the Planet, or reconstructing the foundations and relationships among humans and between humans and the biosphere, which are capable of incrementing a still possible righteous process of social, environmental and ecologic sustainability.

The truth is that we are invaded by daily news, and we can feel climate and nature giving warnings of collapse through extreme floods and droughts, active volcanoes and devastating tsunamis. Speaking of inequality and social exclusion is no longer taboo, but not much is being done to revert this scenario. We are just living with it. The abundance of all sorts of material goods is concentrated in the hands of less than 20 percent of the world's population. But it is not enough to hide the huge contingent of human beings that go to bed on an empty stomach at the end of the day. Destructive productivity and consumption have taken over our lifestyle, generating more and more luxury and waste, destroying life and nature. We hoard individual assets, collective poverty and human misery.

Spicing up the diagnosis there is a crisis of principles and utopias, of imaginary mobilizers. A certain cynicism is spreading like a cultural cancer, destroying the ability to be outraged by a fundamentalist individuality built upon the absolute rule of winning at all costs. The social fabric of social interaction and share, of acknowledging responsibility for the equality of rights for all people, is threatened.

This is the reason why a new form of protest is emerging from the bowels of societies, pointing towards the unacceptable condition of all things. In the midst of protesting groups and social movements, still minorities—outraged in different countries and with different methods of action, occupiers of public spaces, squares and streets, of the most unexpected places, rebellious of all calibers—the common cry is "enough!", "we cannot take this anymore!". Yes, there are many people fighting back, everywhere, but it still does not represent a new historic wave of hope and transformation. Small changes are taking place, but they must be articulated and strengthened, creating irresistible movements, defining a new agenda and a new historic horizon for the world.

This is a civilization crisis. In this crisis, the challenges are planetary, both in terms of how to preserve the Planet's integrity and life for future generations, and in terms of social and environmental injustice, intra and inter present day populations. To speak of a civilization crisis can be a way of replacing the analysis for an empty concept, which hides more than it reveals since it is loaded with ideology. We urgently need to establish analytical systems that dissect and demonstrate the concept of civilization crisis, mostly because this is a condition so that the proposals to overcome the crisis can acquire consistency and understandability, besides the motivating and transforming capacity they bear.

It is worth reminding how unequal the world has become. The issue of social justice is globalized. Today, migrants from all corners of the globe are counted in millions. In general, they are the biggest and more evident expression of the inequality and injustice that rule the world: inequality in terms of life conditions, unequal rights, with growing racism, xenophobia, and intolerance.

2. Fundamentals of a Biocivilization

It is imperative for humankind to think about the basis of a new civilization. At the same time, we need to engage in the long social process of dismantling and rebuilding culture and economy on a social level as well as have the power necessary for the process. The idea of a biocivilization is about searching for a new civilizational paradigm: a concept that is still in an embryonic stage, in the midst of several others, which are also alternatively legitimate. Biocivilization can indicate a direction to go, but not the specific way that we must take. What I propose in this part are some points that may motivate and serve as a script for a more systemic work of analysis and reflection.

Principles and ideas, imagination, understanding and proposals are all necessary but insufficient conditions. All of this requires bearers, collective subjects that see in this set of principles and ideas the expression of the meaning of their existence and engagement, of the utopian horizon to long for, and the possibilities to transform the conditions, relations and structures experienced.

There is no historic change without social subjects to promote it against other social subjects that do not desire it. The alternatives can only be real alternatives if borne by those who mobilize and struggle, from contradictory concrete situations they live in, and from where they build themselves as subjects with an identity and a project, as active citizens. This is a possible task—human history is full of examples—but hard, and time-consuming, for one or more generations.

We are facing a gigantic challenge, of philosophical and political scope, since this is about dismantling presumptions in our thinking and acting that have become common sense and which for this reason shape our minds and organize economy and power in society. We are led to believe that a lack of development, non-development or underdevelopment, is at the root of such ailments. Development is the dream and ideology that dominate planet Earth from north to south and east to west, understood as a rising Gross Domestic Product, possessing and consuming material goods, no matter what (Grzybowski 2012b).

Only now, with the ghost of climate change, has a shadow of a doubt arisen and the ideological and cultural foundation, the principles and ethics of this civilization of productivity and consumption are starting to show gaps. For biocivilization, covering the current situation up in green paint and continue to grow with social exclusion and destruction of the natural common assets is not enough. We must restructure and reorganize the fundaments of human civilization to prevent it from threatening the sustainability of everyone without exclusion, intra and inter generations, for all life forms, as well as of the planet's integrity.

It must be clear that we are here discussing ethical principles and beliefs, which ground, at their core, the relations between humankind and nature, their rich biodiversity, and the relations of humankind with their own social and cultural diversity. Principles and beliefs are the infrastructure of both social ideals and imagination, as well as of things we practice at all levels of life, from power and economy to the individual, group or family daily lives (Jonas 2006). The focus here are principles and beliefs that are already present in a subordinate manner within the civilization in crisis; principles and beliefs that can be incremented as emerging strengths of a new thought and action paradigm, which signals the historic possibility of biocivilization. Yet, this is not about the obvious, as some might think, but about the search for the core of good sense present in the common sense of different cultures, like the great thinker of possible historic change, Antônio Gramsci, has taught us (Gramsci 1981).

2.1. Ethics of the Integrity of Life and the Planet

A core issue, handled by all cosmic visions, relates to our place as natural beings gifted with a conscience. This is not the opportunity to examine such philosophical and theological traditions. Rather, it is important to acknowledge how the vision that established the presumption of separation between humans and biosphere leads to the centrality and domination of humans above all other forms of life. This philosophical presumption—anthropocentrism—is one of the pillars of the dominant civilization. Scientific and technological expansion feeds this presumption and is a condition of industrialization. Undoubtedly, considering ourselves, humans, as absolute masters, and within ourselves distinguishing reason as a basis for objectivity in opposition to and dominating subjectivity (ethics, emotion, affection, enjoyment, fear…), has led to scientific and technical development throughout the ages, but acted against nature and life itself. This constitutes a huge human achievement. We have made science and technology the core principles and upmost expression of rationality. It did not eradicate subjectivity; it subdued it, subordinating ethics itself to rationality (Grzybowski 2011 and 2012b). However, this presumption—rationality—ended up justifying new ways of domination, enslavement, and exploitation of humans by humans.

In the crisis of the dominant civilization, an issue that emerges as a sine qua non condition is the need to restructure and rebuild our relationship with nature. After and above all, we are part of the biosphere. We are nature within ourselves, living nature, gifted with a conscience. Our life is not above nor next to natural logic, but within it. For this reason, we must restructure ourselves as human beings. We are gifted with reason and sensitivity, dependent on each other, multiple and diverse, with the ability to create meanings and directions. Yet we are part of the natural whole and we know how to handle nature, how to share and regenerate it. Future generations have the right to the same natural conditions we have. Moreover, the planet's integrity is a value per se, and it is our duty to preserve it. To interact and exchange with nature is, by definition, living. From a biocivilization perspective, it is in this relationship with nature that we define the sustainability of life and the planet, by adjusting to its conditions and rhythms, following its processes of change, and enriching it, facilitating its renewal and regeneration. Science and technology can be extremely useful, if their use is subjected to the ethics of respect for the integrity of the biosphere, nature, its physical and biodynamic processes, and how it appears on each territory.

From a social-environmental framework, territories are areas of human life, which combine objective conditions—their natural features and what has been established in them by past human occupation—with human action and present projects. These are not physical areas per se, but rather geographic dynamic areas, with a past human history and a history in process, due to current actions. The human use of territory qualifies its organization and offers historic significance to it. We are before a form of occupation and use of natural space, of organizing it as human territory, filled with life and in motion (Santos 1966 and 2001).

The territories can be the path to rebuild the relationship between society and nature, but they must be a path of mutual respect and vital exchanges that reproduce and regenerate, without destroying. This is about making a relocation and rediscovery of a mental and practical path based on the bonds that join us and the natural world, and upon this, the bonds of social living, on a natural and human interdependent planet, from a local to a worldwide scope. We now also know that natural phenomena are interdependent with each other in planetary terms, even if their manifestation is specific to each given territory.

This is the teaching that emerges, within the current crisis, from the cry of those who cannot conceive themselves as independent from their territories, as the original peoples, especially indigenous people and tribes, Brazilian Quilombola communities, wild fruit gatherer groups, peasant communities all around the world. Humankind owes them the preservation of what is left of the planet's biodiversity, given the symbiotic manner in which they live with nature. In them it is also possible to rediscover a culture of social living and respect for nature that does not compromise the different forms of life and their integrity, but benefits from them to live as human beings, as creators of culture, knowledge, senses and communication.

Particularly, the indigenous populations of the Andes are currently bringing us the idea of "*buen vivir*", which is based on people acknowledging themselves as part of nature and seeing in nature a subject with whom to relate, as well as respecting Mother Earth. In fact, their vision and culture combine concepts and practices specific to a society that interacts with all of nature's components (the air, the sun, the moon, the water, the rain, the mountain, animals, plants...) as subjects themselves, just like us, humans. This complexity is difficult to capture and translate into our Eurocentric culture; it is impossible to capture the radicalism of its living philosophy. The fact is that philosophy can inspire us in the reconstruction of ethics and practice to be made by us as humankind in the path to biocivilization.

To become sustainable again, human civilization must give up anthropocentrism as a philosophy, ethics and religion, and to radically change its vision and relationship with nature (Calame 2009). Life, all life forms, have the fundamental right to exist, as well as complex ecological systems, that while interacting among themselves, regulate planet Earth. This must be the founding principle, condition and limitation of human intervention in the relationship with nature and in building flourishing societies.

The first inherent task is to deactivate the machine of production and accumulation of material and financial wealth. The machine is the engine of development. This machine combines the appropriation and limitless use of nature's resources, with domination and exploitation of workers, through privatization, commercialization, and industrialization, incrementing uncontrolled productivity and consumption, all in the name of capitalist hoarding. In spite of being growth-focused and market-regulated, the industrialization machine produces more garbage than useful goods and services (Spratt et al. 2010).

The central ethical issue is: How can we abandon the principles and lifestyle of having more and more, producing more and more luxury and garbage that goes along with environmental destruction? How can we adopt a lifestyle of being more and more happy, more compassionate, more conscious of our responsibilities in regenerating, reproducing and preserving the integrity of the natural basis, sharing it with everyone today, and with future generations, with a planetary vision of interdependence, cooperation, and co-responsibility?

2.2. Ethics of Care, Living Together, and Share

Here we are, facing principles and beliefs that should govern the human infrastructure of economy and power in the path to a biocivilization. In the industrial, productive and consumption-driven civilization, organized according to mercantile value, such principles and beliefs are excluded or minimized. This exclusion ignores virtually all of the human activities involved. Nonetheless, in spite of it all, these are still crucial activities. The activities of care, social living and share refer to the basics of an economy that is focused on life. They are the core economy (Spratt et al. 2010), since real human life is based in those activities.

Care can be viewed as the founding principle, in spite of its interdependence with the other two. Life wouldn't exist without care. It is something immanent to natural life, both in animals and human beings. There's no better example of care than mothers protecting their newborns; and nothing more horrifying than abandonment. Like a continuous thread that accompanies generations, life reproduces and, at the same time, living beings die, in a contradictory process in which life continues through the birth and death of those that enjoy it. All living beings on the planet carry this marvelous fate. And it operates based on the principle of care.

Care is the essential activity of daily life. The feminist movement reminds us that, without care, there wouldn't be any babies or children and life wouldn't reproduce. Besides, without care and love, what would human life be? Without the activities of caring, monitoring, cooking and serving food, washing up, without the domestic economy, human life wouldn't exist. In this space we view as private, the essence of humans is generated. Our elders, parents and grandparents, the sick and the bearers of special needs, they would all be doomed if it weren't for domestic, familiar, and daily care. This vital work is made mostly by women, who carry the burden of the double journey and suffer from male domination. We are, in fact, before an inversion, where the essential—care—is considered private and worthless in our dominant economy, where market occupies a central position. What is worse: our society, by disqualifying care, disqualifies, exploits and dominates women, privatizes the family and, inside it, legitimates male domination.

It would be minimizing and, in a way, a subjection to the principle of market value, to say that this is merely unpaid work only because care denounces and denies the principle of value and wealth in the market capitalist economy, expressed by the Gross Domestic Product. We must therefore erect the principle of care as central to the new economy, to the management of the huge home that is the symbiosis of human life and nature, the indispensable community life, where we live together and everything is shared.

Without care, the atmosphere has been colonized by carbon emissions from large economic corporations, from companies, from the rich and powerful, from consumerism. Today, humankind is threatened as a living species as well as all life forms. Without care, the colonial work of conquering peoples and territories was made and, today, the dispute for the planet's natural resources prevails. In search of greater productivity, without care, we are creating transgenic seeds and destroying the existing biodiversity. Without care, we are polluting water, destroying life in the oceans, cutting away forests and creating deserts. The fact is it becomes impossible to think of sustainability without the principle and ethical value of care.

The principles of living together and share are the corollary of care. Care flourishes with community life and friendship relations. These areas extend care beyond the family in social terms. Cultural life, parties, dreams, imagination and beliefs, that offer direction and meaning to life and love, flourish here. Based on care, cooperation develops and common interests emerge. Living together and sharing are indispensable for communication, for language, for learning. In turn, knowledge wouldn't exist if it weren't for sharing.

There's nothing more aggressive than the dominant style of our cities, made for individual cars, of extreme proximity and kilometric human distance, with security keys and schemes that block and separate buildings within fences and apartment complexes, monitored day and night by private security guards. Luckily, here it is also possible to discover resistance pockets—in the country as in the city, where care, living together, and share flourish—which point towards other possibilities of getting organized for *buen vivir*.

Is there greater denial of humankind than private intellectual property? After all, is it possible to imagine knowledge—as a common asset that is created and not naturally given—as independent from the anonymous contribution of a chain of human beings, from this and past generations, who share their doubts, searches, discoveries, mistakes and successes? Privatizing scientific and technical knowledge can be good for the business of large capitalist corporations, but goes against science and knowledge per se as human cooperative production throughout time (Grzybowski 2010b). Ethical principles and beliefs of care, living together and sharing must be at the very core of the reconstruction of our relation with nature, as indispensable bases of human life, of all life. But they must also be at the core of the new economy and the new power. A sustainable economy is possible only if it is founded upon such principles (Grzybowski 2012a).

2.3. Ethics of "Common Goods"

A new civilizational paradigm will only be possible if we face up to the logic of having more and more material goods of individual consumption and accumulating more and more mercantile wealth as a parameter of happiness. What matters here are the conditions for transformation of the currently dominating system and for the constitution of a new paradigm. In this framework, the issue of common goods acquires strategic relevance. By organizing ourselves around the commons we can create a new way of being and living, both in the relation between humans and in our relation with nature. We'll be facing the possibility to develop biocentrist models of social, cultural, economic and political organization, alternative to the current development (Bollier and Helfrich 2012).

But what are, after all, common goods? Being common is not an *a priori* condition, it is a result. Goods are not common per se, they are socially made common. Common is not an inherent or intrinsic quality of the good (be it natural or produced), but it is a quality that social relation gives it. To generate common goods is a special way of organizing social life (Helfrich et al. 2009).

Commons, more than goods, are all that social relations identify and manage as such. The need which is being felt, desired, and collectively faced leads to the creation of common goods. At the same time, the unruly search for individual capital accumulation has been the most radical form of imprisonment and destruction of common goods. To redeem and regenerate common goods is more than a resistance; it is creating the conditions for another way of life (Grzybowski 2012c).

Humankind has always lived with goods viewed as common. Some of these goods—like water, rivers, oceans, air and atmosphere—are common because they are connected to life, and we cannot conceive life without them. Others are common goods because culture has always deemed them public, including mountains, forests and their fruits, paths and roads, meeting places that originate public squares, holy places like graveyards and places of prayer. Yet another group of goods is considered common because they are a defining part of the social and cultural identity of the group, tribe, or people, like language, music, dancing, singing, and religion. To all of these, we must still add knowledge, in all its varied and rich forms, its communication and practical application to the processes of interaction with nature and of life's organization. These are goods with distinct features. Some are gifts of nature; others are produced and enjoyed collectively. The commons feature grew on a gradual basis, hand in hand with the collective management of these goods. Being part of the group, community or people, also means having the right of sharing these common goods.

But the real story, especially the historic process that created the conditions for the emergence and the development of the industrial capitalist civilization we know, is also one of usurpation by the private imprisonment and appropriation of the common. One of the ways to expand capitalism is to turn common goods into commodities and goods with a market value which is possible only when they become scarce due to privatization. Even different life forms are privatized and commercialized. Conquest, occupation and colonization, based on wars, destruction, and racism, as well as the imposition of rules and standards of domination forced on entire peoples and their territories have been constant in capitalist development. The radical scope of the social resistance caused is related to the undermining of society's common bases that are generated by the process.

De-commoditization and de-commercialization of the commons are crucial conditions to overcome the civilization crisis and to walk towards the search for the sustainable basis of life and the planet. Through social struggle, common goods are concretely and symbolically redeemed, thereby broadening the very comprehensiveness of the common. One of the most evident struggles is perhaps the fight against water privatization, because it is based upon different realities. In all corners of the planet, all populations—in their different manner—have fought for water to remain a common, just as we have explained it. In spite of being diffuse by definition, the atmosphere and the climate are now beginning to occupy a relevant position in the fights for our commons. New concepts like the colonization of atmosphere, oceans, or biodiversity by large capitalist corporations and wealthier societies has gained substance and density. From this premise, these fields emerge as common planetary goods. Struggles like free software (open source) are at the helm of the fight against the privatization of knowledge and for knowledge as a vital common good. With it, the fight against all forms of intellectual property emerges as a condition for the flourishing of common goods and the constitution of a biocivilization. The radicalism of the indigenous vision of *buen vivir* resides in the way it conceives and is related to all nature and to common goods.

Commons are one of the fundaments of biocivilization. To redeem "commons", to expand them, to create new commons are all necessary tasks to build a new civilizational paradigm that opposes the one in crisis. "Commons" do not necessarily deny industrialization, but they subdue it to a logic of collective well-being, and a logic of collective rights to the "commons". Having "commons" at the basis is not being against the benefits and uses they offer, it is merely about imposing and strengthening the principles of care and share. To strengthen the character of common goods is to strengthen sociality, the community spirit, indeed a collective life as an experience that is only fulfilled in the relation with other human beings, with other living beings and with nature in its contradictory and fantastic entirety.

2.4. Ethics of Social, Environmental, and Ecological Justice

Social justice, founded on the acknowledgment of the principle of equality of being human, goes through the most distinct philosophical and religious traditions. Given the reality of social inequality, intra and inter peoples, throughout history, the fight for justice and equality has been the engine of history. Never has humankind been as unequal as in the current context of excluding abundance, of outrageous wealth and unbearable misery, and never has this truth of fighting for justice and equality been so evident.

But what does it mean today to fight for social justice? Upon the deconstruction of real socialism and the superiority of globalized capitalism, the issue of equality and social justice has become even more visible. With the growth of inequality within countries and among them, struggles for equality have intensified; however, they are fragmented. Libertarian and emancipating utopias have lost their charm. Moreover, real socialism presented itself as the alternative to the maximization of productive industrialization ("productive forces"). In practice, social revolutions have accelerated and deepened the destruction of nature. In the emptiness that prevailed, religious and political fundamentalism have become violent and excluding in their own specific ways. Anyhow, struggle against inequalities of all kinds is still a huge flag of unifying potential at a worldwide scale, as illustrated by recent processes like the World Social Forum, and the new and surprising citizen eruptions around the globe. This struggle is closely associated with the emergence of different identities and collective subjects, in a new way of making politics, in this dynamic mosaic of multiple possibilities that planetary citizenship offers.

The problem of social inequality concerns relations of strength, relations of power. Its complexity cannot be reduced to the size of monetary income, no matter how blatant the Gross Domestic Product per capita indicators are. The forms of inequality as forms of social domination are an intrinsic characteristic of an industrially productive and consumption-driven civilization. The society of having and accumulating necessarily breeds exploited, excluded and dominated people, and allows only few to accumulate wealth. In order for this to happen, this "machine" privatizes and commercializes, usurps the common and deprives large layers of the population from means to organize and live autonomously, with no other way of subsistence left than to subject themselves to capitalist exploitation. This form of organization and development template of wealth produces, at the same time, social inequality and environmental inequality. It imposes its ideology of consumption to the entire society, makes it a prisoner of business growth, and perpetuates itself in time.

A dimension that should be incorporated in the re-qualification of the social inequality issue is, precisely, environmental destruction. Humankind has already consumed more natural resources—our ecological footprint—than the planet can endure. Today, we're committing an injustice between generations, because we are not giving nature as we have found it, with regenerative capabilities, to future generations. Environmental destruction should be viewed as an aspect of current social inequality. The destruction is socially unequal with some groups and societies being more responsible than others and, what is worse, it takes place to the detriment of current and future generations.

Therefore, associating the fight for social justice to the fight against environmental destruction is vital, since one depends on the other. In order to face social injustice, it is vital to face environmental destruction and the inherent injustice. It is not one or the other. Rather, it is both at the same time. This is to say, you do not face environmental destruction without facing social injustice. One does not occur without the other and this radically re-qualifies social struggles of our time, in the perspective of biocivilization.

Yet, for a more sustainable and fair world, the unification of social and environmental justice struggles is a necessity, but not enough in light of the new paradigm. We're still in an anthropocentric world, of justice among humans, of current and future generations. But what about nature and its integrity? How much does this affect the struggle for justice among humans?

The review of the relation between society and nature has been considered herein the founding condition for a civilization of life: biocivilization. Thus, the issue calls for an ethical reflection and a reflection of a triple-justice: social, socio-environmental and ecological. After all, is there an issue of ecological ethics, of rights and of nature's justice per se, or not? Is this not what we conclude from the cosmic vision of *buen vivir* and deep ecology, in which nature, its various elements, are subjects with rights? Can we be against the immanent right of seeds and animals to fulfill themselves as living beings, a part of life as it is; or against the right of atmosphere and climate not to be changed? How does it all re-qualify the fundamental fight for social justice? No matter how hard these questions are, the search for the proper answers puts us in the path of biocivilization, even if many generations must still handle them (Grzybowski 2011).

2.5. Ethics of Human Rights and Responsibilities

In our political culture, facing injustice, generated or reproduced, and deepened by what I here call dominant civilization, tends to be associated and mixed up with the very idea of access and assurance of human rights. In spite of the legal definition of such rights being a real and important dimension, it is relevant to consider rights in their legitimacy and their expression in different cultures and realities. The constitution of rights is the process of social dispute, which generates rights based on their inclusion in society and on being a full part of it, acknowledged by all, with no discrimination or inequalities. As part of this process, rights constantly qualify societies in which rights are disputed.

Human rights are not privileges. In order to be rights, they must be equal for all men and women, without any discrimination. If they are fit only for a few, for certain groups, classes or peoples, they are expressions of social privileges associated with power. Thus, it is vital to consider the human conditions in a given society as an expression of social relations of power. The struggle for equal rights, even if such rights are not yet acknowledged, qualifies the struggles, the collective subjects and their promoters as well as it transforms the society, its organization, governance and politics. And with such an understanding of rights—as a common of a political culture of rights under permanent construction and dispute, where equal rights must be for all—they become important in social re-engineering, aiming for the sustainability of life and the planet.

Here's where a fundamental issue arises, one that is present in the current political culture of human rights, but has not been stressed enough. There are no human rights without human responsibilities. I have not forgotten state duties and obligations on the issue of human rights for all. What I want to point out is that rights constitute a social and political relation. In order to be seen as a holder of rights, all rights, the condition is to acknowledge the same entitlement to all others. Human rights—as common—refer to both sides of the egalitarian political relation. That is to say, in order to have rights we must, at the same time, be responsible for the rights of all others. This is a shared relation and, as such, a relation of co-responsibility. The growing awareness of human rights and responsibilities, both intra and inter societies, as well as in the relation with biosphere, sheds light on the fundamental issue of interdependence from the local and territorial to the planetary levels. Rights and responsibilities are based upon the acknowledgment of ecological and social interdependence as unavoidable conditions to re-establishing the basis of sustainability for both life and the planet.

In view of the civilization crisis, there are already initiatives to counteract the definitions of a human rights list (the Universal Declaration, many national and international conventions and treaties) with a new human responsibilities list. This could be used as a reference and fundament for the construction of a new paradigm. The risk that should be avoided is to enclose such a construction within current contradictions of deeply unequal relations. For the status quo of the existing capitalist and industrial-imperialist civilization's power, of the privilege of the wealthy, developed and strong, it will be easy to define responsibilities and allocate them to precisely those who are denied their rights by the system itself.

In the scope of imagination and political philosophy for a biocivilization focused on the inclusion of all as well as on the sustainability of life and the planet, a Charter of Human Responsibilities should be elaborated in relation and in parallel to the reconstruction and strengthening of the Human Rights Charter. Moreover, besides the principles and fundaments developed herein, it will be essential to review human rights and human responsibilities in order to integrate the issue of ecological justice, of the biosphere's right to integrity and of the planet's natural regenerative ability. In this sense, human rights and responsibilities are the pillar of a new paradigm. The idea of a Peoples' Charter, already in democratic construction, follows the lead of the proposal made herein. The Peoples Charter mobilizes and motivates many and distinct collective subjects all around the globe. It is becoming an expression of the diversity of peoples, voices, and cultures, that is to say the territories of what we are as humankind. To transform the definition of human rights and responsibilities into a Peoples Charter for a biocivilization can be a way of connecting and potentiating the powers of living citizenship for the herculean task ahead.

2.6. Ethics of Equality, Respect for Diversity, and Individuality

Here we face principles and values that assemble in themselves humankind's cultural constructions and political conquests. It did not happen all at the same time, nor did it involve all peoples. Its conquest derives from multiple, partly historic disputes throughout human history. This is a historic process in which different social groups and classes, from different generations, have engaged in emancipating social struggles, having one or more of these principles and beliefs as reference, thus outlining the social structures and defining the conditions for future life and action.

Today, it is impossible to think of alternatives for humankind and for its relation with the planet without considering the contradictory articulation of these principles and beliefs. It depends on us, with all those historic conquests, to think about the change that may re-embed human society within the planet's integrity as a sustainability condition. To question ourselves about the basis for biocivilization is to interrogate what we humans are willing to review and renounce for the sake and priority of life as a whole.

Equality as a principle forces us to think in a more holistic and planetary manner, both from a human point of view, intra and inter generations, and from a natural point of view. How can we ensure an equal right to life for all humans and all living beings, while knowing that the struggle between living beings is a condition for life itself? From an ethical point of view, there are no better or worse, superior or inferior beings; there are only living beings that are equally interdependent upon one another.

Diversity as a principle and a belief is a relatively recent statement. It is related to an identity that is about being diverse but simultaneously also about being equal. We have brought to the agora of human struggles the multiple forms of creating identities, cultures and options which cannot now be subjected to overwhelming forms of equality. In fact, for equality to be fair it must respect the diversity. Yet social and cultural diversity cannot be a justification for social inequality (Souza Santos 2011). Diversity, from a natural point of view, is the law of life. It is fulfilled in diversity. That is to say, diversity is part of social ethics, environmental ethics and ecological ethics. That is also the reason why this is a fundament of biocivilization: equality in diversity; diversity opposed to homogenization, both social and ecological; diversity as a condition for sustainable life and the planet's integrity; diversity as a form of fulfillment of social equality. This is valid to face sexism, racism, homophobia, and any other form of discrimination.

It is never too much to remember the importance of conquering and building individuality as a condition for emancipation in human history. Sociality, collectivism and interdependence are vital elements of human life. However, to prevent them from becoming instruments of domination, it is crucial that they are conscientiously applied and that individualities do not disappear in them or because of them. To live is precisely this transaction of desires and individual options, with the desires and options of others; it is acknowledging and sharing common principles and beliefs, common goods, common goals. The individual interdependence is nothing more than the ethical and political affirmation of the singular that is the individual experience of living: each of us as part of the collective. It is quite different from the conservative individualism which denies the dimension of being a part of and depending on a collective, and on building our own individuality based on the collective. Individualism is the affirmation of the self-made men that grounds the dominant capitalist civilization, which is male-dominant, homophobic and racist. The survival of the fittest and relies on the ideal of 'more', that is to say more violent, smarter, more competitive. Individualism is, at the most, the denial of the social, of the principles and beliefs that support the collective and individuality. After all, individuality can only exist based on common principles and beliefs, which acknowledge the same right of individuality to each and all of them without exception.

All of these reflections point towards the issue of culture and the importance of cultural diversity for the sustainability of life and the planet. Culture generates individualities, just as culture still allows for a common humanity to be affirmed and for cultural diversity to flourish. Culture is essential for humans to interact between one another and with nature, to enjoy, preserve and regenerate. A vibrant culture is a diverse culture, not the homogeneity imposed by the current overwhelming globalization. Through a diversified culture which values the potential of the people that constitute it, it is possible to aim for the sustainability of life and the planet. This is one of the dimensions that found society, economy and power for biocivilization.

2.7. Ethics of the Transformation Strategy: the Issue of Democracy and Peace

It is not possible to have a biocivilization without an ethics of peace. This is a fundamental condition relating to all principles and pillars mentioned. The imperialism, nationalism, arsenals, wars and violence internalized in culture, in social structures, in the way of organizing power and economy are the foundations of industrial, productive and consumption-driven civilization. Our civilization feeds on conquests, exploitation, the servility of debt, inequality and social exclusion on a global scale, and the intense use of natural resources. In this sense, peace is not merely a goal for biocivilization; it is an essential condition for sustainability where all life forms have their place.

Here, we enter the question about the right strategy for achieving biocivilization. No doubt, dismantling the current domination, in all its forms, and the transformation of relations and cultures, of minds and hearts, are works of political engineering. This will be defined by the making, the process itself, where the search—bold, generous, and motivated by huge dreams and utopias—mobilizes and creates thrust forces.

There's no historic process without moving forces under dispute. The ethical issue in the strategy to adopt is to make disputes in a constructive manner, renouncing the armed violence of any type and betting on peace. From an ethical point of view, the political strategy possible for biocivilization, in light of the fundaments set therein, relates to uncertain and tortuous paths of democracy through a radicalization and democratization of democracy itself, as claimed in the World Social Forum. This is a task that puts the spotlight on active citizenship (Grzybowski 2010a and 2011).

Here we should clarify, before all, a few presumptions and fundaments of reflection I make on citizenship and the democratic issue (Grzybowski 2013b). Democratization, in its more radical and substantive dimension, is the equalization through political action of the asymmetries and inequalities that exist in society. This is the core of its transforming potential. As such, democracy is a method of political action, of dispute among different forces—and even opposite ones—rather than its result. Better yet, in democracy the purposes are sought, reached and qualified according to the democratic method of struggle, the generator of a collective construction process, result of permanent struggle and negotiation, relative losses and wins for all, none ever definitive. Democracy is not a question of efficiency and results, but of how legitimate the process is to obtain them.

Betting on democratization is betting on the virtuous process generated by the radicalization of the democratic struggle method, which transforms the different social struggles—destructive amongst themselves—into construction forces of possibility, in the difference and opposition, at a given historic moment. This is not about sterilizing social struggles. On the contrary, this is about trying to extract from its contradictions the possible advances in terms of rights and democratization. In these struggles, the different collective subjects are acknowledged and legitimated, according to principles, beliefs, rights and common rules, mediated by institutional political power, as expressions of citizenship. In a pact of permanent creative uncertainties, political power itself is renewed as a correlation of the forces in such dispute. From there, the very project of society emerges, as well as the direction we intend to democratically pursue. The laws and the institutions of the state are adjusted, public policies are formulated, and resources are allocated to their implementation.

All relations in society express relations of power in several degrees and forms. To bring collective subjects that live in such relations to the public arena, according to democratic rules, is the condition for full citizenship. In a permanent dispute, democracy acquires a transforming force when it is strengthened by forces that emerge from the core of civil society. It thus becomes more inclusive and more participative in our multiple diversity. The democratic process always implicates more participation and citizen engagement. The quality of such participation, expressed in the comprehensiveness of the diversity of participating subjects and in the constructive radicalism of the disputes between them, defines, ultimately, the quali-quality of democracy itself.

The fundamental changes in societies must always occur in the state/political power or in economy/market or in both at the same time, as Gramsci reminds us (Gramsci 1978). But neither the state, nor the economy *per se* thrust democratization. In democracy, the instituting and constituting force of processes that push and transform the state and economy derive from the civil society and are expressed through active citizenship.

Citizenship is the fundamental right of all people to have (Arendt 2007), without exception. To acknowledge and to act as a citizen is to see yourself as a holder of rights and acknowledge for yourself the same condition as for all others. This implicates co-responsibility, supported by ethical principles and beliefs of freedom, equality, diversity, solidarity and participation, which make up the unifying social concrete that makes substantive democracy possible.

The locus of citizenship *par excellence* is civil society. I see civil society in its sociological and political sense of a constitutive sphere of social life, between market/economy and state/power. It is a sphere in which contradictions incorporated in relations, structures and processes of societies are expressed in the form of competition, dispute or conflict between different collective subjects, organized as associations, organizations, movements, institutions or hegemonic systems, such as the media, churches and universities. They are the holders of interests, ideas, principles, beliefs, and proposals leading them to disputes, pacts and agreements, seeking puissance. However, the civil society is a public space, more or less developed, depending on the historic conditions of each concrete society. It is neither good nor bad, but it is only historically possible, a product of processes and struggles within the considered society. What characterizes historic civil societies is the state of citizenship, not the other way around (Gramsci 1978, 43–54).

Civil societies expand and gain strength due to citizens' action and participation as social trenches for resistance and action that are articulated in networks, coalitions, platforms and forums. Hence there derives a vision of public interest and common good, the public opinion and democratization "waves", the projects of society that feed citizenship movements on different historic contexts of concrete societies.

For the construction of societies founded on biocivilization, the strategy of democracy can open paths and, in the process, transform the current society—its structure and political culture, the principles and beliefs, the way in which power and economy are organized, their destructive relation with biosphere. In democracy, actions and purposes are based on ethics. Such a methodological basis can transform everything we mentioned above on fundaments of biocivilization into a possible utopia, where we imagine, formulate, and act in view of impossible changes that we intend to make possible. The paths to be built are made as we go along, they cannot be defined *a priori* for all of the planet's territories, with its natural and cultural diversity and its peoples in search of the good life. By connecting and acknowledging the interdependence of everybody, we can build, from the local to the global level, a new architecture of power for biocivilization based on the democratic method and peace.

3. Leads and Misleads of Brazil

The construction of a new paradigm does not occur overnight, it is rather a long and contradictory collective historic process that goes through several generations. We're thus facing something that is unpredictable in terms of results. Even if its starting point is possible to determine and a direction is easy to define, this direction can change. A process like this will necessarily be permeated with conflict, will be disputed, will have forwards and backwards movements, advances and setbacks, strategies and path corrections, discoveries and failures. It will involve groups, communities, social movements and citizen organizations, political forces and power instances, economic, cultural and religious organizations, from the local to the global level.

The world will not change without political will and determination applied to the search of a new paradigm. If one looks at today's crisis, the most probable outcome is that the least bold and non-transforming alterations will prevail: adjusting to the dominant and mitigating its impact, without effectively changing its logic. This is the direction pointed, for example, by the most advanced proposal derived from the industrial capitalist system, the new deal of green economy. This is a new front of capitalist business: to continue to grow and to accumulate, rather than a proposal to transform the economy and the power that supports it according to what is defined here as biocivilization for social and environmental sustainability.

In this third part, I take Brazil as an iconic case and analyze it because here the necessary transition is difficult. My premise is that change must be done here and now, starting immediately from within the system. It involves exploiting its contradictions and potentiating the emergence of new possibilities, launching the seeds and caring for the construction of a virtuous democratic transformations process. We must change everyday consumption, life, work and social living practices. We must change the way we care for the fundamental (Raskin 2009). All this must be made from our territories, our communities, our towns or cities. A virtuous change process such as this is not easy to set off, as I will illustrate based on the situation we now live in Brazil.

3.1 An "Emerging" Country?

My starting point and premise for analysis is the "problematization" of the sense of Brazilian "emergence". In the context of the capitalist world order, when some countries or classes and groups are rising, this necessarily implies that others are going down. There's no place for everybody. After all, this is a system based on market-level competition, where there are winners and losers. In order to have winners, the premise is to have losers. This is a system of accumulating a small group of rich, with the necessary exploitation and domination of many others, always generating excluded and poor, within and between countries. Not to mention the environmental destruction caused by the limitless exploitation of resources that drives competition. Simply look at the history of humankind in the last few centuries to see the succession of powers that are dominant at the economic, political and military level, with wars, conquests and colonization, forced migrations and misery, where a new hegemony meant loss of position as previous hegemonic power.

Globalization accentuated this aspect of emergence by radicalizing the imposition of the same logic on a global scale. Now, even a group of great economical-financial corporations is larger than many countries, redefining the very equation of power and of global governance. The ups and downs of capitalism are turned into a development model.

As I have already stated, I do not think this is the type of emerging Brazil the Brazilian and planetary citizenship need or want when they say, for instance in the World Social Forum, that another world is possible (Grzybowski 2013c). Thus, the emergence should be accompanied by changes in the logic itself, by going from competition to cooperation, by the construction of an alternative model that transforms the unfair and predatory capitalist development and by defining an agenda that moves towards the transition for social and environmental sustainability.

My starting point is to recognize that we are speaking of a Brazil that has changed in some respects, while new contradictions are in operation. I am above all concerned with evaluating the country's political conditions in the face of this new situation. I make this analysis for intervention purposes in order to transform reality.

In Brazil, we are not in that situation of wild dictatorship capitalism without counterweights anymore. Nor are we practicing the submissive liberalism of the adjustment agenda, with reduction of the state, de-regulation, bending of rights and the very free market of the nineteen-nineties. From a point of view of social justice we have made, indeed, very important advances. This includes the creation of millions of jobs with labor rights and with reduction of the informality, a substantial increase of the legal minimum wages, an expansion of social security, a phenomenal expansion of access to credit for the purchase of consumer goods and reasonable inflation, among other changes. We have advanced by bringing to the public agenda the old patriarchy and deep racism that impregnate our daily lives, in the family, in territorial segregation, in work, in public practices and institutions. We have the celebrated Bolsa Família (Family Fund) and derivatives, as politics focused on poverty and hunger. After all, with Bolsa Família, as a public policy, we begin facing what is unacceptable from any point of view and ethical value: that there are people dying of hunger in a country known as one of the main barns of the world.

Nonetheless, we must simultaneously recognize that the improvements in social justice have been made without substantially changing the logic of the capitalist development, its structure and exploitation and added-value concentration process that creates assets and wealth of a small, very small, social class, which, however, is super powerful. The dominant development paradigm among us is still that of growth at any cost, with deeply unequal relationships in social and political terms, based on a pollutant mercantilist, industrialist, productivity-driven and consumerist operation, still of a colonialist and dependent scope, with strategic priority in the production of commodities, that accentuates its predatory character over Planet Earth's great natural patrimony we have to care for. Brazil can now be seen as a late example of social democracy hand in hand with capitalism—for being "low intensity", in fact.

I cannot overemphasize how much Brazil is still a deeply unjust country. In spite of being the sixth largest capitalist economy of the world and in spite of the enormous recent progress induced by the labor party government's active allocation-based policies, we have more than 16 million people living in misery with less than half a Dollar per capita a day, and other 30 million with one Dollar a day at the most. I could list several whopping social inequalities in all fields, including gender and racial inequalities. But maybe the largest contrast that well illustrates the dimension of these inequalities was revealed by the very conservative newspaper *O Globo* on October 15th, 2012. According to *O Globo*, 4,640 Brazilian millionaires (those who have at least 30 million US Dollars in their bank accounts), have wealth that amounts to 865 billion American Dollars (in Brazilian Real this is 1,764 trillion Reais). According to the newspaper, "it is superior to the international reserves of all European Union countries together". The per capita income a day for each member of these very rich families amounts to thousands of Dollars! This is Brazil, using a criterion so typical of a world dominated by markets and money.

I will better illustrate my point of view. From a political perspective, we must consider that the subject of poverty in Brazil works as a political divider in the democratization process and in the development options. The debate on development among us has been dominated by the vision and proposals in relation to how much, as a model and strategy, it is allocation-driven and if it is capable or not of dealing with the enormous poverty and the scandalous inequality. This is the debate between the right and the left that counts in Brazil. This is not so in the environmental issue. The debate of environmental destruction in the political arena, when it exists, tends to be dominated by the issue of social justice. The great political game is made around social justice, where even wide traditionally predatory and conservative sections are using the social argument to continue their business that destroys commons. In Brazil, the debate of alternatives to development, of paradigm change, is still very marginal. Fundamentally—and even more in the governments of the Workers' Party of the last eleven years—development is increasingly desired and this in its form of productive-driven and consumerist development, but with the addition of social inclusion. The logic of conditioning everything to growth as a priority did not change. But bringing the subject of social inclusion as a growth qualifier, no matter how small, it is making a huge difference. There we are.

3.2. Contradictions of the "Neo-Development Trend"

From the point of view of globalization, the success of Brazil has been, until now, based on the great natural patrimony we have. A true return of the economy to the primary sector has occurred, with an increasing exportation of natural resources. The products of the agricultural business, of the soy-corn and meat chains (ox, chicken and pig), more coffee, sugar/ethanol, cotton and eucalyptus cellulose paste, and especially mining, make up to around 60 percent of the Brazilian exports. A differential of Brazil is its diversified industry, especially focused on the domestic market. But its industry has lost against the Chinese imports for years. Definitely, we have chosen a dangerous road of dependence on primary products, which precisely define an underdeveloped capitalist country, just like Celso Furtado always reminded us (Furtado 1971).

I believe that, starting from such presuppositions, we needed to think about Brazil's role in the region and in the world, with the National Bank for Economic and Social Development (BNDES) as main funding institution. Brazil presents elements of colonialism, both internal and external. Internal colonialism is present in the way in which the state handles the issues of Amazon and the natives, the extraction-focused peoples and Quilombolas, where the so-called "national interest"—the economic growth sought after at all costs by the great business community, un-territorialized and even denationalized—is above the respect for the rights, identities and cultures of traditional peoples and the supposedly "immense" territories they control. External colonialism in its aggressive form—similar to any Northern or Chinese multinational—takes place through the purchase of assets, control of natural resources and industrial and commercial expansion in other countries. Our brothers and sisters from the Latin Americas and the peoples of Africa, especially Angola and Mozambique, know this all too well.

To illustrate the contradictions of the new Brazilian development, I will point out a few situations that illustrate the rupture between the social dimension and the environmental dimension causing the growth of an economy that destroys and concentrates at the same time. Of course, the problem is more complex and would demand a complete analysis. However, as an example of the difficult transition for what is called biocivilization here, abandoning the productivity-driven and consumerist development trend, the way Brazil faces the energy, mineral and agricultural business issues is revealing (Grzybowski 2013a).

3.2.1. The Energy Issue

Brazil is quickly advancing, as a true emerging power, towards energy solutions that will make it much more polluted than it currently is. In the case of electric power from to hydroelectric power stations we have a relatively "clean" production matrix, at least if we exclude the environmental and social liability the great dams' implantation has created and continues to create today. Thinking of the future and of the growing demand for energy—because, as we are officially told, we are far from the electric energy consumption pattern of the developed countries—new hydroelectric power stations will need to be built. Today, the vast potential of new energy of this type is concentrated on the great rivers of the Amazon region. Can we imagine what it means to build 40 to 60 hydroelectric power stations of medium and large capacity in a territory like the Amazon? How much flooded land, destroyed forest and impact in the climate and biodiversity? How many devastated territories and indigenous people? How many river populations, leaseholders, and forest fruit gatherers will lose their subsistence? The current drama surrounding Belo Monte illustrates what can happen. I have often said and repeat it here that energy and mining combined with wood and cattle exploitation and soy farming, make the Amazon is the Brazilian spoliation and colonization territory. This is internal colonization of the existing power structure and the economy over the Brazilian people—of Brazilians over Brazilians—that takes place for the benefit of dominant social sections of other areas and great business groups with an eye on the world market and, above all, their own pockets.

In the internal political debate, if it is not possible to implement the project of making the Amazon a great supplier of "sustainable" electric power, the argument cried out as a threat is that we will be forced to build more and more thermoelectrical plants! In practice, however, the construction rhythm of thermoelectrical plants in the country shows that the full steam development promoters' priority strategy is this, regardless from more or less hydroelectric power stations. Obviously, the option of the so called "new development trend" is the dual hydroelectric and thermoelectric power stations, as, in fact, the Decennial Plan for Energy 2021 predicts. And, like a ghost, the threat of nuclear energy hangs above us. The moratorium on nuclear energy, after the great disaster in Japan, is merely temporary. What is incredible is that having twice the sunlight of Germany we are so reticent in using this gift of nature and strategically moving forward in terms of solar energy. The same attention is given to the winds that make our palm trees flutter throughout the over eight thousand kilometers of coast, but… these do not generate much electric power.

At the core of the energy issue it is necessary to point out the strategic position of large constructor firms. Large dams and plants are built because this is a good business for contractors. There are studies showing the potential of small hydroelectric power stations focused on the local needs without significant environmental and social impacts, both in terms of implantation and subsequent transmission of the generated energy. Accounting for it all, the small hydroelectric power station's networks are less invasive and much more productive and democratize the economy as well as increase the sustainability of the territories. Except, that is not exactly what we look for in the development that we have: to look at rivers is to look at a natural resource to exploit, and not an integrating basin, a common good shared by all those who live there. I cannot overemphasize that the option for large hydroelectric dams in Brazil was never taken because this is a renewable energy source, but because it is an expansion front for great businesses, induced by the development-driven state, in alliance with business groups.

Yet the energy weakness of emerging Brazil are the oil beds of the pre-salt. As the debate on how to become independent of the fossil energy matrix—the main source of climate threatening gas emissions—escalates around the world, we are quickly progressing towards dipping our fingers, and even our heads, in oil. It is iconic that the oil is seen and greeted as our manumission letter to enter the exclusive club of developed countries. I see in the oil issue our great political challenge to think about leaving this development trap.

The current estimates of oil reserves of the pre-salt amount to 50 to 100 billion barrels. They are dispersed 800 kilometers along the Brazilian coast and they are between five and seven thousand meters below the sea level. All of this reveals that the technological challenge of extracting this oil is enormous, even more after the huge accident in the Gulf of Mexico. Nonetheless, the Brazilian government decided to face the challenge, and an enormous architecture on a legal, institutional, financial, industrial and operational level is being built. All this to go from the current approximately two million oil barrels a day to more than six million in 2020. Obviously most of it would be for export purposes. Brazil will contribute with more than three million barrels per day to maintain things just as they *already* are in our fossil energy dependent world.

The subject is tragic but it is not simple. Until recently, less than ten years ago, Brazil was a country with an industrialization process depending on oil. Still in the nineteen-fifties, a great mobilization around the campaign "O hil is ours" was led by the President at the time, Vargas, to create Petrobras and the oil monopoly. Many things happened from that time, but even today Petrobras is seen as a model of an entrepreneur and development facilitating institution, besides being a symbol for citizenship in Brazil. Petrobras, with the institutional arrangement made by the Lula government, is in the center of the pre-salt operation that reverses the policy of the previous government where private companies were granted exploitation concessions.. Also, since the Lula Government, a "national component" percentage was established on the enormous demands of ships, drilling rigs and everything else from Petrobras, this reanimated an aggressive naval industry. For the pre-salt only, more than 60 large capacity oil tankers—given the distance from the coast—and more than 60 drilling rigs are needed for extraction of oil in high sea. The trade union movement, cradle of CUT and of the Workers' Party, is today the main support force of the oil project.

But there's more. The debate in Brazil is not about whether it is worthwhile to explore the oil or to leave it where it is, on the contrary: The debate is on how to distribute the oil revenue. A new regulatory law was proposed for the whole sector which brings Petrobras back into the center of the operations. This law instituted a sovereign basis under federal administration for the main revenue, a bit in synchrony with what has been made in Norway for social purposes. But there are royalties. Up until now, only states and municipal districts of the extraction/refinery areas received royalties. With the pre-salt, all the federal units (states and municipalities) in the country want to participate in the feast. The confusion in the dispute for the golden eggs of an oil chicken is limiting the political debate about our future based on fossil energy.

In the energy debate and its relationship with the climate issue, it is relevant to closely observe the role of ethanol for vehicles, an area in which Brazil was pioneer. First of all, I must state that the initial motivation to develop the ethanol technology and production on the basis of the sugarcane wasn't environmental, but commercial. Due to the crisis caused by the increase of oil prices in the nineteen-seventies, which greatly affected the fragile balance of the Brazilian external budget, the military regime decided to bet on a viable gasoline substitute to move cars and, with it, to boost the automotive industries installed in Brazil, the important engine of the "Brazilian economic miracle" of the time.

Ethanol was important in the nineteen-eighties and early nineteen-nineties, but it suffered from the relative reduction of oil prices and, above all, from the discovery of oil in the Brazilian coast, allowing for reducing our dependence on imports. The bright side, in environmental terms, was the maintenance of the ethanol mixture with gasoline—something around 20 percent, on average—that had a clear positive impact in cars' emissions, especially in the cities. But the invention of flexible-fuel cars in the beginning of 2000, gasoline or alcohol-powered, or a mixture of the two, allowed the ethanol production to rise considerably, to the point that the Brazilian government began to boast that they had found the ideal formula to face one of the emissions-villains: the growing fleet of vehicles in the world. Actually, ethanol and biodiesel, as their co-relation, are nothing but agricultural business, one of the most important bases of development of emerging Brazil. Its environmental impact, from an emissions point of view, can even be positive, but its social impact is devastating. This introduces the next question.

3.2.2. The Issue of the Agricultural Business

Brazil today depends a lot on the agricultural business as the force of its presence in the world. Of course this means to transform into "comparative advantages"—according to the hard rule of capitalist market competition—the enormous natural patrimony of Brazil, which we must preserve for the balance of the Planet's environment as a whole. If we add mineral extraction to agricultural business, we have ultimately added, in the so-called commodities, a growing dependence on the Brazilian nature exports (land + mines + water + sun). Capital and work do exist, yes, but at the cost of nature.

At least in the export templates, Brazil clearly returns its economy to the primary sector, as a development strategy. In recent years, such a dependence on primary products is increasing. Yet, this is highly technical natural extractivism. In the case of the agricultural business I stress the use of transgenic seeds and improved breeds, the largest consumption per hectare of pesticides in the world, a lot of machinery, productivity increase per hectare. All those "strengths" do not overcome the fact that we are before an extraction trend based on the "comparative advantages" that destroy biodiversity and forests, that contaminate, that produce processed foods of dubious quality and creates an agriculture dependent of modern landowners, or of large business groups, not at all identified with the rural world. After all, the question is: for whom are these advantages created?

We are in fact before a devastating bomb, socially and environmentally. Great landowners are less than 70 thousand, controlling almost 200 million hectares, one fourth of the national territory, the equivalent to more than 2,800 hectares each, on average. They are faced by almost two million families without land, and another two million with little land. Is there a more excluding business? The agricultural business depends on the control of land and its exploitation free from social and environmental control. The recent debate and fight around the new Forest Code in Brazil was illustrative of the political power of agricultural business. The "rural seats" in the National Congress have power to impose whatever they want, having already imposed upon the Congress and the government anything that matters to them.

We are before a development model of agricultural and livestock production that does not leave much room for the family farmers. They exist in large numbers. They resist, in spite of everything. One of their conquests is the present day is the National Program for the Support to Family Agriculture (PRONAF), basically a form of subsidized credit, in a scale of the most precarious to the economically viable. These differentiated credits began in the nineteen-nineties, after a huge mobilization. With Lula's Government, and now Dilma's, this line of public credit grew immensely, reaching almost 20 billion Brazilian Reais in 2013. Also, since the Lula Government, there's a policy in force that establishes official purchases by the National Company of Provisioning (CONAB) of products from family agriculture for public food programs (asylums, special care centers, etc.), with great economic and social impact no doubt. The requirement to buy one third of the food for school meals (48 million free meals a day at the public schools of the country) from local family agriculture has also been established. These are measures in the scope of the "great transformation". But how much are they changing Brazilian agriculture? It suffices to remember that the agricultural business gets more than 140 billion Brazilian Reais in agricultural credit in 2013, which is seven times more than family agriculture gets.

Another relevant aspect of this issue should be mentioned: land reform for landless families. After the growth of struggle and a memorable campaign, in the beginning of the nineteen-eighties, the land reform entered the political agenda. Since the New Republic—the regime that made the transition from the dictatorship to the democracy, established in 1985—we have land reform rehearsals in Brazil. The democratic Constitution of 1988 established legal principles to accomplish the land reform. The political reality of the country, however, is harder. Little was done in terms of land reform all these years. It is hard to say, but in the Worker's Party governments we were always skating, and preferred to support credit instead of offering an effective program that dismantles the antisocial bomb of the social and environmental predator-landowner. Finally, as a conclusion, we can say that the agricultural business is part of the established power, difficult to change from a perspective of more democratic basis, non-excluding and sustainable.

3.2.3. The "Neo-Extractivism Trend"

As part of the neo-development trend, it is necessary to consider the large investment on extraction. I have already highlighted the oil issue above, but the subject is much wider. Iron ore has been a leader in the Brazilian exports, mostly through the Vale Corporation. The "success" of Vale is officially welcomed, but it is not more than one of the most predatory exploitations in the heart of the Amazon. In the name of development, the iron mountain of Carajás is being transferred abroad, to capitalism hungry for good quality iron ore, especially China. Does this make sense? If it does, of course it has nothing to do with social justice and sustainability of the Amazonian people!

Adding to this, the new Code of Mining tries to potentate the "neo-extraction trend", even if the new law contains a proposal to increase royalties. The new Code searches for ways to grant licenses for mining, despite knowing that the bulk of possible mining areas are part of collective indigenous land. A new threat to rights, all in the name of development, is looming.

An aspect that hasn't been discussed in Brazil, but which is relevant, concerns the expansion of the primary-exporter extraction model to the whole South America area, by the project of the Infrastructural Integration of the South America Region (IIRSA). There, the BNDES, with generous financing for the great Brazilian groups, plays a significant part and shows that expansion for the South America region is part of a government policy supporting Brazilian multinationals.

Many other points could be mentioned here. After all, the "neo-development trend" is not something random, but rather a countrywide project. It is a project that points towards more capitalist growth for income distribution. And robust growth, from five to seven percent a year, as president Dilma herself reminded at the Thematic Social Forum, in Porto Alegre, in the beginning of 2012. Will this be sustainable? How to disable such a growth machine on behalf of the new paradigm, of social and environmental sustainability and, at the same time, priority of life, all life, and good life?

3.3. The Non-Sustainability of Development with Social Justice

The great and surprising mobilizations that occurred in June 2013 in the main cities of the country showed how fragile Brazil as an emerging country is, in spite of its celebrated progress in distributive policies. After all, even with all of the changes in course, what the activate citizenship demanded in the streets were exactly what should be the basic rights in a democratic society: transportation, education, health and safety.

Turning social policies into mere conditionalities—which, in order to be feasible, depend on economic growth—ends up defining its own limit in the development change and in the search for sustainability. Even worse, social policies are no longer a strategy at the service of substantive structures and processes of democratization, both in the economic and political sphere, with the inclusion in full citizenship—its true inspiration.

It is not the universalization of rights and social emancipation that are at stake, but it is just a mitigation of the most perverse effects, without a transformation of the excluding logic at the basis of misery, poverty and inequality. The adopted social policies minimize effects, but do not change their causes (Domingues 2013).

It seems that the larger objective of the social policies that have been adopted is the monetary inclusion in the consumption market. This is certainly urgent and necessary for the millions with no or little income, but it is also insufficient. Having money to pay for private school and a health plan is not the same as having quality public education and a Unified Health System (SUS) guaranteed as a universal right. These are two conceptions and situations that are different from citizenship and socio-environmental sustainability. Having facilitated access to credit and reduced Industrial Production Tax (IPI) to stimulate car sales is not guaranteeing the right to collective mobility in a big city, in fact so critical and such an expression of the social injustice among us. Such a policy deepens yet another aspect of the productive and consumerist industrial development, where cities themselves will no longer be a common, but instead will be more adequate for cars than for citizens. The other side of that kind of development based on the individual car is the most perverse aspect of emissions, with pollution and environmental destruction. Income and credit are feeding and pushing economic growth, the same economy that generates social inequality, poverty and misery, and environmental destruction. Substantially, the policies adopted tend to create consumers and not necessarily citizens. Even in the case of the Family Fund program we are not even close to a universal right to citizenship, a quota for everyone in the quality of shared citizenship, a flag of radical democracy and one of the bases of biocivilization.

This point needs to be very clear. Nothing has been made until now to change the Brazilian tax base which is regressive and deeply unjust, and which generates inequality and destruction. Increasing the income tax with new tax rates for maharajahs, landlords and capitalists is not on Brazil's political agenda. The large fortunes continue to grow and the theme of progressive taxation on inheritances remains untouchable. Land continues to be highly concentrated in the hands of few. There are still symbolic assets, especially knowledge and information that are highly concentrated as well. The policy of introducing quotas for universities is a significant step, because it points in the direction of democratization of access to the public university. Nonetheless, PROUNI, that is scholarships for the poor in the private universities, is not going in the same direction. The democratization of access to information among us wasn't more than the popularization of prepaid mobile phones (of very expensive usage, by the way) and the facilitated purchase of increasingly sophisticated televisions to watch TV Globo and something else from our highly concentrated "private business" media. The massive digital inclusion and the democratization of the large hegemonic systems, especially the large media, illustrate the fear of confronting forces that confuse the citizen's freedom of expression with freedom of communication oligopolies. Thus, as a result of policies that avoid the redistribution of assets, either real or symbolic, the great cancer of social inequality, with its multiple roots and forms, continues to corrode the Brazilian society.

After all, in the progressive political field of the Brazilian society, are we satisfied with dignified precariousness or are we still aiming for dignity in the citizenship condition for all men and women? This is the core subject of this debate. Of course the urgency and precariousness of the poverty situation, of unemployment and lack of income to which millions of Brazilians are condemned, all demand quick action. But the problem is to face emergence in such a way that its generating cause does not reoccur. Is this not the time to ask ourselves what needs and can be changed in economy and in power while we take the ethically and politically correct actions that are necessary to face emergence?

3.4. How to Create the Conditions to Search for the New Paradigm?

In Brazil and neighboring countries, the different waves of democratization of the last three decades, which swept dictatorship away, are losing force. We are no longer in the period of creative democracy, established from the nineteen-eighties, when the contradictions and political disputes led to undeniable conquests of rights and democratic practices to the detriment of an authoritarian and excluding dominant culture. Instead, we are now entering a period of low political intensity democracies, ritualized and with visible loss of democratizing substance—that force emanating from the participative incorporation of the dominated ones in politics, living with inequality and in social exclusion, as citizen subjects, holders of rights. We entered a process of more tensions than progresses, of democracy cut-off by old authoritarianism and populism, without power to transform the existing structures. We are satisfied with distributive policies that are important and necessary, no doubt, but subordinate to the objective of promoting economic growth at all costs. The new development ideology, placed above democracy itself, hovers as a threat, both in terms of social justice and human rights, as well as sustainable administration of territories.

We live in a dangerous moment in which, on one side, the formal legality—or, worse, the judicial subjection of politics due to the interpretation of the law by tribunals—and, on the other, the real power of the great economical-financial corporations both suffocate democracy and are a priority over the instituting and constituent legitimacy of the citizens' struggle, and of active citizenship that sprouts from civil society. We are cornered as citizens. We have victories to celebrate when we look back, but we must mobilize and make pressure again. Only then, pushed by citizenship, will democracy be able to exercise its role. The challenge is to create tension on democracy to make it even more democratic.

As I have written, we need to return to the bases, to do what we did in the resistance and defeat of dictatorship. It is a work of popular and citizen education, according to Paulo Freire's libertarian vision (Freire 1987). Only reality is different. We are in a democracy and with an ample space of freedom. We are, besides, before a reality in which emergencies change and the clearest of challenges are guaranteeing rights. Worse, we now see that it is impossible to move forward in terms of rights without, at the same time, moving forward in terms of sustainability, itself being a right. For this, for social justice and sustainability, with democracy, we need another economy and another power, because development as we understand it is not enough. We need to stop thinking in democratizing development, distributing its benefits, because it needs to be transformed, and alternatives to it must be built.

What is the agenda right here and now? How can we act? What political methods and what pedagogy of hegemony dispute can we invent? What role should active citizenship organizations play in this particular matter? What is true is that we cannot sit quietly waiting. We are before political hypotheses and wagers. Are there real alternatives? Are they viable? What political conditions need to be created? What is positive is that a socio-environmental awareness is growing in Brazil. How much it includes the inevitable social subject, without which there's no viable solution, is not yet clear, at least in the public debate—the one that matters as mobilizing ideology to create political movements capable of accomplishing changes. But we are far from a coherent agenda of viable changes. We have ideas, but they are not articulated. The great take from the streets of June 2013 is somewhat auspicious, but not the least organic. It is more of a citizen explosion in the public space than a movement that carries projects for Brazil.

The larger challenge for democracy and sustainability in Brazil, in the perspective of a transformation that matters, is to define an agenda that is based on the ethical and political foundations of the biocivilization and to conquer hearts and minds for such an agenda. The mobilizing of imagination is the first challenge. It is precisely in this essential respect that the current explosion is exciting. We need to hear and listen to the streets in order to understand and transform the demands of citizenship. Our problem and greatest challenge is of a cultural scope: speaking to people's hearts and minds. Transformation is only possible with motivated citizenship and their actions.

My premise is that the socio-environmental indignation and the insurgencies today, all around Brazil, have the emancipating and constructive potential of a new democratizing wave. The socio-environmental struggles bring our young democracy's greater challenge to the spotlight. The democratization won't move forward in the construction of an inclusive society—without discriminations, of sustainability of life and preservation of nature, of good life—if we do not create the political conditions for a democratic transformation of the industrial-productive and consumerist economic development model, that is socially concentrating, excluding and destructive on an environmental level.

This proposal contains an essential element of the transition to a biocivilization paradigm: relocating and re-territorializing the economy and the power. Going back to seeing ourselves as part of the territories, as our fundamental locus, with specific possibilities and limitations, its conflicts and history. As such it is the path to rebuild the relationship between society and nature. This is a path of mutual respect and vital exchanges that reproduce and regenerate *without* destroying. Based on this we can transform larger economic and political structures of power (nationally, regionally and globally) by making them serve the territories in a subsidiary way. The relationship of citizenship with power and economy, in a democratizing wave that promotes the rights of all before and above the predatory capitalist accumulation, is also a path to be pursued.

The dilemmas of the Brazilian democracy are the other side of the new development strategy, which transforms territories of citizenship into territories to be occupied according to business logic of limitless wealth accumulation. The capital invested in a certain territory, almost always with support from the government, is part of a development strategy that is determined, ultimately, by its valuation rate. Thus, it is mandatory to acknowledge from a citizen's point of view that we are before the reinvention of colonialism, where the occupation of territories is not meant to produce goods and services or to serve the life of the local population, with respect for their conditions and their citizenship rights. For the great economic and financial corporations, territories are nothing but differential for their businesses, a plus in the competition among companies for global markets and growing profits. For them, this is about occupying territories with strategies defined outside and outwards. The specificity of the territories is not a limit, but a competitive advantage in a national and global market. For this, the great projects that colonize territories ignore socio-environmental conditionalities and limits of citizenship rights.

In this context, the character of the disputes within and for the territories is changed. These disputes acquire a dimension that extrapolates the territories themselves. The moving contradictions in territories are part of national and worldwide processes. The active local citizenship, starting from civil society, with their forms and dynamics, reacts and fights against the mercantile and exploratory logic of the great development projects imposed from the outside. This we can see in the indigenous resistance in the Amazon, against the great projects and the agricultural business. Another example are the recent mobilizations in the Brazilian cities against the removal of slums or construction of stadiums for the World Cup. Instead, investing in priorities such as urbanization and urban mobility would be an expression of cities as a common for citizenship.

In the resistance struggle and the search for alternatives, in its territorial specificity, a universalizing dimension is contained in terms of rights, which creates solidarity with all the several fights of Brazil and the world against de-territorialized capitalism and its logic of private appropriation, of commercialization and domain. Fights in territories that emanate from the civil societies organized in such territories, in spite of their fragility, face a development submitted to the market and to great corporations, imposed by the political power of capital and its expression in governmental politics, generator of outwards wealth, leaving destruction, garbage, exclusions and inequalities behind. Today's concrete socio-environmental fights possess a democratic potential since they are all territorialized and, at the same time, of a national, regional and worldwide dimension. They end up being embryos of democratic alternatives to development, focused on the defense and enlargement of citizenship rights, of building sustainability for life and of civil societies themselves, against the economy and the power of globalized capital.

The territorial disputes, as defined here, are everywhere, in the cities and in the field. Once we start mapping the socio-environmental fights in Brazil today, we will see that a kind of moving and active citizenship geopolitics is emerging, with anti-systemic characteristics. Its potential for transformation resides there. The different territorialized fights need to be conceived and convinced of their own potential, connecting, articulating, and creating networks and coalitions, creating forums and platforms, feeding on this new wave of revitalization of the democracy in Brazil.

A new democratizing wave is possible starting from the territories in which local citizenship is organized and where it acts against the lunges of new development trends, from the top down and from the inside out. To transform economy and power with a perspective of sustainability of life and substantive democracy, it is necessary to look at them from the local and territorial demands and possibilities and to incorporate the visions and proposals that emanate from active citizenship in the heart of their civil societies. Economy and democracy need to be re-localized, re-territorialized and to work upwards in a subsidiary manner. To strengthen the socio-environmental conflicts in territories is the path to democratization in current Brazil, because it is where subjects that demand their full citizenship are born, and where the fight for the right to see their rights being acknowledged takes place. In civil societies from territories of citizenship ideas and projects emerge to build a radically inclusive democracy, on the economic, social and cultural level, without inequalities or discriminations of any kind. They emerge as a kind of transforming yeast. This is the social and environmental sustainability towards biocivilization that needs to be strengthened.

Works Cited

Arendt, Hannah (2007). *As orígens do totalitarismo*. São Paulo: Companhia das Letras.
Bollier, David and Silke Helfrich (eds.) (2012). *The wealth of the commons: a world beyond market and state*. Armherst: Levellers Press.
Calame, Pierre (2009). *Essai sur l'oeconomie*. Paris: Ed. Charles Léopold Mayer.
Domingues, José Maurício (2013). O Brasil entre o presente e o futuro. *Le Monde Diplomatique* Brasil. São Paulo: 69, http://www.diplomatique.org.br/artigo.php?id=1397 (04.02.2013).
Freire, Paulo (1987). *Pedagogia do oprimido*. Rio de Janeiro: Paz e Terra.
Furtado, Celso (1971). *Teoria e política do desenvolvimento*. São Paulo: Paz e Terra.
Gramsci, Antônio (1978). *Análise das situações, relações de força*. *Maquiavel, a política e o estado moderno*. Rio de Janeiro: Civilização Brasileira, 43–54.
— (1981). *Concepção dialética da história*. Rio de Janeiro: Civilização Brasileira.
Grzybowski, Cândido (2009). Mudar mentalidade e práticas: um imperativo. *Democracia Viva*, 43, 58–62.
— (2010a). Fórum Social Mundial, a construção de um outro mundo possível. *Democracia Viva*, 44, 66–75.
— (2010b). Cidadania, controle social das CT&I e democratização. *Parcerias Estratégicos*, 15(31), 193–215. http://www.cgee.org.br/parcerias/parcerias.php (10.09.2014).
— (2011). *Caminhos e descaminhos para a biocivilização*. Rio de Janeiro: Ibase. http://www.ibase.br/pt/wp-content/uploads/2011/08/Caminhos-descaminhos.pdf (10.09.2014).
— (2012a). *Cuidar, conviver e compartir*. Rio de Janeiro: Ibase. http://www.ibase.br/pt/2012/03 /cuidar-conviver-e-compartir/ (10.09.2014).
— (2012b). *Ética: fundamentos éticos para a biocivilização, Rio+2.Net*. http://rio20.net/pt-br/propuestas/fundamentos-para-a-biocivilizacao (10.09.2014.
— (2012c). *Os "Bens Comuns"*. Rio de Janeiro: Ibase.
— (2013a) *Brasil: como criar as condições para a "Grande Transição"*. Rio de Janeiro: Canal Ibase. http://www.canalibase.org.br/brasil-como-criar-as-condicoes-para-a-grande-transicao (10.09.2014).
— (2013b). Como radicalizar a democratização? Le Monde Diplomatique Brasil. São Paulo: 72. http://www.diplomatique.org.br/artigo.php?id=1456 (07.02.2013).
— (2013c). *O BNDES nas estratégias do Brasil emergente*. Rio de Janeiro: Ibase.
— (2013d). Que Brasil estamos construindo? In Dawid Bartelelt (ed.). *A "nova classe média" no Brasil como conceito e projeto político*. Rio de Janeiro: Fundação Heinrich Böll, 2013.
Helfrich, Silke et al. (2009). *Biens communs: La Prosperité par le partage*. Berlin: Heinrich Böll Foundation.
Raskin, Paul D. (2009). Planetary praxis: on rhyming hope and history. In Stephen R. Kellert and James Gustave Speth (eds.). *The coming transformations*, 110–146. New Haven: Yale School of Forestry and Environmental Studies.

Santos, Milton (1966). *A natureza do espaço: técnica e tempo, razão e emoção*. São Paulo: Hucitec.

Santos, Milton and M. L. Silveira, (2001). *O Brasil: território e sociedade no início do século XXI*. Rio de Janeiro: Record.

Santos, Boaventura de Souza (2003). *Reconhecer para libertar: os caminhos do cosmopolitismo multicultural*. Rio de Janeiro: Civilização Brasileira.

Sprat et al. (2010). *The great transition*. London: New Economics Foundation.

The Common Good and Constitutionalism in Zambia

Leonard Chiti

1. Introduction

The following essay explores how two key principles of the Catholic Social Teaching (CST) can be employed in resolving national challenges such as high poverty and unemployment levels in a country such as Zambia. It first identifies the common good and human dignity as CST principles that can be employed in contributing to reducing poverty in Zambia. It inquires how the institutionalization of the common good can lead to respect for and the protection of human dignity. Human dignity and the promotion of the common good are important guiding principles that can translate these two abstract values into practice when applied to a context of human suffering (Curran 2002). The inquiry is situated within the Christian faith and draws from both biblical sources and the CST to develop its argument. It begins by reflecting on the vision and purpose of God when God created the universe.

1.1. The Vision of God at Creation

The Hebrew Scriptures assert that at the end of the creative endeavors of God, God proclaimed that all he had created was good (Gen 1:31). Part of that good creation was a human being, made in the image of God (Gen 1:27). A human being possesses intrinsic goodness simply because a human being is created by God. Furthermore, the value of a human being consists in God conferring on it His own imprint of being able to reflect and thereby work out causality and ultimately the existence of God. This value does not arise from any meritorious endeavors on the part of an individual and is not granted by a benevolent force or agent. Consequently, human beings are valued and valuable because God created them in his own image and likeness as thinking, reflective creatures. This is the foundation of human dignity.

According to Gen. 2, at the end of creation God placed the rest of creation into the hands of human beings to care for it (Gen 2:15). This means human beings enjoy a pre-eminent place in the order of creation (Aubert 2003). This can be seen as an invitation from God to human beings to participate in the never ending task of safeguarding the creation of the world. In a sense, to be made in the image of God is to be appointed a steward to care for the rest of creation on behalf of God.

1.2. Evidence from Human History

However, human history frequently seems to show that some human beings have more value than others. This understanding is patently untrue. However, what is true is that in practice not all human beings really possess a dignity and value that comes from God; millions of women and men do not enjoy the respect, protection and promotion of human dignity that is their due. This may in many cases be due to the unjust environment they live in, the way their societies are organized and sometimes to unfortunate accidents of history. This is an affront to human dignity and not in line with God's design of a harmonious universe (Curran 2002).

The truth as proposed here is that human dignity is a fact, proven by introspection, observation and the Christian revelation. The paper will also apply the same logic to regional and global realities. The notion of human dignity gives rise to the imperative to protect and guarantee it. This can be accomplished through the promotion and respect of human rights. Mike Pothier, reflecting on the role of the notion of human dignity in the crafting of the South African constitution concludes that:

"Human dignity is this, an intrinsic quality, which we all have in equal measure, which has a necessary social dimension, and which gives rise to human rights." (Pothier 2006, 30)

In the Catholic tradition, the notion of the common good can be seen as the best guarantor of human rights. Therefore, human dignity is best upheld when just societal structures are put in place to promote the common good. Pothier goes on to say that:

"There is no doubt that the courts will continue to link dignity to the exercise of socio-economic rights, thus making the abstract concept manifest in the lives of ordinary people." (ibid., 28)

This paper agrees entirely with Pothier and desires to link human dignity to the ordinary lives of people by placing it at the center of the protection of human rights, especially those rights that pertain to food, education, health, housing and social protection.

Therefore, a deeper appreciation and practical application of both principles, human dignity and the common good, can bring about a flourishing of the human spirit and improved well-being. In this paper we will draw from the work of the Jesuit Centre for Theological Reflection (JCTR) a Jesuit sponsored faith-based organization (FBO) that has over the years employed CST in addressing social and economic challenges the Zambian State faces. The paper taps into some recent research conducted by the JCTR in selected parts of the country to strengthen its main thesis. The JCTR recognizes that CST can serve as an entry point for Christians who are engaged in public policy work, such as for example constitution making.

It is further suggested that institutional arrangements are the key to translating human dignity and the common good into tangible benefits for the people and thereby enhance the appreciation of human dignity. One such institution is a progressive Bill of Rights in a constitution of a country. In the paper we further explore how these two concepts can be applied in the current quest to craft a durable and progressive constitution in Zambia. It posits that the inclusion of human rights such as the economic, social and cultural (second generation human rights) in the Bill of Rights can help lift many Zambians out of poverty. A progressive Bill of Rights is not only a guarantee that the State will undertake serious efforts to allocate resources for poverty reduction, but it is also a sure way to promote the dignity of the citizens of the country. When a good Bill of Rights is enacted its implementation is key towards achieving human well-being.

1.3. Structure of the Essay

The essay is divided into two broad parts. The first part tackles a local situation, making the case that in Zambia, the institutionalization of second generation human rights is key towards restoring the human dignity of many women and men in that country. Second generation human rights are rights such as access to health, education, employment and housing. They are collectively known as economic, social and cultural rights.

It will begin its exploration by providing basic facts and figures and then introduce the notions of common good and the constitution that guide the reflection thereafter.

Following this, the essay will raise the same argument onto a regional and global level. The idea of human needs being met through the promotion of human rights can be raised at a regional and global level since human rights are universal. This argument will lead us to consider a global common good following from the idea that a common good is best guarantor of human rights and by extension the best way to protect the human dignity.

2. A Description of the Zambian Social Order

This inquiry will undertake a brief theological reflection on a particular context, Zambia. It will employ the methodology of the pastoral cycle in identifying the 'root' problem of human suffering in order to propose that one of the solutions is to incorporate principles of the common good into a Bill of Rights of a constitution. The theological reflection begins with insertion, followed by social analysis and then concludes with the application of theological principles (LoBiondo and Rodriguez 2012).

2.1. Insertion (Location)

The Republic of Zambia became an independent sovereign nation in October 1964. Prior to this event, it was ruled by the United Kingdom. The Republic of Zambia is situated in the southern part of the continent of Africa. It lies between 8 and 18 degrees south of the equator and between 22 and 34 degrees east of the Greenwich line. Zambia is a landlocked country sharing borders with eight countries. These are the Democratic Republic of Congo, DRC, to the North; Tanzania, North-East, Malawi to the east and Mozambique to the South East. Others are Zimbabwe and Botswana to the South, Namibia to the South west and Angola to the west. The country spans 752,614 square kilometers (Republic of Zambia 2010).

2.2. Social Situation Analysis

Zambia is richly endowed with many natural and mineral resources. It has plenty of arable land, fresh water resources, fauna and flora and a stable political climate. However, in spite of its potential wealth, the country faces serious challenges in eradicating human misery. Below an attempt is made to do a brief social (situational) analysis of the state of affairs.

2.2.1. Politics

Since independence in 1964, Zambia has experimented with two political systems. At independence, Zambia was a multiparty state holding regular elections every five years. In 1972, the constitution was amended to proscribe the existence of more than one political party. Zambia became a one-party state similar to many communist-inspired regimes in Eastern Europe of the time.

However, in 1991, the country reverted to a multi-party political system and the party in power, the United National Independence Party (UNIP), lost elections to a newly formed Movement for Multi-Party Democracy (MMD). The MMD ruled Zambia for twenty years before being ousted from power by the Patriotic Front (PF). The PF formed a new government in September 2011.

The PF has by and large continued the political style of government of previous regimes. This includes among other things, attempts to weaken opposition parties, silencing critical voices particularly in civil society and controlling the flow of information through the control of the mainstream print and electronic media.

2.2.2. Economy

Zambia's economic history has somewhat mirrored its political history: after independence, the economy was one of the most buoyant on the continent, as is illustrated by the then strength of its currency, the Kwacha, which at the time was trading favorably against major international currencies such as the US Dollar.

However, in the mid-nineteen-seventies, the economic performance plummeted due to the fall in copper prices (the major foreign exchange earner) and the increase in the prices of petroleum products (Chiti 2008).

This was compounded by mismanagement of state owned enterprises (SOEs) which had replaced previous privately owned companies under a centrally planned and run economy.

The country faced with balance of payment problems turned to international financial institutions, (IFIs), to seek financial support to finance its development programs. However, with copper prices remaining low and production having gone down, the country borrowed heavily and by the beginning of the nineteen-eighties, it was heavily indebted. Financial support from IFIs came with conditions such as de-control of prices, privatization of SOEs and other reforms, which put a severe stress on many families who began to experience the effects of a high cost of living, rising unemployment and other hardships. Many of the reforms fell under the rubric of neoliberal economics or market led economics (Satgar, 2014). The combination of a deteriorating economy and increasing hardships on the population was partly the reason for the change in government that took place in 1991.

Following the change in political leadership in 1991, the new government introduced economic reforms that were designed towards restoring a healthy balance of payments situation, reforming the public sector and attracting direct foreign investments. These measures prepared the country for two fortuitous events in the form of the debt cancellation of 2005 and the rise in copper prices of the early nineteen-nineties. These two factors together combined with better weather conditions contributed to a turnaround in economic performance.

In recent times the economic performance has been impressive, registering average growth rates of 5 percent since 2002. This again is largely due to good copper prices (in the range of 8,000 US Dollar per metric ton). The economy has also been boosted by the construction industry and the services sector (Mutesa 2013). Favorable rainfall patterns since the last major drought in 1992 have also contributed to good economic performance through increased production in the agricultural sector.

2.2.3. Social Aspects

In spite of the potential wealth that exists and the recent robust economic performance, social indicators have largely remained disappointing. Zambia's poverty levels stand at 60 percent of the population with unemployment figures of 13 percent of the adult population. Social services such as education and health, although fairly good on paper, do not inspire confidence given regular reports of some children failing to go school, poor infrastructure and the erratic supply of essential drugs at many health posts (JCTR 2013). A study by the JCTR in Monze, a rural town in the Southern province, shows that, in spite of measures by the government to encourage parents to keep their children in school, slightly over half a million children were taken out of school by their parents (JCTR 2013).

The country continues to face a high HIV/AIDS burden of nearly 12.5 percent (UNAIDS 2014). The cost of living, as calculated by the JCTR, for many households in urban areas remains high, standing at over K3 000 (roughly 600 US Dollars) per month, while average wages for low paid workers stand at slightly over 500 Kwacha (roughly 100 US Dollars) (JCTR 2013). Clearly, the country is experiencing a development paradox in being a potentially rich country but with many poor people. The potential that exists to develop the country has not been exploited fully. The neoliberal economic policies that have produced robust growth have not translated into tangible benefits for the majority of the population. This appears consistent with evidence from other regions in the developing world (Satgar 2014).

2.2.4. Cultural Aspects

Perhaps the most significant and successful feature of the Zambian nation is its unity. Since gaining independence from Great Britain in 1964, Zambia has not experienced serious civil strife. This is in spite of the fact that the country has over 70 ethnic groupings. The country has maintained its motto of "One Zambia, One Nation" which has unified these groups. Further, the philosophy of *ubuntu* signifying humanity and kindness towards others is the glue that keeps the nation together. It is truly the envy of its neighbors in the region.

2.2.5. Ecclesiastical Aspects

The treatment of the ecclesiastical context in this essay will be restricted to the Catholic Church because it is within the Catholic Church that CST emerged and developed. It is also widely used in the Catholic Church.

The Zambia Episcopal Conference (ZEC), the umbrella body of the Catholic Church, is a vibrant faith community. The Catholic Church has provided social services over more than a hundred years, and ZEC has since its inception as the mother body of the Catholic Church continued this service. Many of the current national leaders and other influential Zambians owe their current station in life to this service of the Church in providing a firm foundation for human and national development.

Further, the Catholic Church has been active in promoting social justice as evidenced by its effective work through Caritas, the development wing of the conference and its numerous interventions on political and social issues (Komakoma 2003). The Catholic Church enjoys very good relations with other denominations, especially the Protestant churches.

3. Identification of the Major Challenge

From the brief situation analysis above it is apparent that the nation's major challenge is to translate the potential that exists in terms of wealth into tangible benefits for the majority of its population. Zambia has experienced improving economic indicators but a corresponding rise in social indicators has not been observed. A variety of approaches have been implemented to bring human and social development to Zambians. However, these approaches have yielded mixed results. On the one hand, political independence has been won while on the other hand social development has lagged behind.

3.1. A Development Paradox

The brief situation analysis conducted above has clearly demonstrated that in spite of immense potential that exists in Zambia to grow as a prosperous country and the existence of a stable and peaceful nation and recent robust economic performance, the majority of the country's population does not enjoy a decent and adequate standard of living.

Some people have likened Zambia's developmental paradox to that of people sitting on a mountain of gold while starving (Chiti 2013).[1] Many Zambians yearn to live a fulfilled life. They desire to have an adequate

---

[1] Conversations with colleagues at a workshop on the Global Common Good, October 2013.

standard of living that includes good access to food, housing, education for their children and medical services. However, the fulfillment of these desires continues to elude them.

3.2. Judgment

The situation described above can be seen to contradict the vision and purpose of God when God created the universe. Furthermore, this situation is scandalous given the potential of the nation to meet the needs of its population.

Many explanations have been advanced to explain why the country cannot bring about social and human development to its people in tandem with economic development. Often, the popular and conventional explanation of this situation is couched in technical terms. For instance, one national development document, which guided the economic and political processes of the country between 2006 and 2011, the Fifth National Development Plan (FNDP), explained this problem by a lack of 'linkages between capital intensive sectors that have driven growth and the rest of the economy (Republic of Zambia 2006).

However, it is increasingly being recognized that technical solutions alone cannot bring about the desired change. Consequently, the solution to the problem need not always be technical. Normative approaches can also contribute towards resolving crucial national problems. In this paper we will not go into those explanations. However, we shall highlight one possible way for alleviating the country's paradoxical situation.

Real, authentic and sustainable development can only occur in Zambia if the country adopts normative approaches to developing in tandem with technical ones. In a country that has declared itself Christian and reinforced this declaration in the preamble of the country's current constitution; normative issues should be taken seriously in its development agenda. Even though this declaration is controversial, it is nonetheless important to back it up with attempts to conduct national affairs in a Christian way. In the Catholic faith tradition this vision is obviously founded on the Christian scriptures and the social teaching of the Church.

3.3. Reflection: A Christian Vision of Real, Authentic, and Sustainable Development

In this paper we will make a strong case for the alignment of national development efforts to Christian values and principles in order resolve the challenge of human misery amidst plenty. This can be done by adopting a Christian vision of development. The Christian vision of authentic development is firmly founded on God's purpose at creation. God created a human being in his likeness to enjoy the fruits of this earth and thereby reflect his full glory. The Christian scriptures narrates that God out of God's own volition put in place the earth and the universe. This is contained in one of the important parts of the scriptures, which is the book of Genesis. The first two chapters of this book present two traditions that explain the origins of the universe and the human community. The climax of God's creative act is the creation of the human being. God confers on the human being a pre-eminent place in the whole of creation. It reads: "God places the human creature at the center and summit of the created order."

This followed from God's own election that human kind amid all of creation is created in God's own image (Genesis 1 and 2). The pre-eminent place given to human kind by God reflects God's desire that human beings share a dignity that only comes from God by virtue of God's creative act (Genesis 1:27). Made in the image and likeness of God, every human being has basic rights and corresponding duties (Henriot 2001). This notion of human dignity will henceforth become the supreme reference point in the continuing quest to realize God's design of history. It can be argued that in the Christian tradition, the imperative to defend human dignity is the fulcrum around which all human endeavors revolve (Working Group on Human Dignity and Human Rights). It follows then that every human endeavor and institution should emulate God's desire to showcase the dignity of women and men.

4. Human Dignity: Theological and Philosophical Foundation for Human Development

St Irenaeus from the second century reminds us that: "The glory of God is man fully alive." (Marshall 2013, 1) This profound statement links the flourishing of the human condition to the glory of God. This glory is reflected in a human being whose dignity is respected and protected. The converse can also be stated, that when the human condition does not reach its full flourishing, then God's design is frustrated. Human dignity, as already stated, arises not from any human quality or accomplishment nor is it a consequence of any human achievement or attainment. Instead, it is a generous creative endowment from the Creator (Working group on Human Dignity and Human Rights 2012). God further endows the human being with a capacity to think, reflect and love. This sets the human apart from other creatures. Therefore, "being in the image of God the human individual possesses the dignity of a person, who is not just something, but someone." (Pontifical Council for Justice and Peace 2004, 108) This dignity proceeding from God means that no authority or power other than the Creator himself can detract or degrade its value (Mannion 2007). Similarly, human beings and institutions can only cooperate with God when they uphold God's intention in creating human beings. The primary responsibility of any power or authority then becomes to protect and promote this dignity.

This being the case, human dignity becomes a point of reference in any endeavor to promote the flourishing of the human spirit. Anything that detracts from this possibility becomes an affront to human dignity and goes against God's design. The same notion becomes an operating principle in the quest to realize the vision of God: a human being that reflects God's glory. This point is well summed up by Curran who states that:

"[…] God made the human person as master of all earthly creatures to subdue them and use them for God's glory." (Curran 2002, 132)

The protection and promotion of human dignity is the foundation of a human-centered development. Development in the Catholic imagination always has as its goal the flourishing of the human spirit and the protection of human dignity. The suffering of millions of women and men in Zambia through high poverty levels is a distortion of human dignity. Nwaigbo claims that:

"Wherever there is injustice, it is definite that the right and dignity of a human person is not respected and often abused." (Nwaigbo 2012, 22)

The suffering of people from lack of access to food, employment, shelter, clean environment as is the case in Zambia is testament to Nwaigbo's claim.

Human dignity and its concomitant rights do not exist in a vacuum. The intention of this paper is to establish a clear link between human dignity and human rights in their legal-institutional context. According to Pothier, the existence and nature of human dignity implies the existence and demand for respect of human rights. Pothier is drawing his conclusion from the teaching proposed by the Pontifical Council for Justice and Peace which states that:

"the identification and proclamation of human rights is one of the most significant attempts to respond effectively to the inescapable demands of human dignity."(Pontifical Council for Justice and Peace 2004; para 152f.)

Another way of stating the same claim is by suggesting that human rights address situations, arising from human interventions or otherwise, where human beings are unable to live to the full according to their human dignity or realize the full potential of their humanity. Respecting and promoting human rights guards against this (ab) use of power. Respecting human rights and particularly those that contribute to the full flourishing of human beings such as food, water, shelter and employment protects human dignity. The vision of Irenaeus stated above (Marshall 2013) can be realized when human rights are fully implemented to enable human beings to access the conditions that lead to well-being.

Human beings can only enjoy abundant life in an environment where they can exercise their human rights, and the more fully they can exercise these rights, the more fully or abundant their lives will be; that is, their lives will be more in accord with what God wants and what the message of the Christian faith proclaims.

The theological reflection sketched above sets the stage for an identification of a critical matter that will later become the focus for the application of CST teaching on human dignity and human rights. It will also be the locus around which we will develop the argument that human dignity is best promoted through the institutionalization of the common good. The imperative to protect and promote human dignity and human rights emerges from a crisis situation that lays bare the challenge to be tackled.

4.1. The Role of Human Dignity in the Evolution of the Catholic Social Teaching

Before moving into the main thesis of institutionalizing the common good, it is helpful to locate the place and role of human dignity in the corpus of the social teaching of the Church. CST is a body of wisdom that has evolved over a long period of time to provide principles and values to guide the Christian quest to protect and promote human dignity. CST is mainly derived from Scripture, plus the teaching of the Catholic Church, particularly its popes, on the social issues of any given time. It is meant to help Christians examine social, economic, political and cultural matters. "Catholic social teaching focuses primarily on changing institutions and structures." (Curran 2002, 45) CST helps members of the church to reflect on the social and economic challenges of any given era. CST provides guidance on how actions of individuals and groups, local and national leaders, government and non-government actors should contribute to the shaping of just societies, economies, political and legal systems (Chiti 2011). Such guidance proceeds from the truth that "…God-given dignity of the human person has been a central point in Catholic Social Teaching" (Curran 2002, 132).

Central to the CST is the human person (Pontifical Council for Justice and Peace 2004, 580). CST is a vehicle that helps Christians translate God's vision for the universe and human being into a given time and space.

CST roots human dignity in the principle that every person is the living image of a God whose infinity cannot be captured in any single entity or representation (Kelly 2011). It relies on an understanding of human dignity as a gift given freely by God. It is not dependent on any human characteristics or achievement (ibid.).

4.2. Human Dignity and the Rights-based Approach to Development

Flowing from the inherent and inalienable quality of a human being is the notion of human rights. "Respect for human dignity is the basis of all the particular human rights to which individuals have a claim and which they have a duty to uphold" (Hogan 1998, 41). That human beings are created in the image of God is a foundation upon which the notion of right emerges (Donahue 2005). The promotion of human rights serves the protection of human dignity. This is because human rights are 'premised' on the equal worth of every human being. (Häusermann 1998) This draws heavily from international human rights instruments such as the Universal Declaration of Human Rights of 1948. Since 1948, important developments in the appreciation of human rights have evolved. Today, there is wide spread consensus the world over that human rights are universal, interdependent, equal, interrelated and indivisible (World Conference on Human Rights 1993). Consequently, viewing human development from this perspective has become an established norm.

Pope Paul VI defined development as a "transition from less human conditions to those which are more human" (Pope Paul 1967, n 20). To be more human means to have one's dignity respected. This also includes being able to bring one's individual humanity to the fulfillment of what it is capable of and in the process to experience satisfaction and some sense of personal fulfillment. In this sense, one's dignity is promoted through the promotion of human rights. A rights-based approach to development will ensure that human beings have access to those conditions of life that enhance human dignity.

CST, which defines the common good as the "sum total of social conditions which allow people, either as groups or as individuals, to reach their fulfilment more fully and more easily" (Pontifical Council for Justice and Peace 2004, 93) that lead to a fulfilled life, finds a rights-based approach to development in tandem with the intentions of God. A rights-based approach to development culminates in the attainment and enjoyment of human rights and brings out a situation in which the human dignity of every person is recognized and respected. This can only happen where every person can give full expression to the practice and attainment of human rights.

Thus, the rights-based approach to development reinforces the promotion of the common good. CST asserts that the whole social order and its development must invariably work for the benefit of the human person, since the human person comes before every political, economic, scientific, social and cultural consideration (Second Vatican Council 1965). Social structures in society should serve the human being and promote the dignity of every man and woman. Amongst other things this would entail creating the conditions where the poorer members of our population have access to clean water, sanitation, health and education (Mulima 2007).

4.3. Human Rights in the Catholic Social Teaching

The concept of human rights within CST reached a clear articulation, elaboration and systematic treatment around the time of Pope John XXIII (Hogan 1998). Writing in *Pacem in Terris*, the Pope proclaims that: "[A] well-ordered society requires that men [and women] recognize and observe their mutual rights and duties." (John XXIII 1963, 31)

This teaching was elaborated further in subsequent social encyclicals such as *Gaudium et Spes* and *Populorum Progressio*. *Pacem in Terris* presents a comprehensive list of rights which include among others: The rights to life; bodily integrity, food, clothing, shelter, medical care, employment, a just wage, education, to mention but a few (Hogan 1998). It can be observed that this listing of rights corresponds to the aspirations of many people world over. Observance and promotion of these kinds of rights would indeed lead to improved human well-being.

The foregoing sought to demonstrate that in the Catholic imagination, human dignity is a central facet of the creative action of God. It represents a Christian vision of the universe. Human dignity is an imprint of God's own image. Any other creature in material creation, be it animate or inanimate, does not enjoy this privileged status. However, throughout history the design of God has either been ignored, forgotten or frustrated. Consequently, human dignity in many cases has suffered irreparable damage.

5. Human Rights and Constitutionalism

Thus far, we have treated God's vision of the universe through creation; the place of human beings in that creation and the value of the human being subsisting in God's design. We have also introduced the notions of human rights and the rights-based approach to development. It will be the object of this paragraph to place the preceding discussion within the notion of the common good as it relates to economic, social and cultural rights. We will state that the promotion of a common good is one of the best guarantors for human rights. This will then establish a link to a constitution through the provision of a progressive Bill of Rights. Finally, we argue that human dignity is protected through an institutionalization of the common good in a Bill of Rights.

5.1. Social Structures in Society

Any given society is organized in a particular way in order to provide for its people's needs and advance their aspirations. It puts in place structures which can be referred to as institutions that define a particular way of being a nation. Such structures include but are not limited to politics, economics, social, cultural and religious structures. Political, economic, social and cultural structures are established in such a way that they serve the interests of the nation. In contemporary language social structures can be equated to institutions. Some institutions are private while others are public. One such institution (social structure) is a constitution.

At the beginning of this essay, an attempt was made to sketch the social conditions that make up the Zambian nation. It was observed that the structures in place are not serving the enhancement of human dignity.

5.2. The Role of the Constitution

A constitution encapsulates the needs and aspirations of citizens of any society. Simply put, a constitution is the "supreme law of the land" (The Human rights Commission 2008). A constitution is not only the supreme law of the land but it is also a tool that guides the nation in attending to any challenges that may arise.

One prominent Zambian lawyer articulated the challenge facing Zambia in the following words:

"The challenge facing Zambia, following the new democracy, is building a country that is fair to all its citizens; a country in which all individuals feel and know that they are valued members of society and that they have rights in respect of human dignity, development, equality and freedom. As the supreme law of the land, the Constitution needs to reflect these democratic principles." (Mung'omba 2005, 1)

A good constitution ensures that provisions are made to enable people to access and enjoy conditions that promote the fullness of life. It is for this reason that particular attention is paid to provisions within the constitution that allow the enjoyment of human rights. Human rights in many constitutions are especially provided for in a section referred to as a Bill of Rights. Such a section contains a comprehensive listing of fundamental rights and freedoms conferred to all the citizens of the country.

5.3. Economic, Social and Cultural Human Rights – Second Generation Human Rights

One set of rights that need to be emphasized in a good constitution is the second generation of human rights referred to as economic, social and cultural rights. These rights are necessary for creating conditions that are adequate to meeting physical, moral and biological requirements for every category of person. Their objective is to ensure that every person has access to resources and opportunities necessary for an adequate standard of living (JCTR 2004). These rights which include the right to food, water, education, health and a clean environment are meant to guarantee that every citizen has access to the basic social services that their human dignity requires.

Many nation states have signed up to the international covenant for economic, social and cultural rights. However, not all have integrated them into their national constitutions. Zambia is such a state and is yet to integrate these rights. In the current constitution, these rights are provided for in a section that deals with directive principles of state policy and are therefore not justiciable. In addition to this, a recent cross section research in selected parts of Zambia showed that the government is not doing enough to educate its citizens on their rights (JCTR 2013). There is a pressing need to move such human rights into a Bill of Rights. This can only be achieved by carrying out constitutional reforms.

5.4. Economic, Social and Cultural Human Rights and *Pacem in Terris*

Articles 23, 25, and 26 of the Universal Declaration of Human Rights from 1948 acknowledges the importance of ESCRs by providing for the right to employment, education and an adequate standard of living (including access to food, clothing, housing and medical care and necessary social services, and the right to security in the event of unemployment, sickness, disability, widowhood, old age or other lack of livelihood in circumstances beyond one's control). It is interesting to see that a similar list of human rights is provided for in the Social encyclical *Pacem in Terris* dating from 1963. The Universal Declaration of Human Rights and the encyclical *Pacem in Terris* were developed at a time when the world was recovering from the terrible human tragedy caused by the Second World War. Both had as a motivation the prevention of similar catastrophes in future. Therefore, both sought to protect human dignity and to provide conditions that would lead to the complete realization of the fullness of life. The aim was that no person or group of people be discriminated against on any basis whatsoever.

The foregoing has attempted to define some guiding principles drawn from the Christian faith in general and the Catholic Social teaching in particular, as well as contemporary developments in the understanding of human rights in order to prepare the stage to demonstrate why it is imperative to have a good constitution in Zambia. Zambia needs a constitution that can help the majority of Zambians recover their God-given human dignity. The next section will attempt to link these normative and primary principles to an important exercise of crafting a new constitution in Zambia.

6. The Common Good and Constitutionalism in Zambia

Thus far in this essay, a significant amount of space has been dedicated to a discussion on human dignity. The point has been to demonstrate that in any undertaking or human endeavor, the Christian vision takes as a point of departure the recognition and promotion of human dignity. This is seen to be in line with the design of God at the beginning of creation.

It is the firm belief of the author that individual rights are always experienced within the context of the promotion of the common good. This is consistent with the social teaching of the church (Aubert 2003). In the following paragraphs, an attempt will be made to link the common good to the enhancement of human dignity through the enjoyment of human rights and to locate the common good within the exercise of making a constitution in a country such as Zambia.

6.1. The Common Good

CST defines the common good as: the "sum total of all those conditions of social living—economic, political, and cultural—which allow people, either as groups or as individuals, to reach their fulfillment more fully and more easily" (Pontifical Council for Justice and Peace 2004 93).

The common good according to CST describes a situation where men and women have access to opportunities and facilities to enhance their well-being. The promotion of the common good has as its goal the perfection and fulfillment of the human person. This perfection and fulfillment relates to God's original design when he formed women and men in his likeness. It reflects the glory of God.

This perfection and fulfillment will be met when human needs are met. Human needs can be met when human rights are protected. From the discussion above, the common good can be restated as the sum total of those social structures that go towards enhancing the human dignity. Social structures work towards putting in place economic, social, political and cultural conditions that contribute to the improvement of the living standards of the people. The CST definition of the common good can be translated in terms that speak to a contemporary situation of lack of an institutionalized system to enable women and men "readily and fully to achieve the perfection of the human condition." (Compendium, 2014)

The previous section made the case that having a progressive Bill of Rights will assure opportunities for people to access the basic goods and services needed to move "from conditions that are less human to those conditions that are more human." (Paul VI 1967, n20) This was earlier seen as the Christian vision of development as articulated in the encyclical *Populorum Progressio*.

This resonates well with the rights-based approach to development which considers that rights can promote development. These rights are contained in the body of second generation of human rights conventions such as the right to food, housing and employment. Therefore, it can be observed that the promotion of economic, social and cultural rights can aid the promotion of the common good. The promotion of the common good in turn leads to authentic human development. Authentic human development can ultimately promote human dignity. In other words true development can only occur when a comprehensive body of individual rights is incorporated in a Bill of Rights so that such rights become justiciable. The State will be obliged to provide for these rights in much the same way as it provides or facilitates the enjoyment of civil and political rights.

"The protection and promotion of the inviolable rights of man rank among the essential duties of governments" (Vatican Council II, 6). This means when the State fails to show real commitment towards providing for such rights, individual citizens can appeal to the courts of law for redress. This is one reason why the promotion of the common good can be greatly enhanced with a good constitution which is a basic framework for guaranteeing human rights. In this sense the drafting and enactment of a good constitution with a progressive bill of rights can be related to the promotion of human dignity.

6.3. The Common Good and the Need for a New Constitution in Zambia

In the case of Zambia, many Zambian governments since the early nineteen-seventies have attempted to craft a constitution acceptable to the Zambian people. In the last twenty years alone the country has on several occasions attempted to draw up a new constitution. Many of these attempts have failed because no sufficient consideration was given to ensuring that there were provisions in the constitution that would promote the common good and to having sufficient guarantees to protect and promote human dignity.

The current constitution is an outcome of several amendments to the independence constitution of 1964. It has resulted from several amendments taken *ad hoc* to address specific issues that have arisen at different times in Zambia's fifty years of independence. For instance, in 1972, the constitution was amended to accommodate a socialist inspired republic. In 1991, an article forbidding the existence of multiple parties was removed to pave way for a multi-party political system. Further in 1996, the then President inserted two clauses in the constitution that forbade Zambians whose parents were born outside the country ineligible to run for President. The second insertion relates to the declaration of Zambia as a Christian nation.

Many people believe that a completely new home-grown constitution is important. Successive governments from 1991, when the country reverted to multi-party politics from a socialist type of government, have set up constitution review commissions (CRCs) to canvass people's views in an effort to put together a 'people-driven' constitution.

7. The JCTR's Engagement in the Constitution-Making Process in Zambia

The foregoing has attempted to demonstrate that having a progressive Bill of Rights in a constitution can contribute to the promotion of the common good. The common good, it has been stated, has strong links with those human rights that directly meet the needs of the poor. The following will endeavor to show that applying CST principles in practice takes the form of a team of actors inspired by the values and principles of the CST acting in tandem with like-minded stakeholders.

The JCTR, one of the most active civil society groups campaigning for a new constitution, believes that the principles and values of CST can contribute towards ensuring that the legal and constitutional frameworks are just and meet the needs and aspirations of the people. A progressive Bill of Rights can guarantee access to "those conditions […] that allow women and men to more fully and more readily achieve the perfection of their lives." (Pontifical Council for Justice and Peace 2004 93)

The JCTR is a faith-based organization that promotes study and action on contemporary issues in Zambia. It was founded in 1988 to serve as a center that promotes theological understanding of current challenges in Zambia. The mission to promote the fullness of life is in line with the mission of Jesus Christ, which in John 10:10 is stated as "I have come that they might have life and have it abundantly."

The mission of Christ can be translated into modern parlance as a quest to improve the quality of life of people. In the gospel according to Luke, Jesus inaugurates his mission by quoting prophet Isaiah and appropriating the words of the prophet to himself. Thus for Jesus, his mission was in favor of the poor, the sick, those in jail or suffering from other human ailments. He would go about changing their life conditions in a physical and spiritual sense. Thus, the promotion of the fullness of life leads to the protection of human dignity. The bedrock of the JCTR's work is the application of the principles of the CST to contemporary social analysis in order to generate actions which address the challenges faced by many Zambians. The JCTR moves from a study or reflection on first principles to advocating for the setting up of institutions to mediate the movement from theory to action and to motivating actors to intervene in a given context.

The JCTR has been very interested and active in ensuring that a new constitution is enacted. It has contributed to the efforts of crafting a constitution through submissions to CRCs of the past. In recent times, the JCTR led a coalition of civil society organizations (CSOs), to ensure that issues that meet the will and aspirations of Zambians are included in a new constitution. This comes out of a conviction that human dignity can best be promoted in Zambia by having a Constitution that obligates the State to undertake serious measures to promote the common good.

The JCTR's interest in constitution-making stems from its conviction that a constitution is among the best guarantors of human dignity and an effective instrument to protect and promote human rights. A good constitution inspires the citizens of a country to work towards a common vision. Citizens can align their efforts and endeavors towards a mutually shared goal under the banner of national development. Consequently, having a constitution that embraces the Christian vision of development can galvanize national efforts towards paying special attention to the needs of those who cannot help themselves to enjoy a full life. The special attention paid to vulnerable members of our communities is also in line with another principle of CST, which is the option for the poor. In other words, a constitution can in this sense, contribute towards mobilizing national efforts to enhance human dignity by promoting the conditions necessary for the exercise of human rights, that is by promoting the common good.

Individual human rights can best be experienced in the context of the promotion of the common good. A good Bill of Rights in line with CST will contribute towards realizing those conditions of social living, which make it possible for every man and woman to realize the perfection of their humanity. This conviction follows from the teaching of scripture that human beings are made in the image and likeness of God (Genesis 1:27). The teaching of scripture implies that every human being should be able to realize the fullness of their humanity, because they are made in the image and likeness of God. This creative act of God is the foundation of the protection and promotion of human rights. It should be the inspiration of any national developmental efforts.

The JCTR believes that a good constitution will outline the duties and rights of citizens and guarantee the protection and promotion of human rights. The purpose of a good constitution is to define and outline the duties, rights and functions of government and its various organs. It forms an institutional framework that can serve as a basis for the resolution of the many challenges facing a country. This can be done primarily by enshrining in the constitution a progressive Bill of Rights.

7.1. Bill of Rights

The Bill of Rights is an important section of the constitution that outlines the fundamental rights and freedoms of all citizens. The JCTR believes that there can be no integral, sustainable development, as articulated by Pope Pius VI, in *Populorum Progressio*, unless a progressive Bill of Rights is included in the constitution. This Bill of Rights must contain economic, social and cultural rights (Henriot 2008).

Individual rights are always experienced within the context of the promotion of the common good (Mater et Magistra 1961, 65). It is the heart of a constitution. A progressive Bill of Rights is the life-blood of the constitution and by extension the life-blood of the nation. And just as the heart of a human being gives it the life-giving blood, so will a Bill of Rights give the inspiration to a nation to consider the interests and needs of all as a communal undertaking. A constitution that has a good Bill of Rights compels duty-bearers to assure rights-holders that they will enjoy the conditions that make for decent lives. The current Bill of Rights in the Zambian constitution does not include economic, social and cultural rights. While it includes all civil and political rights it completely leaves out economic, social and cultural rights.

For instance, in the 1996 amended constitution, part III of the Constitution of Zambia provides for rights such as:

1. Life, liberty, security of the person and protection of the law;
2. Freedom of conscience, expression, assembly, movement and association;
3. Protection of young persons from exploitation;
4. Protection for the privacy of his home and other property and from deprivation of property without compensation.

In the context of high poverty levels and wide inequalities it is imperative that the State undertake to provide conditions and services to ameliorate the suffering of the majority of its citizens. The incorporation of economic, social and cultural rights will ensure that the State "undertakes to take steps individually and through international co-operation, to the maximum of its available resources, with a view to achieving progressively the full realization of the rights recognized in the present covenant by all appropriate means, including particularly the adoption of legislative measures" (International Covenant on Economic, Social and Cultural rights (ICESCR), art

2(1)). Economic, social and cultural rights should aim at ensuring that every citizen of our country has access to resources, opportunities and essentials for an adequate standard of living (Zambian Civil Organizations 2005). This is what the promotion of the common good entails.

If economic, social and cultural rights are included in the Bill of Rights, the government will be obliged to make clear efforts to meet people's basic needs.

In the proposed constitution which is in draft form, the Constitution provides in clause 62, for rights such as:

(1) A person has the right to
(a) The highest attainable standard of health, which includes the right to healthcare services.
(b) Accessible and adequate housing.
(c) Be free from hunger to have access to adequate food of acceptable quality.
(d) Clean and safe water in adequate quantities and to reasonable standards of sanitation.
(e) Social security, protection, and education (Republic of Zambia 2012, 38).

The above rights are missing from the current constitution of Zambia. If the rights proposed above were to be enshrined in the new Bill of Rights of the Zambian constitution, they could facilitate a significant improvement in the lives of millions of Zambians. This class of rights obligates the government, private enterprises and individuals to respect, protect, and promote the full realization of human dignity. And the above rights represent the sum or part of the sum of those conditions that can lead to the fulfillment and perfection of people's lives, the common good.

8. The Common Good and a Good Constitution

CST reminds us that the State exists to promote the common good. Thus, pursuit of the common good ensures that social conditions are such that every person both benefits from and contributes to the fullness of life. It is when the common good is being pursued that persons can satisfy their own individual needs, especially those that exceed their own capacities to provide for themselves. This is why the JCTR believes that one of the most important ways to promote the common good is to put in place a good constitution that will include economic, social and cultural rights in a Bill of Rights.

Working to put in place a good constitution that reflects the will and desires of citizens is an excellent vehicle of applying the teaching of CST. CST's emphasis on human rights arises from its concern for the dignity of every human person. CST believes that the role of public authorities such as governments is to promote the common good. It follows from this that a good constitution can ensure that the common good is enhanced to meet the challenges and needs of the people. A good constitution is thus an expression of the pursuit of the common good by all citizens. In this respect, a good constitution serves the people. It puts people at the center and ensures that institutions of governance and every other activity are geared towards serving people.

9. The Concept of a Global Common Good

At this juncture in this investigation, is it possible to speak of a global common good? What would a global common good look like? Does a global common good require institutions to be promoted? In an attempt to reflect on the above questions, we will briefly recall conversations that have taken place over the last 20 years on a matter that has come to be known as 'globalization'.

9.1. Globalization

Globalization is a complex notion. It has been defined in a variety of ways and thus constitutes a multi-dimensional notion that can mean many things to many people. Gavin Kitching, while acknowledging the difficulties involved in finding one universal definition for globalization, offers a helpful way of looking at the phenomenon. He describes globalization as a process leading sometimes to a 'global economy' where goods and services are produced globally, consumed globally and distributed globally (Kitching 2001). Even Kitching finds the definition inadequate. However, we can adopt it in our present exercise as a heuristic device towards analyzing what a global common good can be.

The process of Globalization is today accepted without too much difficulty. There is plenty of evidence that many processes in the world today have assumed a global dimension. For instance, advances in information and communication technologies (ICTs) have brought about unprecedented opportunities for instant communication across the globe. It is now taken for granted that an individual residing in China can easily pick up a mobile phone, or open a computer and communicate with someone as far removed from his place of domicile as Chile. Such a conversation might involve negotiation on a business matter or a transfer of money. The world has, to some degree, become a global village. The world has become interconnected and interdependent more than ever before. This phenomenon brings with it a good side and a bad side. Supporters of globalization tend to uphold its positive benefits while detractors tend to focus on its bad side. Many people believe the world has become a global village partly because of the process of globalization. This is positive insofar as it brings people together and facilitates exchange. However, becoming a global village notwithstanding, the process of globalization has its share of critics.

There is no denying that globalization has aided the advancement of the human race. However, it has come under heavy criticism from some quarters. One of the most cited criticisms of globalization is that it is promoting only one version of civilization, namely that of North America. Another concern leveled at the process of globalization today is the asymmetrical flow of goods and services, which tend to move in one direction and not the other. It is a recognized feature of the global economy that manufactured goods tend to flow from the North to the South and raw materials tend to flow in the other direction. This phenomenon has not helped many developing nations to compete favorably in the global economy and reap desired results. Rather, it has helped developed economies to entrench their hegemony over less developed ones. This is a clear case of injustice in economic relations across the globe. More generally, the greatest criticism of globalization targets its uneven effects both across and within countries. Some members of local populations benefit more from globalization than others. It is also a fact that some regions or countries benefit more from globalization than others (Kitching 2001).

Some critics such as Satgar have even gone so far as to blame globalization as the main cause of the impoverishment of some segments of populations in places such as South Africa. He cites the insistence by dominant groups in South Africa and elsewhere on the efficacy of neoliberal economic policies to improve living standards and reduce poverty as a cause of the lack of progress in alleviating the suffering of the people (Satgar 2014). This view has been shared by many other third world intellectuals who have argued that in the late nineteen-eighties and early nineteen-nineties major neoliberal multilateral institutions such as the World Bank and the International Monetary Fund contributed to the sufferings of millions of people across much of the developing world by imposing neoliberal economic measures such as privatization, decontrol of prices and deregulation of markets including labor markets. In sum, even though globalization has many good sides, not every woman or man has access to the good side. Instead, there are millions of women and men who only experience the bad side of globalization. Seen at a global level, globalization for the most part has benefited a few regions around the world while others have experienced the bad side of globalization more than its good side. The developing world tends to experience less of the positive side of globalization and more of its negative side, while the developed world experiences more of the positive side of globalization and less of its negative side. Clearly, the task then is to promote a more equitable distribution of the benefits of globalization. At the same time, it is important to minimize the bad side particularly in regions of the world that bear the brunt of the globalization process. This calls for the development of a global ethic that will contribute towards the reduction of inequalities and level the playing field in terms of allowing equitable participation of individuals and communities in the process of globalization.

9.2. Globalization and the Global Common Good

Following from the conclusion of the last section it is clear that a different approach needs to be taken to ensure that the benefits of globalization are shared equitably within nations and across the globe. The process of globalization perhaps gives us a glimpse of what many citizens aspire to, which is to share in the goods of the earth regardless of being domiciled in different geographic locations. However, as has been pointed out in the section above, very few get to experience 'life in a global village'.

One of the factors giving rise to this uneven distribution of the benefits of globalization is lack of a global ethic to guide the relations and exchanges of globalization. Globalization and its concomitant neoliberal economic paradigm is underpinned by the notion of methodological individualism. This individualistic ethic posits that, as one individual acts in a self-interested fashion and given a particular set of circumstances that allows such an individual to expend his or her endeavors in an unfettered way, such an individual, while prospering, would contribute to a 'trickle down' effect whereby many others would benefit from his or her entrepreneurship. Behind economic globalization lies this individualistic ethic. It is not surprising then to note that globalization tends to benefit some, a few, while leaving out many others. What this clearly points to is the need for a 'global' ethic to guide the distribution of the goods of globalization. In this essay we refer to such a global ethic as a global common good.

9.3. The Global Common Good

Arising from the discussion above and referring to the normative discussions, one can begin to define a global common good as a set of circumstances, earlier referred to as structures, which ensure that conditions exist in a global village that lead to the flourishing of the human spirit and the security of peoples' livelihoods. Such a description of a global common good should be treated with some caution. This is because unlike the "common good" which has a firm foundation in CST, a global common good has not reached an advanced and systematic treatment. However, this should not prevent some discussions of a global common good, given that the theme our paper is underpinned by a desire to serve human dignity through the promotion of human rights. Therefore, in the absence of a 'definition' of the global common good, this author is inclined to raise the discussion on the common good as it pertains to a local environment to a higher level, which is the global reality.

10. International (Global) Human Rights— Instruments in the Service of a Global Good

The discussion in sections 4 and 5 on the importance of institutionalizing human rights to gain some traction on poverty eradication also revealed another important role of institutions. It was shown that a progressive Bill of Rights that includes second generation human rights can mediate positive social change in a country such as Zambia.

Indeed, institutions can play the role of mediating social change. Institutions are a vehicle in that they transmute lofty values and principles into concrete actions. They enable actors at different levels of society to translate visions and goals through strategies and plans into programs that can be carried out at the lowest level of society. Institutions can help put into practice another important CST principle which is subsidiarity. This promotes action at lower levels of society by locally based actors while leaving centrally located actors to focus on the promotion of the common good.

World history shows that at different times in history institutions have emerged that sought to facilitate positive change. One of the oldest institutions that has played a critical mediating role in world history is the Catholic Church. The Church not only transmits the good news that human beings can be redeemed from their self-centeredness and live in harmony with one another but has at different times facilitated practical ways of resolving non-spiritual challenges. The aforementioned CST is the primary mechanism for dealing with pressing matters such as poverty alleviation and the promotion of good governance. It can then be argued that mediating institutions are the key towards resolving critical challenges.

When it comes to promoting a global common good it is important to have key mediating institutions. In the area of human rights the world community has developed key institutions and international human rights instruments that should facilitate the development of a global common good. The Human Rights Council (HRC), part of the United Nations, is a body that seeks to induce respect for and to promote human rights. Using the argument in part 1 as an analogy, it can be argued that when the HRC plays its role of facilitating good performance in human rights application to various human problems it is promoting the global common good.

The following sections will briefly highlight some of the international institutions that have been serving a global common good. They will take an analogous approach by using insights drawn from the first part and applying them at regional and global levels.

10.1. Human rights at regional and global levels

As pointed out earlier, ESCRs are among the fundamental human rights that have been included in the Universal Declaration of Human Rights (1948). There, ESCRs are defined as those human rights relating to the workplace, social security, family life, participation in cultural life, and access to housing, food, water, health care and education.

At a continental or regional level, the African Charter of Human and Peoples Rights (1981) is an institution charged with the responsibility of promoting African peoples and human rights. Africans value communal life and individuals find their fulfillment in community life in as much as the community benefits from the endowments and endeavors of individual members. A famous African saying celebrates this communal ethic in the following saying: "I am because you are."

This saying encapsulates the philosophy of *ubuntu* in that members of a community recognize that meeting the needs of individuals builds a community, and that a community is built by the contribution of its parts (Mahajan, 2009). In fact, Mahajan describes *ubuntu*, in terms strikingly similar to the notion of the common good. "It [Ubuntu] represents humanness, sharing, community or humanity toward others." (ibid)

The common good is built or promoted when the interests of others rank as high as an individual's interest. This notion and other African values find their institutional expressions in the African Charter of Human and Peoples' Rights. This charter is fundamental to the African Union, a political grouping of African states that has come together to promote what might be called 'African common good.' The charter promotes second generation human rights discussed in some detail above.

10.2. International human rights covenants

At the global stage, many nations have signed up to the International Covenant on Economic, Social and Cultural rights (ICESCRs) of the United Nations. However, as noted by some scholars, the institutionalization of these rights in domestic laws varies and in many cases leaves much to be desired.

In her foreword in *Economic, Social and Cultural Rights,* Virginia Dandan argues that "for too many states and even human rights NGOs, ESCRs have long been considered secondary to civil and political rights. While law and policy have widely recognized these rights, it remains far too easy for Governments to ignore their freely-undertaken obligations to secure these rights for those most in need."(Leckie and Gallagher, 1995, 6) It has been argued above that the situation highlighted by Virginia Dandan is currently the status quo in the Zambian case.

10.3. Institutionalizing international human rights

The foregoing suggests that a global common good is possible and can be mediated by regional and global institutions. Institutions such as the United Nations, the World Bank, the International Monetary Fund, the World Trade Organization, to name but a few, could become important promoters of a global common good. At the moment they are perceived by some as serving the interests of some parts of the world as opposed to others.

One important critic of the above institutions is the anti-capitalist social movement called the World Social Forum. It coined a phrase that suggested that "another world is possible" (Stiglitz 2006). It is calling attention to the fact that the neoliberal ideology need not be the only vehicle for delivering development to the majority of the citizens of the world. It is critical to look beyond this ideology and find appropriate ideologies that are country specific to drive the development agenda. Unfortunately, in recent times this movement has run out of steam. However, the quest to move away from rigid conservative economic approaches to resolving world poverty remains imperative.

11. Conclusion

The Christian faith tradition posits that God created the human person and endowed such a being with an inherent and inalienable dignity. This dignity can be debased but not destroyed. The obligation to protect and promote human dignity lies squarely on society. Society can enhance human dignity by putting in place structures and institutions to achieve this goal.

A good constitution is one such structure that can enhance human dignity. This can be done by ensuring that the Bill of Rights which is the heart of any constitution has as comprehensive and adequate a provision of basic rights so as to assure a full life for all inhabitants of a given society. CST provides good principles and values that can assure such a state of affairs. The common good is a key value that can ensure that human dignity reflects the Godhead in society.

Works Cited

The African Forum for Catholic Social Teachings (2006). *Constitution-Making and Human Dignity*. Harare: AFCAST.

Aubert, Roger (2003). *Catholic Social Teaching: A Historical Perspective*. Milwaukee: Marquette University Press.

Chiti, Leonard (2008). *Zambia's diversification debate*. Master's thesis, School of Oriental and African Studies, London.

— (2011). "The Basic Needs Basket and the Catholic Social Teaching." http://dottrinasocialedellachiesa.net/wp-content/uploads/2011/05/CHITI.pdf (5.10.2014).

Vatican Council II (1965). *Declaration on Religious Liberty. Dignitatis humanae*.

Curran, Charles, E. (2002) *Catholic Social Teaching: A historical, theological and ethical analysis*. Washington, DC: Georgetown University Press.

Donahue, John, SJ (2005). "The Bible and the Catholic Social Teaching." In Kenneth Himes (ed.). *Modern Catholic Social Teaching: Commentaries and Interpretations*, 9–40. Washington DC: Georgetown University Press.

Falconer, Alan D. (1987). "Human Rights." In *The New Dictionary of Theology*. Dublin: Gill and MacMillan.

Häusermann, Julia (1998). *Rights and Humanity, a rights based approach to development* London: Rights and Humanity.

Henriot, Peter (2001). "Easter Hope for a new Constitution." Address to SAPN in Lusaka Zambia, Zambia.

Henriot, Peter (2008). "True Freedom cannot be realized in Zambia without Economic, Social and Cultural rights in the New Constitution." Address to the Economic Association of Zambia, Lusaka, Zambia, May 2008.

Hogan, Linda, (1998). *Human Rights*, Dublin: Trocaire.

Human Rights Commission, (2008), *Constitutionalism and Human Rights; 2008 State of Human rights in Zambia*, Lusaka: Human rights commission.

Jesuit Centre for Theological Reflection (2013). *Rural Basket Report.* Lusaka: JCTR.
— (2013). *Urban Basic Needs Basket,* Lusaka: JCTR.
— (2013). *Research on Economic, Social and Cultural Rights,* Lusaka: JCTR.
Kelly, Michael, (2011). *Catholic Social Teaching and the Aids Epidemic,* Lusaka: JCTR.
Kitching, Gavin (2001). *Seeking social justice through globalization.* Pennsylvania: Pennsylvania State University Press.
Komakoma, Joseph, (2003). *The Social Teaching of the Catholic Bishops and other Christian leaders in Zambia.* Ndola: Mission Press.
Leckie, Scott and Anne Gallagher (2006). *Economic, Social and Cultural Rights; A legal resource guide.* Pennsylvania: University of Pennsylvania Press.
LoBiondo and Rodriguez (2012), *Development, Values and the Meaning of Globalization.* Washington, DC: The Woodstock Theological Center.
Mahajan, Vijay (2009). *Africa Rising; How 900 million African consumers offer more than you think.* New Jersey: Pearson.
Mannion Gerard, (2007). "Working and Being: Social Justice and a theology of Workers." In Philomena Cullen, Bernard Hoose, and Gerard Mannion (eds.). *Catholic Social Justice,* 89–126. London: T&T Clark.
Mulima Akapelwa, (2007). "Human Rights: A Contemporary Development Challenge." In Internet Jesuit Center for Development (ed.). *The Development of Peoples; Challenges for today and tomorrow,* 153–164. Dublin: Columba Press.
Marshall, Taylor, (2013). „The Glory of God is man fully alive: Did St Iraeneus Really say that?" http://taylormarshall.com/2013/the-glory-of -God-is-man-alive-did.html (05.10.2014).
Mutesa, Fred (2013). *Situational Analysis,* unpublished manuscript.
Nwaigbo, Ferdinand, (2012). "Integral Human and New Evangelization." *African Eccleisal Review* 54 (2), 14–47.
Paul VI, (1967). *On the Development of Peoples.* Rome: Acta Apostolicae Sedis, 59.
Pontifical Council for Justice and Peace (2004). *The Compendium of the Social Doctrine of the Church.* Rome: Liberia Editrice Vaticana.
Pothier, Mike (2006). "Constitution making and Human dignity: the South African experience." In The African Forum for Catholic Social Teachings (ed.), *Constitution-Making and Human Dignity,* 22–32. Harare: AFCAST.
Republic of Zambia (2008). *The Fifth National Development Plan, Progress Report.* Lusaka: GRZ.
— (2012). *First Draft of the Constitution of Zambia,* Lusaka: Republic of Zambia.
Satgar, Vishwas (2014). *The Solidarity economy, alternative, emerging theory and practice.* Pietermaritzburg: University of Kwazulu Natal Press.
Stiglitz, Joseph (2006). *Making Globalisation Work.* New York: W. W. Norton.
Zambian Civil Society organizations (2005). *Parallel report, Economic, Social and cultural rights.* Lusaka.

The Global Common Good and the Governance of the Mining Sector in the Democratic Republic of Congo

Ferdinand Muhigirwa Rusembuka

In our globalized world, the governance of natural resources is considered as one of the major economic, social and environmental challenges for integral human development. If one looks closely at the current management of natural resources, one discovers an urgent need for a transparent, accountable and equitable management of natural resources in the world and especially in Africa, which accounts for 40 percent of the world's known gold reserves, and 80–90 percent of the chromium and platinum group metals (McKinsey Global Institute 2010, 3). Across Africa, democracy is sinking deeper roots and the accountability that comes with it strengthens the management of natural resources. Economic governance continues to improve as Africa is now seen as having the greatest overall investment potential of all emerging economies globally, with seven of the ten fastest growing economies from 2011 to 2015 in Sub-Saharan Africa: Ethiopia, Mozambique, Tanzania, Democratic Republic of Congo (DRC), Ghana, Zambia and Nigeria (African Development Bank 2012, 2). However, despite these positive macroeconomics indicators, nine African resource-rich out of the twelve countries are at the bottom of the UN's 2013 Human Development Index.

The DRC is regarded as one of the potentially richest countries in the world. It is endowed with 155 million hectares of tropical forest in the world, with agriculture resource estimated at 80 million hectares of arable land; with hydroelectricity Inga power capacity of approximately 100,000 MW, with 55 percent of Africa's reserves of fresh water and with a very rich abundance of around 1,100 different minerals (World Bank 2008). How is it possible that the DRC as one of the potentially richest countries in the world is among the poorest countries on the planet? How can we overcome the resource paradox: resource wealth amid human poverty? How can we promote a better management of the DRC's abundant natural resources to reduce poverty and improve the quality of life of the people?

How can a better governance of the DRC's extractive industry[1] contribute to the global common good? To respond to these important questions, one has to understand the governance of the mining sector in the Democratic Republic of Congo and its contribution to the global common good. In this paper, I will examine, first, the state of the Congolese mining sector; second, the roles and strategies of the stakeholders; third, the global dimensions of Congolese natural resources; fourth, some insights on global common good and close fifth, with perspectives and recommendations.

1. The State of the Governance of the Congolese Mining Sector

In the following section, I will highlight the main features of Democratic Republic of Congo's economy with a growth in gross domestic product, an increase in mining production, a poor human development index and the negative environmental and social impacts of the industrial mining sector.

1.1. Main Features of DRC's Economy

Africa's economy is getting better because of improved macroeconomic policies, increased investment in infrastructure, institutional development, a deepening of financial systems and rising productivity. "Defying the predictions of those who believe that Africa is gripped by a 'resource curse', many resource-rich countries have sustained high growth and improved their citizens' daily lives" (Africa Progress Panel 2013, 96). Despite a weaker global economy with the economic and financial international crisis, Sub-Saharan Africa's growth has remained robust, "averaging more than 5 percent annually over the past 10 years. In 2012, several countries have reached growth by at least 6 percent" (ibid., 14).

Apart from building manufacturing industries, improved management of mining resources could provide the revenues needed for investment in agriculture, food security, employment, infrastructure, health and educa-

---

[1] In this paper, it is about extractive industry and not about artisanal and small scale mining which in DRC has an estimated 3 artisanal miners.

tion. One can hope that African Minerals Development Center—the chief organ to drive continent-wide implementation of the Africa Mining Vision 2050, adopted in February 2009 by the African Union Heads of States and governments—will promote "transparent, equitable and optimal exploitation of mineral resources to underpin broad-based sustainable growth and socio-economic development"(ibid., 96).

The DRC is the third largest country in Africa and the largest among the members nations of the Southern Africa Development Community (SADC). In the mining sector, DRC is the largest producer of cobalt globally, accounting for about 55 percent of the global output in 2012 according to the US Geological Survey Mineral Commodity Summaries 2013 report. It was the second largest producer of industrial diamonds in 2012, contributing about 21 percent of global production. Furthermore, the country boasts some of the highest quality copper reserves globally, with some of the mines estimated to contain grades above 5 percent. The country received about 8 billion Dollars in investment during 2009–2012 (KPMG Global Mining Institute 2014, 2) with the majority being invested in the mining sector. According to Mupepele Monti (2012, 290ff.), the Democratic Republic of Congo is the world leader with three quarter of global cobalt reserves (45 percent), the 3rd largest global iron reserves (5.83 percent), the 2nd largest global copper reserves, the world leader in industrial diamonds (80 percent), holds the 3rd place for pyrochlore (with 6.63 percent of world reserves), 4th place for copper (10.77 percent of world reserves), 5th place for coltan, 7th place for gold and 8th place for tungsten. Within Africa, the DRC ranks as 2nd largest for coal, 5th for gas methane and 6th for oil.

Despite its abundant resource wealth, the majority of the population remains desperately poor, with an estimated GDP per capita of just 241 Dollars in 2013 according to the IMF's most recent estimates (October 2013). According to the 2014 UNDP Human Development Index, the DRC ranks second to last, 186 out of 187 countries. The World Bank's Doing Business 2014 report ranks DRC at the 183rd position out of 189 countries. The Ibrahim Index of Africa Governance ranks DRC 47th out of 52 countries. DRC's poverty rate is 71 percent. The main paradox is the coexistence of the geological scandal and the scandal of poverty.

However, Democratic Republic of Congo's economy has been characterized since the nineteen-eighties by the burden of the external debt which reached 12.3 billion Dollars. On July 1st, 2010, the IMF and the Bank's

International Development Association decided to cancel all external debt after the implementation of the policy measures required to reach the completion point. As a result, DRC will no longer face heavy debt service in relation to its revenues and foreign exchange resources.

A positive economic indicator to be mentioned is a growth in GDP of 7.2 percent in 2012 which reached 8.1 percent in 2013, thanks to mining, trade, construction and agriculture. Also, the "rationalization of macroeconomic policy and stable commodity prices helped to contain inflation, which stood at 1.1 percent, against 2.7 percent in 2012 and a target of 4.0 percent in 2013. Proper coordination of fiscal and monetary policies and the rally in export earnings have also increased foreign exchange reserves at the central bank. Growth performance is expected to reach 8.5 percent in 2014 and 8.6 percent in 2015. It will be driven by mining production (copper, cobalt and gold), the (re-)construction of roads and the energy infrastructure as well as the impact of the agricultural campaign launched in 2012" (African Development Bank, 2014).

There have been several studies and reports on the state of the extractive industry in the DRC[2]. The mining sector is currently challenged by illegal exploitation, the propensity to fraud and corruption, the geological and mining information systems, the cross-border smuggling of minerals, lack of transparency and accountability, insufficient skills for innovation, tax evasion and armed conflict. There are approximately 300 mining companies (in exploration and in production) in the DRC. The major mining companies like Freeport McMoran, Glencore, Lundin Mining, China Railway Group, Eurasian Natural Resource Corporation, Anvil Mining Congo and African Minerals are listed on the stock exchanges in London, Toronto, Hong Kong and New York. There is an increase in mining production: in 2012, DRC was the largest global cobalt producer, the 3rd tantalum

---

2 Among these one may name the UN Panel of Experts Reports on the Illegal Exploitation of Natural Resources in 2003, 2008, 2009, 2010, 2011, 2012, 2013; the Duncan & Allen reports of January 2005, the Lutundula report of July 2005, the review of mining contracts, 5 case studies by Kalala Budimbwa of September 2006, the report on 12 mining contracts of November 2007, the Ropes and Gray report of December 2007, the Mutamba report of September 2009 the report of the Government Committee on the review of mining contracts in the DRC of November 2011, and the analytical study of the DRC Senate on the contribution of the mining sector to the budget of the DRC of July 2013.

produce globally, the 7th tin producer globally, the 8th copper producer globally and the 10th highest gold reserve globally.

Also small-scale mining, despite its production and contribution to the Congolese mining sector, does not lead to significant economic growth for the livelihoods of the local community as testified by a traditional chief[3].

While the macroeconomic indicators are positive and despite its increase in mining production, the social situation in the DRC remains worrying. The labor market remains very small even if the mining sector is the second employer in the DRC with around 50,000 formal employees according to the Oxford Policy Management Report from October 2013. Rampant malnutrition is one of the leading causes of death. Nearly 5 million children remain outside the school system, the quality of which is also questionable. The major challenge facing the country is to ensure that the economy contributes to the human development of the people.

The mining sector is still considered to be the engine of the Congolese economy. In 2010, it constituted 12 percent of GDP and 50 percent of export revenues. In 2012, the contribution of the mining sector to the national budget was around 10 percent (or 800 million Dollars). Despite this major contribution to GDP, the mining sector's contribution to growth and to the national budget remains low, taking into account the increase in mining production and the tax potential.

If we look at current revenues in the mining sector, in 2012, the main sources of mining revenues, in order of size, are as follows: tax on the remuneration of Congolese nationals and foreigners (29 percent), mining royalties (23.23 percent), customs import duties (12.17 percent), value added tax (11.79 percent), income tax (7.36 percent) and annual surface rights by mine (5.59 percent). The return constituted by the main levies specific to the sector (taxes on income and mining royalties) remains low despite an improvement in world prices and an increase in mining production.[4]

---

3 Before 2010, every young person was an artisanal miner and was happy. Since the arrival of the Resource Mining Company, there is no great interest in artisanal mining for the people in the village. Because the Resource Mining Company does not fulfill the requirements contained in the Memorandum of Understanding. This testimony was collected by an Arrupe Research and Training Center staff member in July 2014 during an investigation on conflict minerals in Kalemie, Katanga (DRC).

4 The taxes paid by mining companies not are significant according to the government. One of the objectives of the revision of the June 2002 Mining Code is to increase the taxes from the mining sector. The 2012 report of DRC to ITIE board showed that there

1.2. Environmental and Social Impacts of the Industrial Mining Sector

Environmental governance can be defined as a set of processes, rules, practices and institutions that contribute to the protection, management, conservation and use of biodiversity, ecosystems and various kinds of renewable and nonrenewable natural resources in a way that reconciles sustainable development and poverty reduction. Mining still is a high-risk activity for the environment and the livelihood of the local population living in the area where the mining activities are taking place. In the DRC the 2011 Act on the environment has set up basic principles and policies for the protection, management and conservation of the environment.

The July Congolese Mining Code of 2002 and the Regulations of 2003 stipulate environmental obligations to be fulfilled by mining industries in order to respect and protect the environment. Here are some of these environmental obligations:

- an obligation placed on applicants for mining rights to present an environmental impact assessment and an environmental management plan of the project before they can obtain an operating license (Articles 15, 69, 71, 73, 204 of the Mining Code)[5];
- an obligation for companies in the exploration phase to establish a plan of mitigation and rehabilitation of the environment (Article 203 of the Code), and to undergo an environmental audit every two years (Article 459 of the Regulations);
- an obligation to provide a financial security guarantee that would permit the state to make good any environmental damage in case the company is unable to do so at the end of the project, in the light of regular inspections of mining environmental administration (Article 461 of the Mining Regulations).

The industrial mining sector also has a number of negative impacts at the socio-cultural level, such as the exploitation of man by man, family imbalance, immorality, pollution of the environment, water, air, rivers as well

---

is more transparency both on the part of the mining companies and the Congolese financial institution. This is why on July the ITIE both accepted DRC as a valid member.

5 To obtain a license, a mining title, every mining company should present documents of the environmental impact assessment of its mining project, showing how the company will reduce the negative environmental impact of during the extraction and production phase. This document must be approved by the national DRC minister of mines.

as the relocation of many villages and cemeteries. A study conducted by a group of local researchers in 2012, organized by the Carter Center, analyzed the impacts of two mining investments on the quality of life of the local communities in Lubumbashi: those of Chemaf and Ruashi Mining (Carter Center, 2012). The study identified general trends linked to a lack of consultation, information and access to justice for people living near the sites (the Ruashi case). In the case of the Chemaf mining company, there were serious problems relating to the pollution of water, soil and plants.

In DRC, like in many African countries, the environmental impact assessment and social impact assessment are poorly done. For this reason, "the Yale 2010 Environmental Performance Index listed SubSaharan Africa as the weakest region by far in terms of its environmental management capacity, with countries from the region accounting for 30 of the bottom 50 spots in the list; and for every one of the last six places" (Africa Progress Panel 2013, 87).

2. Roles and Strategies of the Congolese State

In this section dealing with the roles and strategies of the Congolese state, I will lay special emphasis on the role and the strategies of the Congolese state. I will examine the policies, the legislation and administration of the DRC's government in relation to the governance of the mining sector. In DRC, different stakeholders like the Government, the private sector and civil society play a major role in the governance of the mining sector.

The exploitation of natural resources in DRC is a major national issue. The number of new mining companies and local communities affected by the exploitation of resources in the DRC continues to rise. In theory, all of the different stakeholders should act in accordance with Article 58 of the Constitution of the DRC of 18 February 2006, according to which "all Congolese have the right to enjoy the wealth of the nation. The State has the duty to redistribute the wealth of the nation equitably and to guarantee the right to development".

2.1. Government Policy

The DRC Government Program for 2012–2016 set the following objectives: to continue and finalize institutional reforms in order to strengthen the effectiveness of the state; to consolidate the stability of the macroeconomic framework and to boost growth and the creation of employment; to continue the construction and modernization of basic infrastructure (communication channels, schools and hospitals); to improve the living conditions of the population; to strengthen human capital and turn Congolese civil society into a pool of new citizenship; and to strengthen diplomacy and development cooperation.

This program includes a section dealing with the governance of natural resources. According to this section, the foundation on which the social and economic progress of our country is built is a combination of developing processing industries, particularly in the agro-industrial sector, of processing primary products, and of structuring or industralizing. The strategy of developing the industrial sector will focus particularly on the creation of special economic zones, in which—depending on the specific features of each region (availability of raw materials, qualification of the labor force)—processing industries and/or structuring industries will be installed. The DRC joined the Extractive Industries Transparency Initiative (EITI) in 2005, the Kimberley Process (also in 2005), the regional certification system of the International Conference on the Great Lakes Region (ICGLR) in December 2010, and the Organization for the Harmonization of Business Law in Africa (OHADA) in September 2012.

At the conference on good governance and transparency in the DRC's mining sector held on 30 January 2013 in Lubumbashi (Katanga), the Congolese Prime Minister declared that "the main objective of the government will be to stimulate mining production by existing businesses or to start up production with a view to supporting growth and employment."[6] In fact, growth in the Congolese mining production is already evidenced given that copper production increased from 10,000 tons in 2003 to around 940,000

---

6 Mining products objectives are made up as follows: Copper: 500,000 tons in 2011 to 1,500,000 tons by the end of 2015; Cobalt: 120,000 tons in 2011 to 180,000 tons in 2015; Zinc: 19,000 tons in 2010 to 60,000 tons in 2015, Gold: 5,000 Kg in 2011 to 12,000 Kg in 2015, Diamonds: 22 million to 27 million carat in 2015; Coltan: 500 tons per year between 2012-2016, Wolframite: 1,200 tons per year between 2012-2016, tin: 10,000 tons per year between 2012-2016.

tons in 2013 while cobalt production increased from 4,000 tons in 2003 to around 100,000 tons in 2012. The Government's program for 2012–2016 aims at increasing the contribution of the mining sector to the national budget from 9 percent in 2010 to 25 percent in 2016, and the contribution to GDP from 12 percent in 2010 to 20 percent in 2016.

Mention should be made of the signing of the matrix of economic governance between the government, the World Bank and the IMF to ensure the traceability and certification of certain minerals, the 3Ts (tantalum, tin, tungsten) and gold. These efforts are facing the reality of fraud, corruption and tax evasion that must be fought in order to promote transparency and accountability in the mining sector. "With some of the world's richest mineral resources, the DRC appears to be losing out because state companies are systematically undervaluing assets. Concessions have been sold on terms that appear to generate large profits for foreign investors, most of them registered in offshore centers, with commensurate losses for public finance" (Africa Progress Panel 2013, 55).

2.2. Congolese Legislation and Administration

The DRC Mining Code of July 2002 lays down the legal and regulatory framework not only for the tax regime, but also for all the other elements of the management of the mines in the DRC. This Mining Code expresses the various national, regional and international calls and commitments approved by the Democratic Republic of Congo in order to improve the business climate and to promote responsible, effective and sustainable governance in the mining sector.

In order to ensure that the Congolese people actually enjoy the mining resources of their country, it seems to me that it is necessary to revise the July 2002 Mining Code. Why? Firstly, because the implementation of the 2002 Mining Code did not improve the livelihood of the local people; secondly, the new Mining Code must take into account the decentralization process prescribed by the Constitution of 18 February 2006 (articles 2, 9, 58); thirdly, the new Mining Code should include some provisions of SADC (Southern African Development Community) Mining Protocol and the African Mining Vision.

If legislation in response to the challenges of the democratization and sustainable development of the country is progressing along the right tracks, a significant part of the task has yet to be completed if we are to see it actually put into practice by the various stakeholders, in particular by the Ministry of Mines and its main services (both national and provincial) in charge of the management of the mining sector.

2.3. Private Sector

There are two main organizations coordinating the private sector in the DRC: the Federation of the Congolese Companies (FEC) and the Chamber of Mines. The FEC is a patronal union and a non-profit organization. It coordinates all the companies involved in trade, industry, agriculture and crafts. The Chamber of Mines is the main minerals industry association. It represents the collective interests of companies involved in mineral exploration.

The private sector is a key player in the good governance of mineral resources, essential to promoting peace, reducing poverty, and combating corruption and impunity. By implementing a genuine policy of social responsibility, companies will contribute to the social, environmental and economic development of the state and the population. Economically and socially, the mining code defines the appropriate role of mining companies. They thus have the obligation to "improve the well-being of local communities in implementing economic and social development programs and to compensate people when moving their place of residence" (Article 452).

During their work on the revision of the Mining Code, 40 civil society organizations involved in natural resource issues raised the following shortcomings with regard to corporate social responsibility: the lack of respect for the rights of local communities; the lack of a sustainable development plan aimed at improving the economic and social well-being of the communities affected by mining projects during and after operations; the lack of economic justice with regard to the wages of people working in the companies[7]; the lack of public consultation when the environmental and social impact assessments were being carried out; the failure to implement mitigation and rehabilitation plans; negative environmental impacts from mining companies like the pollution of water and air in Lubumbashi and Kolwezi; displacement of families, villages, communities and the lack

---

7 The Governor of Katanga, Moise Katumbi Chapwe, asked mining companies in Katanga to pay workers at least US$100 per month.

of fair compensation to these communities with Banro Corporation in Twangiza (South Kivu). In general, most of the mining companies do not assume their social, economic and environmental obligations towards local communities. It is thus necessary to implement a genuine policy of corporate social responsibility so that companies contribute to the social, environmental, economic and financial state and the population.

2.4. Civil Society Organizations

In the DRC, the number of non-governmental organizations (NGOs) is estimated at over 9,000. Among the thousands of NGOs, there are about fifty working in the field of natural resources. Their effectiveness on the ground depends largely on their training and the expertise of their members. One challenge is the capacity building of their members working in the governance of natural resources sector.[8] It should also work in synergy with organizations interested in these issues, creating advocacy networks at national, continental and international levels.

The NGOs involved in issues of natural resources in 2012 until 2014, took an active part in the ongoing revision of the Mining Law of 2002 by analyzing the mining law and by highlighting the weaknesses of the latter. They proposed 44 amendments to the government and Parliament concerning the vision of mining, the corporate social responsibility of mining companies, the mining law, taxation and the environmental obligations (Propositions d'amendements sur la revision du Code Minier, 2012).

Well-trained NGOs engaged in natural resource issues should work in partnership with the government and the private sector, requiring the State to better regulate the mining sector and from the private sector to fulfill its corporate social responsibility. *Vis-à-vis* the local communities, civil society organizations, should be involved in reinforcing the capacities of local people, empowering them, raising their awareness and responsibility, helping them to become the owners of their sustainable local development within the mining area.

---

8 An initiative in 2011 to fill the gap was the creation of a school for transparency Congolese civil society coordinated by GIZ, CEPAS, Carter Center, Revenue Watch Institute, DAI and ASADHO. The first two weeks of training took place in Kinshasa Cepas and Carter Center, but could not continue due to lack of financial resources.

3. Global Dimensions of Congolese Natural Resources

In this section, I argue that an improved management of Congo's natural resources, namely mines, energy, forest, water and land has potential global dimensions and can contribute to the building up of the global common good for humanity.

3.1. Mining Sector

Experts consider that the current mining industrialization allows the DRC to gradually regain a leading position as one of the great mining powers of the world. With more than 90 percent of the world's cobalt production, it is already by far the world's leading producer of this metal. Industrial extensions underway at Tenke Fungurume Mining, Katanga Copper Mining, and Boss Mining will further consolidate the production of cobalt which is expected to stabilize at around 1,500,00 tons by 2015. Production of copper, of which cobalt is an associated element, is also growing strongly with 522,000 tons in 2011, 600,000 tons in 2012 and 940,000 tons in 2013. It should, however, reach a peak of 2 million tons in 2020, making the DRC number two in the world behind Chile, which has 38 percent, thus becoming one of the top five producers in the world (Mupepele Monti 2012, 297).

In the gold sector, the recovery together with industrial production prospects at AngloGold Ashanti, Kibali Gold, Mwana Africa and Banro Corporation should allow the DRC to reach a peak of 30 tons of gold per annum by 2020, thus becoming the 10th largest producer in the world (ibid.). Capacity constraints and, in many cases, a lack of political leadership and poor management remain barriers to a more effective social and environmental impact management.

3.2. Energy Sector

The DRC has significant hydroelectric resources. The Congo River is the second largest in the world measured by rate of discharge (40,000 cubic meters/second) after the Amazon (200,000 cubic meters/second) but the

Congo's rate of discharge is more regular than that of the Amazon because the Congo follows a course both sides of the Equator.

Its exploitable energy potential for the production of hydroelectricity is estimated at 774,000 kilowatts per hour, equivalent to 66 percent of the potential of Central Africa, 35 percent of the overall potential of the African continent and 8 percent of the annual production potential of the planet. But only 3 percent of this potential is currently 'on line' with a coverage of less than 10 percent across the nation as a whole (World Bank, 2014). The DRC occupies third place in the world after the People's Republic of China and Canada with regard to hydroelectric power. Its potential is equivalent to an exploitable power capacity of approximately 100,000 megawatt of which almost half (44,000 megawatts) is derived from just one site, Inga, which makes this the largest reserve of hydroelectric power in the world. Thus the best solution to the energy deficit that hinders the continent's economic growth might come from the DRC.

The Grand Inga project[9] seeks to harness the potential of the Congo River, sub-Saharan Africa's greatest waterway. International bodies such as the Southern Africa Development Community (SADC), the New Partnership for Africa's Development (NEPAD) and the World Energy Council (WEC) as well as the Central African Power Pool consider it one of the highest priority projects in Africa. The Grand Inga project forms part of a larger endeavor to tap the hydropower potential of the Congo River. "The broader Grand Inga plan is designed to generate 40,000 megawatts, which would be twice the size of the Three Gorges dam in China. US companies have pledged 14 billion Dollars in new projects for Africa during the summit, including the US-backed 'Power Africa' initiative to expand electricity generation across the continent"[10]. The next phase of the Grand Inga project, Inga 3, is expected to cost 12 billion Dollars and produce around 4,800 megawatt of electricity. The formation of public-private partnership arrangements (Agence Ecofin 2011) is envisaged by joining together sub-regional and regional organizations in the electrical energy sector, including

---

9 Two existing dams, Inga 1 and 2, have been in operation since 1972 and 1982 respectively, together generating nearly 1 800 MW.

10 Some financial institutions have committed to support the Inga 3 Project, Three consortiums, from China, Spain and South Korea, have indicated they intend to bid for the Inga 3 project, The World Bank has approved a 70 million Dollar grant to DRC (World Bank 2014b).

the Southern African Power Pool (SAPP), the Central African Power Pool (CAPP) and the Eastern Africa Power Pool (EAPP).

3.3. Environmental Sector

The country contains a large forested area estimated to be around 155 million hectares in size, which is the second biggest expanse of tropical forest in the world. As such, since 2002 the country has been working on implementing its priority reform agenda for the next 20 years with a view to achieving the sustainable management of its forests. Among the various advances, one should also count the large scale protection of natural forests which, in time, should extend to some 40 million hectares, compared to the current figure of 28 million hectares, or 17 percent of the national territory.

The Democratic Republic of Congo is committed to environmental and climate change issues as its forests account for 60 percent of those in the Congo basin and 10 percent of the world's tropical forests. In addition, "the trees in Congolese forests contain 140 giga tons of carbon, making the DRC one of the largest carbons sinks in the world. That is why the DRC is one of the African countries that has made the greatest progress with regard to preparing the REDD strategy" (United Nations Economic and Social Council 2013).

With 47 percent of the forests in Africa and the role that these play in biodiversity, the DRC is a major player in environmental matters. Its tourist sites, especially those that feature its fauna and flora, also make the country an actor in this sector (Enerunga 2004). The Congo basin is the watershed of the Congo River in Africa. It is the second largest river basin in the world, after the Amazon. As is the case with the Amazon basin, it houses one of the richest dense tropical forests in the world in terms of biodiversity and, like the Amazon basin, is suffering deforestation. It covers a surface area of 3,730,500 square kilometers, extending into the following countries: Angola, Burundi, Cameroon, Gabon, Central African Republic, Republic of the Congo, Democratic Republic of the Congo, Rwanda, Tanzania and Zambia.

For these reasons, "the Africa Mining Vision calls for a transparent and inclusive mining sector that is environmentally and socially responsible [...] which provides lasting benefits to the community and pursues an integrated view of the rights of various stakeholders. The document also highlights the critical role of public participation in assessing environmental and social impacts. Translating this compelling vision into practice is vital if Africa is to reap the benefits of the extractive industry boom; the social and environmental" (Africa Progress Panel 2013, 86).

3.4. Agricultural Sector

The Democratic Republic of Congo's arable land is estimated at 80 million hectares, the number two in the world after Brazil. The land can potentially feed two billion souls on our planet, equivalent to Africa (918,014,166 inhabitants) plus the Americas (902,157,549 inhabitants) or Africa plus Europe (734,129,205 inhabitants) plus Oceania (33,594,581 inhabitants) (Kyalangilwa 2008). The amount of arable land represents 34 percent of the surface area of the national territory.

With the amount of arable land available in 2018, central Africa will be able to ensure the sovereignty and food security of its populations that will number more or less 150 million inhabitants. By this time, the DRC will have only 35.2 million of its 80 million hectares of arable land in production. Western powers, very concerned as they are by the gradual fall in oil production, are considering intensifying the production of biofuels. The countries seen as having the necessary agricultural potential are Brazil and the DRC.

3.5. Aquatic Sector

The DRC is sometimes referred to as the "water tower of Africa" since it is home to more than 50 percent of Africa's surface water reserves (UNEP 2011, 4, 10). There are regular and abundant rainfalls and the Congo River has the largest discharge volume in Africa (ibid., 9f.). Paradoxically, only around 26 percent of the total population have access to drinking water (ibid., 27). Taking into account the DRC's current population growth rate of about 3 percent a year, 72 million people will need to be provided with drinking water within the next 18 years. Because of this low level of provision, the drinking water supply and sanitation sector is the subject of much attention from donors, the Congolese authorities and actors within civil society.

During the course of the 'Decade for Water' (1981–1990), Africa has experienced an improvement in water supply, with coverage increasing from 32 percent to 46 percent while, in the case of sanitation, the increase was from 28 percent to 36 percent. Since the end of the decade, however, there has been an absence of growth, and it is the case that more people lack adequate services today than in 1990. In 1994, 381 million people (which correspond to 54 percent of Africa's population) did not always have access to drinking water and 464 million (66 percent) did not have access to sanitation facilities.

These agreements are not part of international law, but they fall under the framework of the Helsinki Rules on the Uses of the Waters of International Rivers. This international guideline adopted by the International Law Association at the 52nd conference held at Helsinki in August 1966 and is now widely implemented in international agreements. Given the inequality of water resources and water consumption in the world, it seems necessary to reconcile the respective needs of farms, local inhabitants and industry. With its Water Partnership Program, the World Bank has been seeking to establish an analytical approach at a global level under which water would be considered a social, economic and ecological good, and the focus would be on establishing an effective technical and institutional framework (World Bank 2014a).

4. Insights on the Global Common Good

After explaining the global dimensions of the Congolese mining resources which can contribute to the building up of the global common good, I would like to share some insights and make explicit, first, my understanding of the notion of integral human development as developed in *Popolorum Progressio* and; second, show how the management of mining resources can be considered a mixed blessing for communities.

4.1. Integral Human Development

Different ideas come to mind with regard to the current practice of development. In fact, the notion of development in our globalized world is characterized by economic growth, environmental degradation, an economy of exchange, free trade, free competition, growing consumerism, wealth concentration, "excessive inequalities of economic power" (Paul VI 1967, para 58), "an economic dictatorship" (ibid., para 59), "the scandal of glaring inequalities" (ibid., para 10) or "the unmerited misery and the inhuman principles of individualism" (ibid., para 67).

The notion of development today is closely connected with the economic and financial international crisis. The link between financial development and economic growth explores the manner in which financial development contributes to economic development. One way of viewing the relationship between the two is to assess the manner in which the human and capital investments can be channeled so that they can produce tangible results that promote economic development. "The grave economic and financial crisis gripping the world today springs from multiple causes. Opinions on the number and significance of these causes vary widely. Some commentators focus above all on certain errors that they consider to be inherent in the economic and financial policies. Others stress the structural weaknesses of political, economic and financial institutions. Still others say that the causes are ethical breakdowns occurring at all levels of a world economy that is increasingly dominated by utilitarianism and materialism. At every stage of the crisis, one might discover particular technical errors intertwined with certain ethical orientations" (Pontifical Council for Justice and Peace, para 2).

A Christian vision of development, articulated by the Catholic Social Doctrine, can help us grasp some insights on the global common good. What is suggested about development, in Populorum Progressio, is neither knowledge nor know-how. It is a vision, a perspective of development. Paul VI states that "development cannot be limited to mere economic growth. In order to be authentic, it must be complete: integral, that is, it has to promote the good of every person and of the whole person" (Paul VI 1967, para 14). As an eminent specialist he has also very rightly and emphatically declared: "we do not believe in separating the economic from the human, or development from the civilizations in which it exists. What we hold important is human being, each human being and each group of human beings, and we even include the whole of humanity" (ibid.).

This vision of development will lead to "the fullness of authentic development, a development which is for each and all the transition from less human conditions to those which are more human" (ibid., para 20). By less human conditions, Paul VI means "oppressive social structures, whether due to the abuses of ownership or to the abuses of power, to the exploitation of workers or to unjust transactions". Conditions that are more human are by contrast "the passage from misery towards the possession of necessities, victory over social scourges, the growth of knowledge, the acquisition of culture, increased esteem for the dignity of others, the turning toward the spirit of poverty, cooperation for the common good, the will and desire for peace, the acknowledgment by men of supreme values, and of God their source and their finality" (ibid., para 21).

Authentic human development is not reduced to simple economic growth. It embraces concerns for all aspects of the lives of peoples. To the peoples who benefit from it, it brings the means of self-betterment and spiritual growth. There can be no progress towards the authentic complete development of human beings without the simultaneous development of the global common good in the spirit of solidarity, mutual support and accountability. Thus, human fulfillment constitutes, as it were, a challenge and an ideal. "But there is much more: this harmonious enrichment of nature by personal and responsible effort is ordered to a further perfection. The need for answers that is not just sectored and isolated, but systematic and integrated, rich in solidarity and subsidiary and geared to the universal common good" (ibid., para 6). A global common good needs a free, stable world economic and financial system at the service of the real economy for all human beings.

Today, the global financial and economic crisis only stresses the importance of finding a way to sustainable and responsible economic activity. To reach this objective, spirituality and ethics have to be restored as a counterbalance to economics and politics. One might therefore conclude with the words of the Pontifical Council for Justice and Peace: "The primacy of the spiritual and of ethics needs to be restored and, with them, the primacy of politics—which is responsible for the common good—over the economy and finance. Economics and finance need to be brought back within the boundaries of their real vocation and function, including their social function, in consideration of their obvious responsibilities to society—for example, that of nourishing markets and financial institutions which are really at the service of the person and are capable of responding to the needs of the common good and universal brotherhood" (Pontifical Council for Justice and Peace, para 10).

4.2. Mixed Blessing for Communities

Resolution 1803 (XVII), adopted by the General Assembly of the United Nations, on December 14th, 1962 provides that States and international organizations shall strictly and conscientiously respect the sovereignty of peoples and nations over their natural wealth and resources in accordance with the UN Charter and the principles contained in the resolution. These principles are set out in eight articles concerning, *inter alia*, the exploration, development and disposition of natural resources, nationalization and expropriation, foreign investment, the sharing of profits, and other related issues. This prerogative is also confirmed in Article 2 of the Charter of Economic Rights and Duties of States which states that "every State has and shall freely exercise full permanent sovereignty, including possession, use and disposal, over all its wealth, natural resources and economic activities".

If one applies this to the case of the mining companies in the DRC, several points can be noted. On the one hand, there have been some 'blessings' with mining operations for local communities in creating jobs, building of some medical centers and hospitals, primary and secondary schools and roads. Some mining companies are contributing to food security by being involved in the agricultural sector like the Katanga province.[11]

On the other hand, in the management of mining activities, "the environmental and social impacts of mining are often poorly understood or perceived as long-term and distant. Many communities continue to experience displacement without adequate information, compensation or recourse to the rule of law as a result of extractive industry investment" (Africa Progress Panel 2013, 87). The majority of the population stays poor and suffers from human rights violations, from polluted air and water, from erosion of forests and soil as well as from toxic and nuclear deposits. "But the operations have wider effects on local communities, which often

---

[11] Moise Katumbi Chapwe, the Governor of the Katanga province has asked the major mining companies to cultivate 500 hectares.

feel excluded from the benefits and the wealth that extractive industries generate, and harmed by the disruption or ecological impacts of extraction" (Africa Progress Panel 2013, 34). This is why the Africa Mining Vision 2050 calls on governments to harness the potential of extractive and artisanal mining, "to improve rural livelihoods, to stimulate entrepreneurship in a socially responsible manner, to promote local and integrated national development as well as regional cooperation" (ibid., 35), managing social and environmental outcomes for increased impact and benefit of the communities and the investors.

I think that a bottom-up and people-centered approach for new democratic procedures is needed in order to sustain the global common good where local communities live out the values of participation, social inclusion, information and solidarity. Social and economic well-being of people should include and sustain democratic procedures in the memorandum of understanding between mining companies and local communities. One can rightly question the saying: What is useful for the individual leads to the good of the community.

One cannot ignore that individual utility or interest do not always promote the common good. In many cases a spirit of solidarity, sharing, cooperation and humanity is called for to transcend personal utility or particular interests for the good of the community. Taking into account the poor socioeconomic situation of the people in the DRC and that up to now local people are not really getting a fair share from mining industry, solidarity is limited to one's family, one's ethnic group, one's tribes or one's community.

Natural resource management can affect social conflict through many different channels. In the Eastern part of the Democratic Republic of the Congo, armed local militia, linked in some cases to neighboring countries, have used mineral revenues of tantalum, tin, tungsten and gold to finance their military operations and to commit human rights abuses and sexual based violence. The ICGLR has set up the six tools[12] of the Regional Initiative against the Illegal Exploitation of Natural Resources. The OECD has drawn up Due Diligence Guidance for Responsible Supply Chains of Minerals from Conflict-Affected and High-Risk Areas. The Due Diligence

---

12 The six tools are: (1) the mechanism for regional certification; (2) harmonization of national legislation; (3) the regional data-base on the flow of minerals; (4) the formalization of the artisanal mining sector; (5) the promotion of the Extractive Industries Transparency Initiative (ITIE); and (6) the early warning mechanism.

Guidance is supported on the ground by the work of the Bundesanstalt für Geowissensschaften und Rohstoffe (BGR)[13], PROMINES[14], USAID and GIZ. Mining companies sourcing from conflict-affected areas in the Democratic Republic of the Congo should consider the new Congolese mining code (art. 8), the OECD Due Diligence and the Dodd-Frank Act as opportunities to mitigate the risk of financing conflicts, to cut off the financial sources of armed and militia, to fight human rights violations and to make multinationals and small scale mining accountable in proving that the origin of minerals from eastern Congo are conflict-free and to control the compliance with the product regulation and the payment of taxes.

4.3. Global Common Good

The common good is common insofar as it is available for all, shared and enjoyed by all. Natural and mineral resources of the DRC are a common good for all the Congolese, men and women, as affirmed in article 58 of the DRC Constitution of 18 February 2006: "All Congolese have the right to enjoy the wealth of the nation. The State has the duty to redistribute the wealth of the nation equitably and to guarantee the right to development." Article 59 of the same Constitution states that "all Congolese have the right to enjoy the common heritage of humankind. The state has the duty to facilitate their enjoyment." Common good corresponds to "fullness of life", "*promotion humaine*", "*buen vivir*", the fullness of human dignity, the improvement of the quality of life for all, for every human being.

Global common good includes the values of inclusion, participation, ecological sustainability, social and economic well-being and solidarity. Every individual and every community shares in promoting and preserving the common good. To be faithful to their human and ethical vocation, communities should take the lead in asking whether the human family has adequate means at its disposal to achieve the global common good. "Recognizing the primacy of being over having and of ethics over the economy, the world's peoples ought to adopt an ethic of solidarity to fuel their action. This implies abandoning all forms of petty selfishness and embracing

---

13 Since 2009, BGR supports the DRC Ministry of Mines to develop a mineral certification system for tin, tantalum, tungsten and gold.

14 Promines is a mining project of the Congolese government financed by the World Bank (50 million Dollars) and DFID (40 million Dollars).

the logic of the global common good which transcends merely passing and limited interests. In a word, they ought to have a keen sense of belonging to the human family, which means sharing in the common dignity of all human beings." (Pontifical Council for Justice and Peace 2011, 47—own emphasis)

More than a mere concept, global common good is rather a question of vision, a question of building a world where every person, no matter what his race, religion or nationality, can live a fully human life, "freed from servitude imposed on him by other persons or by natural forces over which he has not sufficient control; a world where freedom is not an empty word" (Paul VI 1967, para 20).

To promote global common good in a new economic world requires more than mere changes or accommodations but rather bold and creative reforms in three areas, namely free competition, free trade and external debt.[15] First, the "economy of exchange can no longer be based solely on the law of free competition, a law which, in its turn, too often creates an economic dictatorship" (ibid., para 59—own emphasis). In trade between developed and underdeveloped economies, conditions are too disparate and the degrees of genuine freedom available too unequal. The wealth of the rich and the dominion of the strong are increasing, while the poor are left in their misery and adding to the servitude of the oppressed. The free competition of the market, as it operates now cannot contribute in a meaningful way to the global common good.

Secondly, the rule of free trade, taken by it, is no longer able to govern international relations. It has shown its limits with the current economic and financial crisis. "The advantages of free trade are certainly evident when the parties involved are not affected by any excessive inequalities of economic power" (ibid., para 58). There are excessive inequalities that lead to trade among industrially developed countries and developing countries. In fact, highly industrialized nations export for the most part manufactured goods, while countries with less developed economies have only food, fibers and other raw materials to sell.

As a result of technical progress the value of manufactured goods is rapidly increasing and its producers can always find an adequate market. On the other hand, "raw materials produced by under-developed countries in Africa are subject to wide and sudden fluctuations in price, a state of

---

15 For the 3 economic areas, I am largely inspired by an article I wrote on "Development and good governance in the DRC" (Muhigirwa Rusembuka 2008, 626–636).

affairs far removed from the progressively increasing value of industrial products" (ibid., para 57). This means that the efforts made to assist African developing nations on a financial and technical basis are illusory if their benefits are almost nullified as a consequence of the unequal trade relations existing between rich and poor countries.

Thirdly, another obstacle in promoting global common good is the burden of external debt. In fact, "developing countries will no longer risk being overwhelmed by debts whose repayment swallows up the greater part of their gains" (ibid., para 54). Interest rates and time for repayment of the loan could be so arranged as not to be too great a burden on either party, taking into account free gifts, interest-free or low-interest loans, and the time needed for liquidating the debts. And the receiving countries could demand that there be no interference in their political life or subversion of their social structures.

An immense and constant amount of work is to be done towards the integral development of peoples and of every person. The three bold and creative reforms in free competition, free trade and external debt must be re-thought in order to promote global common good which includes integral human development, transcends national goods and promotes a sustainable common good at the local, regional, continental and global levels.

5. Perspectives and Recommendations

For the governance of natural resources, the following perspectives and recommendations[16], if implemented in an effective way, can contribute to building up a new world where global common good is not an utopia, but becomes a reality, a shared value cherished and lived out by many people:

- To protect the dignity of each human person and the rights of communities affected by extractive industry investments, and to respect the environment by assessing the potential social and environmental im-

---

16 The main recommendations come from part V of the recommendations made by the Africa Progress Panel, entitled "Shared agenda for change that benefit all" (Africa Progress Panel 2013, 92-98).

pacts of extractive industry activities, with an emphasis on the improvement of the quality of life of the people and the communities.
- To strengthen and to sustain democratic procedures requiring multinationals to fulfill corporate social responsibility in the economic, social and environmental areas and to re-locate political power in the hands of the people.
- "To conceive of a new world with the creation of a world public authority at the service of the common good" (Pontifical Council for Justice and Peace 2011, 13—own emphasis) which integrates their respective sovereignties and economies of nations for the common good of peoples. It is the task of today's generation to create the new world dynamics for the achievement of a global common good today and for future generations.
- To strengthen African government's transparency and accountability to their citizens. "For too long, African governments have been responding to externally driven transparency agendas. They have been following, not leading." (Africa Progress Panel 2013, 6). It is time to set up rules and mechanisms in order to promote transparency and accountability, and to reduce the gap between the wealth generated by mining resources and the well-being of the African people.
- To adopt a global common standard for extractive transparency: All countries should implement the project-by-project disclosure standards embodied in the US Dodd-Frank Act, the OECD Due Diligence Guidance for Responsible Supply Chains of Minerals, the African Mining Vision, the six tools of the ICGRL, applying them to all extractive industry and to artisanal mining.
- To ensure equity in public spending by strengthening countries committed to fair and transparent equity in mining activities for socioeconomic benefits for the people: "African governments should harness the potential for social transformation created by increased revenue flows. Finance generated by the development of minerals should be directed towards the investments in health, education and social protection needed to expand opportunity, and towards the infrastructure needed to sustain dynamic growth" (Africa Progress Panel 2013, 93).

6. Conclusion

To conclude, the establishment of good governance in the DRC's mining sector will remain a dead letter without a shared strategic vision of the authentic development of the DRC, without effective political will, without the establishment of the rule of law and a democratic culture, without the adoption and implementation of strategies and consistent measures, and without stakeholders in the mining sector playing their part. The achievement of better governance of mining resources will impact positively on the common global good of the Congolese people at national, provincial and local level.

To promote equity in extractive industries in the world, transparency and accountability remain the twin pillars of good governance. "Taken together, they are the foundation for trust in government and effective management of natural resources—and that foundation needs to be strengthened" (ibid., 54). Extractive industries could become a dynamic source of growth for the national economy. What is missing, in many resource-rich countries, is a regulatory institutional environment that attracts investment, protects human rights, respects environmental obligations and promotes health and education.

A good governance of DRC's natural resources in general, particularly the management of its mining resources, of electrical energy from the Inga dam, of its abundant freshwater reserves, of its 80 million hectares of arable land, of its 155 million hectare expanse of forest, of its cultural heritage sites, could contribute to the promotion of the common good in Africa and to the global common good.

In our globalized world, we urgently need people who have the courage and the willingness to serve and to promote the global common good. "The time has come to conceive of institutions with universal competence, now that vital goods shared by the entire human family are at stake, goods which individual States cannot promote and protect by themselves" (Pontifical Council for Justice and Peace 2011, para 12). Cooperation and interdependence between nations and peoples are needed to give birth to and to achieve a global common good for today and for future generations.

Works Cited

African Development Bank Group (2012). "Governors' Dialogue—Long-Term Strategy 2022 Issues Paper." http://www.afdb.org/fileadmin/uploads/afdb/Documents/PolicyDocuments/LTS%20Issues%20Paper%20for%20 Governors%20Dialogue.pdf (16.09.2014).

African Development Bank Group (2014). "Democratic Republic of Congo Economic Outlook." http://www.afdb.org/en/countries/central-africa/democratic-republic-of-congo/democratic-republic-of-congoeconomic-outlook/(16.09.2014).

Africa Progress Panel (2013). Africa Progress Report 2013: "Equity in Extractives: Stewarding Africa's Natural Resources for all." http://africaprogresspanel.org/publications/policy-papers/africa-progressreport-2013/ (16.09.2014).

Agence Ecofin (2011). "Inga: La solution pour eclairer enfin l'Afrique." http://www.agenceecofin.com/inga/2509-1421-inga-la-solutionpour-eclairer-enfin-l-afrique (12.11.2014).

Enerunga, Anselme (2004). "Preserving Biodiversity in the Democratic Republic of the Congo through an Integrated Forest Policy Approach." Paper presented at the UNESCO conference on "Promoting and Preserving Congolese Heritage—Linking Biological and Cultural Diversity", September 16/17, in Paris, France.

KPMG Global Mining Institute (2014). "Democratic Republic of Congo. Country Mining Guide." http://www.kpmg.com/mining (12.11.2014).

Kyalangilwa, Joseph M. (2008). "La République démocratique du Congo peut nourrir toute l'Afrique et les pays de l'Union européenne." In *Horizons et Débats* 8 (27).

McKinsey Global Institute (2010). "Lions on the move: The progress and potential of African economies." http://www.mckinsey.com/insights/africa/lions_on_the_move (12.11.2014).

Muhigirwa Rusembuka, Ferdinand (2007). "Peace and Development in Africa." In International Jesuit Network for Development (ed.). *The Development of Peoples. Challenges for today and tomorrow. Essays to mark the Fourtieth Anniversary of Populorum Progressio*, 54–68. Dublin: Columbia Press.

Muhigirwa Rusembuka, Ferdinand (2008). "Development and Good Governance in the DRC." In Manfred Schulz (ed.), Entwicklungsträger in der DR Kongo, 626-636. Berlin: Spektrum.

Mupepele Monti, Léonide (2012). *Industries minérales congolaises. Chiffres et défis, volume 1*. Paris: Editions L'Harmattan.

Paul VI (1967). *Populorum Progressio*. http://www.vatican.va/holy_father/paul_vi/encyclicals/documents/hf_pvi_enc_26031967_populorum_en.html (16.09.2014.).

Pontifical Council for Justice and Peace (2011). "Towards reforming the international financial and monetary systems in the context of global public authority."

http://www.vatican.va/roman_curia/pontifical_councils/justpeace/documents/rc_pc_justpeace_doc_20111024_nota_en.html#1._Economic_Development_and_Inequalities%20%2816.09.2014%29

United Nations Economic and Social Council (2013). "Forêts: le fnuf considère la RDC comme 'un des plus grands puits de carbone au monde ' et les grands groupes qui exigent l'exécution des engagements liés à la 'crise forestière." http://www.un.org/News/frpress/docs/2013/ENVDEV1348.doc.htm (16.09.2014).

United Nations Environment Program (2011). "Water Issues in the Democratic Republic of the Congo: Challenges and Opportunities." http://postconflict.unep.ch/publications/UNEP_DRC_water.pdf (12.11.2014).

World Bank (2008). "Democratic Republic of Congo: Growth with Governance in the Mining Sector." Report No. 43402-ZR.

World Bank (2014a). "Water Partnership Program." http://water.worldbank.org/wpp (16.09.2014).

World Bank (2014b). "World Bank Group Supports DRC with Technical Assistance for Preparation of Inga 3 BC Hydropower Development." http://www.worldbank.org/en/news/pressrelease/2014/03/20/world-bank-group-supports-drc-with-technicalassistance-for-preparation-of-inga-3-bc-hydropower-development (16.09.2014).

World Bank (2014c). "Transformational Hydropower Development Project Paves the Way for 9 Million People in the Democratic Republic of Congo to Gain Access to Electricity." http://www.worldbank.org/en/news/feature/201403/20/transformationalhydropower-development-project-paves-the-way-for-9-million-people-inthe-democratic-republic-of-congo-to-gain-access-to-electricity (16.09.2014).

Recasting the Development Approach in Indonesia

B. Herry-Priyono

The late Clifford Geertz, an eminent cultural anthropologist whose 'thick description approach' has become part of ethnomethodology, wrote in the early nineteenth-seventies an essay on the mood of the new nations "from Congo to Guyana" in the wake of their independence between 1945 and 1968. As a specialist on Indonesia he captured the mood of the new country under his analytical lens:

"Considering all that independence seemed to promise—popular rule, rapid economic growth, social equality, cultural regeneration, national greatness and, above all, an end to the ascendancy of the West—it is not surprising that its actual advent has been anticlimactic. It is not that nothing has happened, that a new era has not been entered. Rather, that era having been entered, it is necessary now to live in it rather than merely imagine it, and that is inevitably a deflating experience" (Geertz 1973, 234f.).

When the Republic of Indonesia was declared independent by its nationalist fighters in 1945, it inherited both a *beamtenstaat* (bureaucratic state) of the colonial past and a paralyzed state-sector economy as the only aspiration focus for the ascending social classes. Geertz's portrayal captures the ensuing plight of development in Indonesia. As always, history does not consult the convenience of the nationalists. The new nation soon inherited debts totaling approximately 4.3 billion guilders (Kahin 1952, 443). Debt servicing was one of the major problems of how to generate capital for development. The Dutch ex-colony was "saddled with economies which had never been intended to have an internal dynamic of their own or to have powers for self-generation" (Palmer 1978, 13).

This was a predicament that would haunt the development story in Indonesia for many decades to come. From the onset of the new Republic, economic problems had always loomed large on the landscape. When 'development' was used as a catch-all term for the nation building process, its notion slipped into its unfortunate identification with economic development. There is nothing distinctively Indonesian about it. Similar tendencies happened elsewhere.

This study is an attempt to reflect upon this legacy in present-day Indonesia, with special attention to the way the problem has affected the struggle for the common good—no doubt we need to distinguish between genealogy and causality. In particular, this paper will address the following questions. First, how was the notion of development being understood in the differing trajectories of politico-economic conditions? Second, in what way is the idea as well as the conduct of development in present-day Indonesia to be understood? Third, how should this conduct of development be critically re-envisioned in relation to the idea of the common good?

In the light of these questions, this study will suggest the following argument. The key to allying the conduct of development to the idea of the common good rests on the struggle to transform its approach, in that the rent-seeking character of development in Indonesia needs to be replaced with genuine community development. This may appear straightforward at first glance. As will be shown, however, this line of proposal involves some conceptual recasting that is likely to be at the core of any agenda to forge beneficial links between development and the common good.

This study will be organized into three parts. The first section deals with a genealogy of how the notion of development has been understood in Indonesia. Since genealogy is not the principal aim, what will be presented is necessarily schematic and serves only insofar as it helps us understand the main issue under question. The second section will discuss how development in Indonesia has gradually degenerated into its present-day rent-seeking character. In this part we will be presented with the current problems as to why the present conduct is detrimental to the idea of development, let alone to that of the common good. The third part will outline a conceptual proposal as how to envision the direction of necessary changes.

1. Trajectory of the Meanings of Development

What Geertz calls "deflating experience" in the above quote involves all kinds of twists and turns that characterize any historical process, but the following portrayal seems apt to describe what befell Indonesia: "The general forward motion of the nation as a whole has been replaced by a complex, uneven, and many-directioned movement by its various parts, which conduces to a sense less of progress than of agitated stagnation" (Geertz 1973, 236f.). To oversimplify the chaotic nature of the process, there are at least three points worth noting.

First, having captured the Dutch-controlled colonial state apparatus, the nationalist urban middle classes moved upward to occupy the leadership of the new Republic. The colonial legacy of the state sector and the absence of domestic entrepreneurial classes left a deep mark on the kind of political economy the country had when it commenced its affairs in the late nineteen-forties. There was a striking continuity in the predominance of the state sector, especially state administration, as the focus for economic and social aspirations. Industry declined from 12 to 10 percent of national income between 1953 and 1958, export crops collapsed from 12.4 to 6.8 percent, and its overcrowded civil employees were underpaid and bitterly divided along ideological lines (Robison 1986, 64). It was in this sector, as it was during the pre-independence period, that the major segments of the nationalist urban middle classes were located.

Second, the post-independence period up until 1966 was characterized by a pattern in which the middle-turned-upper class and the new middle classes organized themselves through an experiment in parliamentary liberal politics to establish their rule. Unlike the archetypal model where local bourgeoisie ascended to national dominance through their monetary capital, here we see a case where groups of middle-class individuals, whose political economy was based not on money but on administrative niches, tried to establish a political leadership. Despite being couched in populist rhetoric, their attempts to create a domestic bourgeoisie unmistakably suggest a quest for an economic basis for their newly acquired administrative powers. Their economic nationalism not only ended in failure but became a precursor to a political force that would shape the Indonesian political economy between 1966 and 1998, namely the military.

How it happened turned out to be the bloodiest era in post-independence Indonesia. By early 1965, the price of petrol skyrocketed from 4. to 250 Indonesian rupiah, train fares fourfold, telecommunication and postal charges tenfold, and inflation ran at the rate of 500 to 600 percent in mid-1966 (World Bank 1966; Crouch 1978, 165; Hill 1994, 88). It was in this condition that President Sukarno's power declined rapidly and two forces faced each other in a violent struggle: the Communist Party and the Army. The major segments of the middle classes, politico-bureaucrats and merchants were increasingly allied with the anti-communist Army. When the final confrontation took place from September 30, 1965 onward, nothing could be ascertained as to which camp started the putsch and which the counter-coup. What was clear is that in the ensuing years the Army led a series of head-hunting campaigns against the communists or suspected communists. This period was known as the years of pogrom, with approximately 400,000 to a million Indonesians massacred (Green 1990, 61). Thus was the end of a turbulent era.

Third, the defeat of communist and radical nationalist forces also marked an exit of populist politics. To distinguish itself from the displaced regime, the new government called itself the Orde Baru (New Order). The military, especially the Army, led by the new president, General Soeharto, quickly sought technical assistance from the so-called 'technocrats', an epitome not of the middle classes but of Western economic orthodoxy.[1] Trained in the tradition of neo-classical economics, their remedy for the debacle was direct: a resort to foreign capital. The military, untutored in the art of economic policy, provided political machinery for the "growth ethos" of the technocrats inexperienced in *realpolitik*. The momentous event which had a causal significance was a closed-door conference in Geneva, Switzerland, in November 1967, in which James A. Linen, then the president of Time-Life Corporation, organized a meeting between the Indonesian technocrats and ministers and the world's top business executives. The latter included oil companies and banks, General Motors, British Leyland, Imperial Chemical Industries, British-American Tobacco, American Express, the International Paper Corporation, US Steel, Siemens, Goodyear, etc. (Winters 1996, 56-76).

---

[1] By the time of their ascendancy to ministerial posts, the technocrats were mostly professors at the Faculty of Economics, University of Indonesia, Jakarta. As they did most of their advanced studies at the University of California, Berkeley, USA, this handful of professors-turned-technocrats, who were concentrated at the BAPPENAS (the National Development Planning Board), were later popularly known as the 'Berkeley Mafia' (Bresnan 1993, Ch. 3; Winters 1996, 75).

Table 1: *Dynamics of the Indonesian political economy*

Period	Macro-Economic Conditions	Models of Political Economy
1967–1973	Initial Industrialisation	Economic Liberalism: • Open-door policy to foreign capital • Import Substitution Industrialisation (ISI) in intermediate and capital goods sectors
1974–1981	Oil Boom	Economic Nationalism: • Restrictions on foreign capital • State-led deepening of ISI • Priority policy for indigenous industrialists
1982–1986	Post-Oil Recession	Structural Adjustment: • Allopathy against oil slump, devaluation • First deregulation, financial and tax reforms • Multinationalisation
1987–1997	Export Industrialisation	Deregulation and Liberalisation: • Export and investment policy • Second financial, fiscal, investment reforms • Diversification

Source: Sato (1994, 126, table 9). The table is an adjusted summary of Sato's more elaborate table.

There are roughly four periods through which the New Order regime underwent major politico-economic changes, which in many respects can be seen as four strategies of development adopted by the regime. Table 1 summarizes the pattern. What concerns us here is the way the notion of development in Indonesia from 1966 onward was deeply shaped by the idiom of economic growth, whose attainment was in turn pursued in direct response to the structural conditions of the global political economy. In particular, the period between 1982 and 1986 was crucial. The policy shift in this period was triggered less by voluntaristic reasons than by changes in the global economic climate which forced the New Order regime to make structural adjustments. With the collapse of oil prices, the government was gradually deprived of the main sources of development funds. Oil prices slumped from 34.53 US Dollars per barrel in 1982 to 29.53 Dollars in 1983 and by 1993 plummeted to 16.58 Dollars (Petroleum Report of Indonesia 1993; Barnes 1995, 22f.). It was during this period that a series of fundamental trade, investment, financial and fiscal reforms began in earnest, all leading toward what was subsequently known as structural adjustments: deregulation, liberalization and privatization.

With the collapse of revenue luxury from high oil prices also ended the commanding prestige of civil service as the coveted sources of employment and social status: "As the old status concerns were blown away by the new status supplied and fed by money, new recruits flooded the professions—from the civilian bureaucracy, the army, from upwardly mobile petty commercial and well-off peasant circles as well as from aristocratic families for whom high finance, corporate boards, and the professional *haut monde* now seemed sensible substitutes for the increasingly declassed government service" (Lev 1990, 30). This was the period of rapid growth of private business within the increasingly privatized economy. Indeed, capitalism was losing its improbability in Indonesia (McVey 1992, 33). The country, classified as a "chronic dropout" during the mid-nineteen-sixties (Higgins 1968), was by the late nineteen eighties seen as one among a select group of developing countries destined to become a developed one.

Fourth, the period from 1998 up to the present has witnessed no clear pattern. When the East Asian financial crisis hit Indonesia in July 1997, the Soeharto regime was about to rule the country for the seventh consecutive term. By early 1998, amidst the worsening economic conditions and the mounting protests from university students and other popular groups, the regime began to show its political fatigue. Its fall on May 21, 1998, brought relief as much as angst: the departure of the dictator was the relief, the imminent rise of civil disorder the angst. With the end of the thirty-two years of heavy-handed rule, all kinds of permissiveness sprang up, from the burgeoning of graft and corruption to the virulence of sectarian violence, from the abandonment of health care services to the rampant plundering of development budget. It is within this condition that the problems of development in present-day Indonesia need to be understood.

The term 'development' has its notional evolution along the above trajectory. There is a specific word in Indonesian, *pembangunan*, which is generally rendered into English as 'development'. It is made up of the verb *bangun* (to build, awaken) and a combination of a prefix (pe) and a suffix (an), which changes the verb into a noun. The word can mean two things: the first meaning is associated with physical processes (for example *pembangunan jembatan*, bridge construction), whereas the second with a state or process more abstract than its English equivalent, referring to awakening or emergence. It is this second meaning that has been the predominant semantic of 'development' in Indonesia. With awakening or emergence as the main outlook, the term "prescribes both the nation's destination and the path by which that objective will be reached, and is the most unambiguous example of a common purpose binding together the diverse peoples of the archipelago" (Chalmers 1997, 2). It is *pembangunan* which provides an overall idiom for any leaders in Indonesia to operate. Therefore, it has been somewhat paradoxical that the issue of development has continued to revolve narrowly around debates over economic policy objectives.

Before the term 'development' gained currency in the aftermath of World War II, Western-educated nationalists in Indonesia used it to evoke their struggle against imperialism. The struggle involved the issue of *ekonomi kolonial* (colonial economy) as opposed to *ekonomi nasional* (national economy) as part of the independence aspirations. Indeed, the question of the economy always loomed large in the minds of the early nationalists who were well versed in the anti-imperialist ideas of Lenin and Bukharin (Kahin 1952, 50–53; Sutter 1959, 687–693). However, since national economy was a state of hope rather than actuality, the advent of independence in the nineteen-forties was then haunted by the question of how to do it. Their ideological poise led to "populist developmentalism" which entailed heavy state involvement at the moments when the entire state apparatus was still in an infancy stage. In real terms, the campaign for populist developmentalism took the form of what was called 'Indonesianization': the transfer of industrial foreign ownership into indigenous hands, material expansion and economic diversification (Feith 1962, 373f.). The close association between the notion of development and anti-colonial struggle for independence gave way to the former's identification with the process of nation-building.

A wave of tensions immediately arose. By the time the independence was won, most leaders were committed to implementing a liberal-democratic political system that ran counter to the communitarian idea of the economy. It was against this backdrop that the idea of economic progress was pursued through heavy reliance on state-owned companies, with an eye on nurturing an indigenous bourgeoisie. The heart of the program were racially biased policies in favor of giving credits, contracts and protection for indigenous merchants. The program soon failed, less because of the weak entrepreneurial ethos than due to the nature of factional politics during this period. Instead of an indigenous bourgeoisie, what emerged was a group of "license brokers and political fixers" (Robison 1986, 45). The country was on the brink of collapse. The idea of development as a nation-building process was nowhere visible and the climate was poisoned with agitated power struggle.

It was in this climate that the military and its economic technocrats stepped in. Their marriage of convenience would catapult the idea of development into a mystified national ideology. Development process was conducted strictly according to the so-called Five-Year Plans (Repelita), the first of which was drawn up in 1968. Since then all policy objectives were justified by 'development' as the principal idiom. In President Soeharto's words that would be repeated over and over in his addresses to the whole nation:

> "I feel it necessary now to speak with you directly about the policies that have been adopted by the government, because I know that development is not something that happens just because of a command. Development can only succeed if the people work enthusiastically and participate in implementing development. I believe that all of you, the whole people, will take part in development because you know clearly the direction in which we are heading." (Soeharto 1970, 54)[2]

The ensuing development mobilization yielded quick results. From being the world's largest importer of rice in the nineteen-seventies, the country gained rice self-sufficiency in the early nineteen-eighties. Between 1966 and 1990 manufacturing rose from 8 to 20 percent of the Gross Domestic Product. Primary education was improved steadily and by 1990 literacy rates for those over fifty years of age reached more than 80 percent (Hill 1994; Jones and Hull 1994, Fig 3.4). As expected, all this process was accompanied by a growing gap between the rich and the poor. It did not take long for the critics to raise their dissenting voices. The democratic-socialist camps re-entered the arena. Criticisms were directed less against the overall development design itself, for "the Five-Year Plan is better than previous plans". Rather, they were directed against a "too strong faith in market mechanism" and regional development that began to resemble center-periphery relations in the dependentista theory, a critical view of development as de-development or under-development (Sumawinata 1997 [1968], 61). A chorus of criticisms was also directed against the authoritarian *cum comprador* character of the regime that began to show up, in which "those who benefit from these activities are the big-shots and members of their families—wives, relatives, children, nephews, close friends and cliques; children and wives have been made directors, members of the board and

---

[2] Several cited documents on the development debate in Indonesia during this period are taken from a collection compiled by Chalmers and Hadiz (1997).

shareholders in all sorts of foreign and domestic joint ventures" (Enggak Bahau'ddin 1974, 64f.).

With the revenue windfall brought about by rising oil prices in the first half of the nineteen-seventies, the New Order's authoritarian confidence was also on the rise. During this period, development agenda was pursued in a language of the modernization theories widely popular in the nineteen-sixties and nineteen-seventies (cf. Peet and Hartwick 2009, 103–140). The way development was understood as modernization is illustrated in the following idiom:

"As a developing country, Indonesia is still always confronted with the problem of having to decide how to shape its future. The appropriate policy is what is generally called modernization [...]. The challenge of modernization is something that developing countries cannot ignore... [T]his doctrine approaches modernization from two complementary and mutually reinforcing directions..., the security approach and the prosperity approach. [...] For Indonesian society, which is still largely traditional, modernization involves changing and renewing its value system. Modernization thus entails changing those norms which are no longer socially functional, or hinder change. Change should be comprehensive. [...] For socio-cultural change, modernization demands an open attitude to foreign influences and cultures, as well as the strong support of progressive leaders who can promote the work ethic and a spirit of progress." (Moertopo 1997 [1972], 75ff.)

In policy terms, it was nothing other than a state-led industrialization through planned sectoral targeting (Soehoed 1997 [1977], 85). When oil prices started to fall in 1982 and continued to slump until the early nineteen-nineties, the so-called 'Development Regime' began to be hard-pressed by the rule of structural adjustment pursued by international agencies like the World Bank and the International Monetary Fund (IMF). The policy question was plain: how to integrate the Indonesian economy into the global economy.

"There are compelling reasons for a substantial reform of economic policy in Indonesia. Present policies have [...] encouraged a highly inefficient form of industrialization protected by high trade barriers and extensive subsidies. A sharp break with this cycle of expanding intervention is required. Market interventions should be carried out in a way that makes their costs highly visible and uses market mechanisms in enforcing efficiency. The move toward greater reliance on market mechanisms should be carried out in a comprehensive program of deregulation and elimination of market interventions." (World Bank 1981, 96f.)

Much stronger pressures were posed by the World Bank in the ensuing years, as "Indonesia's resource prospects have worsened considerably [...]

as a consequence of the worst international recession" (World Bank 1983, 98). There was also a need "to foster the development of a broad-based and internationally competitive industrial sector leading to a rapid and sustainable growth of non-oil exports" (World Bank 1985, 101). It was in this climate that development programs began to falter. 'Development' remained the policy idiom but its dirigiste character was gradually overtaken by the expansion of the private business sector and its substance eclipsed by the deregulation-liberalization-privatization fever. By the late nineteen-eighties the term 'development' was already poisoned with a toxic meaning due to its close association with the draconian character of the regime. Terms like 'developmentalism' or 'developmentalist approach' were viewed as coterminous with authoritarianism and became a target for intellectual derision.[3]

When the 1997 Asian financial crisis hit Indonesia, the development infrastructure that was gradually deserted during the market-driven structural adjustment period in the mid nineteen nineties was further unraveled. Like many other products of policy-speak, structural adjustment did not signify a reality as much as a false hope for what used to be promised by development. Indeed, as the post-1998 alternate regimes offered little more than mere opening for procedural democracy, what seemed unbearable in the past began to appear desirable. The purposeless character of the Indonesian political economy after 1998 was such that a yearning has since been brewing for a strong leadership capable of bringing 'development' back in. Development was unpalatable in the past, development is desirable now. The present is caught between regret and longing.

It is instructive to witness that the longing for development has been growing at the moments of its absence. This may indicate that there is something precious at the heart of development, in spite of the fact that its merit has been tainted by the exploits of the New Order regime. Not only does the concept of development give an idea of improvement of the quality of life but also a purposeful direction for the nation as a whole. This is apparently the idea held dear by the founders of Indonesia. It is a general meaning of "development that was embedded in the older idea of progress, that there was an unfolding of potential and that the new was a purposeful improvement on the old" (Cowen and Shenton 1996, ix). This general meaning could be stretched back to "the rise of man" or perhaps

---

3 For various critiques of the conduct of the New Order regime and its developmentalist ideology, see Budiman (1990).

"the emergence of modern states in Europe around the sixteenth century" (Gasper 2004, 33).

What concerns us is a much more specific meaning of development which began to gain semantic currency in the aftermath of World War II.[4] Within this category there is a bewildering variety of definitions that amount to "seven of the hundreds of definitions of development" (ibid., 2). Each offers its own perspective, but what runs common in all these post-war definitions of development is the idea of "the exercise of trusteeship over society; trusteeship is the intent which is expressed, by one source of agency, to develop the capacities of another" (ibid., ix). In short, the exercise of development trusteeship is "embedded in the predicate of social and political order" that is the government of a nation-state (ibid., 7).

It is within this idea of trusteeship that debates continue over what development pertains to. Is it little more than the Westernization of the world? Is it modernization of traditional societies, with or without the Western images of modernity? Or is it part of the trajectory of capitalism whose development necessitates under-development of poor and near-poor countries?[5] To these competing theoretical perspectives can be added debates over perimeters, which in turn involve the problems of the sufficiency or insufficiency of economic growth, gross domestic product (GDP) or gross national product (GNP), basic needs approach, capability approach as reflected in the Human Development Index (HDI) and the so-called happiness index, etc.

Despite disagreements, there seems to be a loose concordance that development concerns the idea of improvement of life quality. The point of contention, rather, lies in how best to approach the notion of 'improvement'. In many respects, the idea of the common good has always been implied in the idea of development. But how the idea of development, in real terms, is beneficially connected to the common good is a question of what Cowen and Shenton refer to as the problem of agency in the exercise of development trusteeship. Since the exercise of trusteeship is in practice embedded in the conduct of government, the question then involves not only how to ensure the link between the art of government and develop-

---

4 For a critical survey of the genealogy and meanings of 'development' in the history of ideas, see Cowen and Shenton (1996).
5 For a survey of these contending theoretical paradigms of development, see Peet and Hartwick (2009).

ment for the common good, but also how to ensure optimal participation of development beneficiaries in the art of government.

This last point seems crucial to understanding the widespread disenchantment of the term 'development' among the Indonesians in the past two decades. It is the exercise of trusteeship that was increasingly abused by the New Order authoritarian regime. With the ousting of the dictatorship in 1998, the story of three-decade directed development ended on a low note. Since then there have been hardly any significant attempts to address its defects and regenerate its virtues in a programmatic way.

2. Development versus Rent-Seeking Activities

The key to understanding the current problems of development in Indonesia is the captive nature of both the idea and conduct of development. Captive to what? There are many aspects, ranging from the sheer incompetence of policy makers to the currency of the market-driven model of transformation since the nineteen-nineties. However, this study will focus only on one specific factor that is rarely mentioned but, in my view, is robust to explain the current predicament of development in Indonesia.

The thrust of the argument can be boiled down to the following point. Despite being invoked as the rationale for policy making, what is widely claimed as development has increasingly degenerated into rent-seeking exploitation. Its most rampant form involves the plundering of development budget by businesses, politicians and government officials; hence the endemic nature of corruption in Indonesia. Any agenda to forge a virtuous link between development and the common good can hardly avoid this problem.

A brief clarification of the term 'rent-seeking' is warranted. Although the term 'rent' has always been with us, the notion 'rent-seeking' only began to gain currency in the economics literature in the nineteen-seventies (Buchanan 1980, 3). The concept was first developed in relation to the libertarian bent of the so-called Public Choice Theory. In advancing the libertarian cause of the free-market doctrines, it argues that, among others, regulatory prerogatives "imply arbitrary and/or artificial scarcity created by government; [s]uch scarcity implies the potential emergence of rents, which in turn implies rent-seeking activity" (Buchanan 1980, 9).[6] Rent-seeking is "the activity of wasting resources in competing for artificially contrived transfers", or "the expenditure of scarce resources to capture an artificially created transfer" (Tollison 1982, 577, 278). In short, government regulatory capacities are a nemesis of economic efficiency and free-market optimum.

This libertarian notion of rent-seeking has been subjected to several criticisms, some of which argue that there are many types of rent and not all are necessarily detrimental. For instance, state exclusive rights over scarce natural resources (natural resources rent) are likely to be beneficial and socially desirable (Khan 2000a, 65).[7] It is not the theoretical debate that concerns us here. Rather, among many types of rent-seeking, the most relevant for this study is the plundering of development budget through various pursuits of commercial contract to businesses, in which the involvement of government officials and politicians is an integral factor.

---

6 To further explain the meaning of rent-seeking, Buchanan used this illustration: "Suppose that a courtier persuades the queen to grant him a royal monopoly to sell playing cards throughout the kingdom. The courtier so favored will capture sizable monopoly profits or economic rents, and this will be observed by other persons who might like to enter the industry. But their entry is effectively prevented by enforcement of the royal monopoly privilege. [...] The potential entrants are not likely to sit quietly by and allow the favored one among their number to enjoy his differentially advantageous position. Instead of passive observation, potential entrants will engage in rent seeking. They will invest effort, time, and other productive resources in varying attempts to shift the queen's favor toward their own cause. Promotion, advertising, flattery, persuasion, cajolery – these and other attributes will characterize rent-seeking behavior." (Buchanan 1980, 7f.)

7 One of many criticisms was suggested by Mushtaq Khan and others: "Rent-seeking theories were initially constructed by liberal economists who wished to show that state intervention induced additional rent-seeking costs by artificially creating rents (Krueger 1974; Posner 1975; Buchanan 1980). These arguments were meant to strengthen the case for free markets where, in theory, no one would earn any rents. [...] Since a deviation from this condition signals inefficiency in the simple neo-classical model, all rents are sometimes associated with inefficiently operating markets. [...] That is a bit like asking what the world would look like in the absence of all friction. None of the structures and activities which we know might be viable in the absence of all friction, and, similarly, no institutions and rights might survive if all rent-seeking expenditures really disappeared. [...] The no-rent model remains compelling not because the evidence supports it, but because its policy implications are much simpler to understand." (Khan 2000a and Khan 2000b, 6, 67, 79, 141) For another similarly engaging critique of the neo-classical model of rent-seeking, see Przeworski and Wallerstein (1986, 221–228).

"Leaks are funds siphoned informally from budgetary or project revenues. At each step along the way in the collection of revenues and the disbursement of expenditures in and out of the state budget, a percentage is extracted as something like an unofficial fee for service. In 1993, economist and former minister Sumitro Djojohadikusumo estimated that the national budget incurred leakages of around 30 percent each year. In 2003, Minister for Planning Kwik Kian Gie more conservatively estimated budget leakages as at least 20 percent." (Dick and Mulholland 2011, 69)

As is immediately clear, this type of rent-seeking exploit obviously overlaps with the issue of corruption. Indeed, the problem has predominantly been cast in the language of corruption (Aspinall and van Klinken 2011, 3). However, what I am aiming at here is less the issue of corruption than the rigging of development budgets and processes through business contracts which then subvert the conduct of development.

If development involves concerted efforts for life improvement, and if so-called life improvement includes the life ecology in its entirety, then development cannot but cover the entire dimensions of both societal and individual life. In practical terms, development then involves concerted efforts for quality improvement in public health, environmental condition, education, people's purchasing capacity, physical infrastructure, etc. All this cannot but be reflected in the budgetary exercise of development trusteeship, which in turn is reflected in the way government manages its budget for development. No doubt the budgetary exercise is not the only area of development trusteeship, but the way the act of development trusteeship is exercised can certainly be gauged from the management of its development budget.

Let us start with physical infrastructure. Infrastructure development covers vast areas of construction: highways, roads, bridges, airports and seaports, irrigation systems, water supply, power stations, telecommunication networks, hospitals, clinics, schools, offices, housing, etc. The most important actors of rent-seeking are construction industries in collusion with both local and national state officials and politicians. It is estimated that "80 percent of building contractors depend entirely on government work" financed by infrastructure development funds (World Bank 2001, 21). In budgetary terms, this involves a staggering amount. For example, the infrastructure development budget in 2004 amounted to 62 trillion Indonesian rupiah (6.8 billion US Dollars). At the local level, most of these funds were spent on building basic transportation facilities (24.7 percent), housing and settlement (7.46 percent), regional development (7.31 percent), natural resources and irrigation (3.50 percent); little of it was spent on education and culture. Indeed, "construction projects are a major focus of collusive and predatory behavior, and *kontraktor* (contractors) are often prominent not only in business but also in politics. Provincial and district parliaments are full of contractors who live on building projects they themselves decide on. Contractors are prominent in the campaign teams for directly elected district heads and governors." (van Klinken and Aspinall 2011, 140, 143)

In skimming-off the infrastructure development budget, all imaginable schemes are employed: from outright budgetary mark-up to cutting-down the quality of the work and materials, from bribing tendering committees to sheer fabrication of the projects for plunder. Often the entire local government and parliamentary committees are bought out. It comes as no surprise that '*proyek*' (project) has become a dirty word among ordinary Indonesians today. The following vivid account from a contractor illustrates the point:

"You have to have insiders, people in the tendering committee or among the kepala dinas. You approach the people in the committee. [...] The key is you have to know the character of the people there. For example, if one likes girls on a Saturday night, then we'll take him to Medan on Saturday night. We'll take him to a hotel and give him a woman so that tomorrow he'll love us. If he likes entertainment, we'll give him entertainment. If another one likes fighting cocks, I'll go out and buy him a big rooster in a cage and bring it round to his house on a Sunday. If another likes to eat venison, we go and find venison and bring it to him. The key is that we must be able to read the character of other people. He won't ask for it, we need to be able ourselves to know what he likes. That's the general pattern. And how much does all this cost? Well, if the project is 1 billion, then 100 million is pretty reasonable. That's not a written rule but, yes, it's about 10 percent." (cited in van Klinken and Aspinall 2011, 155f.)[8]

What is recounted above is the normal pattern. But what really takes place goes even further in the form of sheer invention of construction projects *ex nihilo*. In such cases the needs of the local communities are made up to appear imminent. An inflated amount of development budgets is then proposed either by the contractors, government officials or politicians. The government officials guard the administrative gates, the politicians the

---

[8] The account is an excerpt from a confidential interview as part of an ethnographic research conducted by Edward Aspinall in 2008 in Aceh, a province that was devastated by tsunami in December 2004.

legislative processes, the contractors carry out the projects. All kinds of illicit payments are involved at every turn, from conception to completion. It is true that the locals may also reap the benefit of this rent-seeking exploit, but what they get is more externalities than development. With poor or much reduced quality of the materials and work, another string of projects is bound to be cooked up for repair or re-construction in the ensuing few months and years.

The same pattern can be extended to an area so much cherished in any development agenda: education. Although the plundering in this area is perpetrated less nakedly than that in the infrastructure sector, what happens is no less pervasive. Again, collusion between businesses, government bureaucrats and politicians is the rule. One example is a book procurement scandal that broke out in 2000. The case began as a Book Reading Development Project (BRPD) launched by the Ministry of Education in 1995. The aim of the project was to provide books to junior high schools. The total budget of the project was 132.5 million US Dollars.

The project involved Regional Offices of the Ministry of Education organizing book procurement. At least 19 percent of the budget was fraudulently distributed to various parties: 10 percent went to local project leaders, 5 percent to the Directorate General of Basic and Intermediary Education, 1 percent to the World Bank staff, 1 percent to the book center of the Ministry of Education, 1 percent to the State Treasury Office, another 1 percent to other parties. Still, every printing firm that won some slices of contract had to purchase printing paper from a designated company (PT. Pinasti) at 20 percent more than the market prices. The way the budget was siphoned off also involved many top publishing firms in Indonesia (Danang Widoyoko 2011, 176). In a recent investigation conducted by The Indonesia Corruption Watch, the biggest component of education budgets plundered through rent-seeking exploits between 2003 and 2013 were funds for what in Indonesia is called Bantuan Operasional Sekolah (School Operational Assistance). These education funds are directly delivered to all elementary and secondary schools in the country and are meant to be spent directly for repairing and improving school infrastructure (ACDP Indonesia 2013).

Budgets for public health are another lucrative target for plunder. Its *modus operandi* varies according to the arising opportunities in the provision of medical equipment and drugs, capacity-building, grants for public hospitals/clinics, specific programs in nutrition and vaccination, etc. In all this, the involvement of pharmaceutical companies, government officials from the Ministry of Health, national and local politicians and medical doctors is rampant. The way development budgets are siphoned off need not involve all these parties, for it is commonplace that the skimming-off is done at the first step of budgeting process. In 2011, I had a privilege of supervising a survey conducted by DEMOS (a Jakarta-based independent research organization) on the state of economic, cultural and social human rights in six sampled districts across the country. Among the research's agenda was an inquiry into the way expenditure for public health was reflected in the local government's budget.

What is officially written on the budgetary sheet conceals more than it reveals. The case of the district of Mimika in West Papua is instructive. It was officially written (official version) that office or administrative budget made up of 59.30 percent, whereas that for public health expenditure was 40.70 percent of the total. After being re-examined (DEMOS version), the budget for public health ended up with a bare 15.95 percent of the total, whereas that for office/administrative expenditure amounted to 84.05 percent. The figures have not even involved what occurred at the stage of budget realization phase but remained as the state of budget as officially approved.

How did it happen? A great deal of spending that actually belonged to administrative expenditure was put on the development expenditure entries, such as meeting allowance, office uniform, personal computer, etc. Still, the procurement involved in administrative expenditure was also marred with rent-seeking exploits involving officials, businesses, politicians, medical doctors and other parties. The same survey found a similar pattern of malpractices in the area of education and human resources development (DEMOS 2011). All this has been the rule rather than an exception up until the present day.

In mid-2012, an investigation based on a set of data from the State Audit Agency found the following pattern in the ten most corrupt state agencies. The Ministry of Education and Ministry of Health ranked third and fourth respectively in terms of their proneness to rent-seeking, whereas the Ministry of Religious Affairs occupied the eighth place (FITRA 2012). What is telling about this pattern is that almost all state agencies charged with development programs have become regular avenues for rent-seeking. As of March 2011, for instance, 155 regional officials, including 17 governors, had been named graft suspects, most of them involved in what this study calls rent-seeking. Only less than 5 percent of 525 provincial, district and city administrations were declared clean by the State Audit Agency (*Jakarta Post* 2011a, 6).

Gone is the era when development was conducted in a guided if authoritarian way. This may explain why since 1998 there has been a growing nostalgia for a strong political leadership capable of undertaking a well-coordinated development program. This should not be taken as a desire for a return to dictatorship or as an approval of similar rent-seeking pursuits during the New Order regime. Rather, the problem seems to lie in the differences in magnitude: rent-seeking was centralized then, it is decentralized and more endemic now. The growing clamors for corruption eradication can be taken as a direct product of this endemic and decentralized nature of rent-seeking exploits.

Graph 1: Poverty-eradication budget versus property rates.

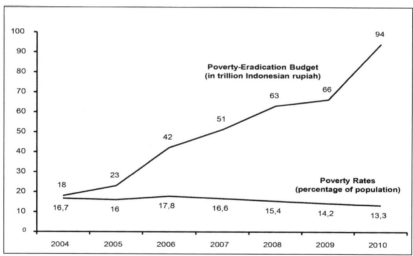

Source: Bureau of National Statistics (various years)

There is a vivid way of capturing the problem. Despite continuous debates over the nature of development, poverty eradication is always on top of any development agenda. The above graph 1 shows how so-called rent-seeking pursuits may have been detrimentally associated with poverty rates. Graph 1 reveals an irony. The period spanned from 2004 to 2010, and the criterion adopted was a conservative standard of poverty between 0.75 and

1 US Dollar/day, much below the international standard. As is clear from the figures, the steady increases in poverty-eradication budget are hardly associated with poverty rates reduction. It comes as no surprise therefore that there has been a poignant anecdote circulating among critics and policy insiders alike: the paltry decline in poverty rates over the years have more to do with the natural drive of the poor to escape poverty rather than with the government's poverty-eradication program; hence the irrelevance of the program.

As noted, the figures use the lowest standard of poverty. If the standard is raised to 2 Dollars/day, the picture is more staggering. Indeed, using the standard of living costs on less than 2 Dollars/day in 2006, the World Bank came up with a figure of 49 percent (110.74 million) of Indonesians living in poverty (World Bank 2006). This means that almost half of Indonesians lived in poverty in 2006 (Indonesian population in 2006: 226 million). As expected, disparities between the rich and the poor have been steadily on the rise. The Gini Index, a measure of economic gap, shows a worsening trend: 33.1 in 2002, 39.4 in 2007, and 41.3 in 2011 (World Bank 2012).[9]

Such criticism may sound harsh, but it rightly points to the absence of development. Apparently in a move to appear respectable, the government recently launched a massive economic development program called MP3EI (Masterplan for Acceleration and Expansion of Indonesia Economic Development 2011–2025). The master-plan divides Indonesia into six so-called "development corridors".

Each corridor is assigned to specialize in specific products with its comparative and competitive advantages. The Sumatra Corridor (1) would be "a center for production and processing of natural resources and as the nation's energy reserves", the Java Corridor (2) "a driver for national industry and service products", the Kalimantan Corridor (3) "a center for production and processing of national mining and energy reserves", the Sulawesi Corridor (4) "a center for production and processing of national agricultural, plantation, fishery, oil and gas, and mining", the Bali-Nusa Tenggara Corridor (5) "a gateway for tourism and national food support", and the Papua-Maluku Corridor (6) "a center for development of food, fisheries, energy, and national mining" (Coordinating Ministry for Economic Affairs 2011, 46f.).

---

9 All data on the Gini Index for Indonesia in comparison with other countries can be found at the World Bank website: http://data.worldbank.org/SI.POV.GINI.

In some respects, the document can be seen as the most extensive development roadmap produced since 1998. In other respects, however, the document has less to do with development than with opening all the gates of boundless resources and potentials in Indonesia for global investment. In the language of the same document:

"Indonesia will need to embrace a new way of thinking, [...] a new way of conducting business. To foster the economic growth, [...] it will depend on the private sector participation which includes state-owned enterprises and private domestic and foreign investors. It contains the main direction of development for specific economic activities, including infrastructure needs and recommendations for change of regulations as well as to initiate the need of new regulations to push for acceleration and expansion of investment" (ibid., 20, 23).

It did not take long to encounter its ugly face. It was within the MP3EI scheme that in August 2012 the Papua-Maluku Corridor (6) launched a colossal initiative called The Merauke Integrated Food and Energy Estate (MIFEE). As noted, the Papua-Maluku Corridor is assigned to specialize in the "development of food, fisheries, energy, and national mining". Merauke is a district on the south-western tip of Papua, a vast territory of approximately 4.5 million hectares (45.071 square kilometers). In this district lives one of many ethnic groups in Papua, the peoples of Malind-Anim, inhabiting community lands for many generations. It is the Malind-Anim areas that have been the main target of land acquisition for the MIFEE project. Since its launching in 2012, the MIFEE authority has issued contract licenses for many food-processing and mining companies to start their businesses on a vast territory covering more than 2.3 million hectares.

As happens in many areas in Indonesia, a string of controversies soon broke out, revolving around the issue of land ownership, which further involved a series of atrocities ranging from the use of violence, thuggery, frauds, bribery to all kinds of manipulation. Usually people from a certain company that has secured license would come to the local communities, flanked by government officials, police and often military forces. A draft of agreement is then presented to purposely selected community representatives who can hardly read or write. Then "consenting" signatures are secured, some manipulative twists and turns are done, a certain amount of money is handed over, and the ownership of the community lands has "legally" changed. One example of such ploy reads as follows: "The First Party hereby agrees to provide and ensure the release and handover to the

Second Party the ownership of community lands of 36.892 hectares in total and all things attached to the lands" (Siti Rakhma Marry 2012).[10]

As recounted by the locals, "we don't know what MIFEE is; when we go to Merauke, we hear something called MIFEE, and we thought it is an environmental program". Any protests are dealt with harshly either through more violence, bribery or divide-and-rule tactics. Strictly speaking, various malpractices involved in the MIFEE may not be called rent-seeking yet they are no less predatory and parasitic, and the process eventually also involves many exploits integral to rent-seeking activities.

Figure 1: Deforestation in Kalamantan, Indonesia

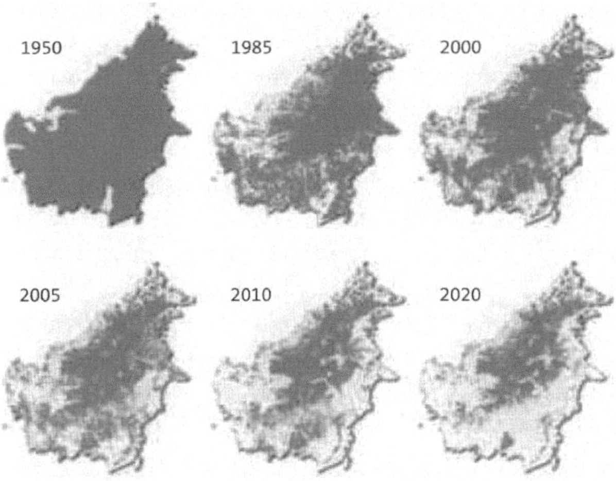

Source: UNDP (2012, 6)

The MIFFE case can be taken as representative of the conduct of development in present-day Indonesia. Predictably, it has grave impacts on the state of environment. Between 12 and 15 million hectares of forest areas in Indonesia are deforested each year, equivalent to 36 football fields

---

10 This account is based on an ethnographic research conducted by Siti Rakhma Marry in mid-2011 in Merauke, Papua. The agreement formula is taken from a legal document for the agreement between several Malind-Anim village communities and PT. Rajawali (a food company) which secured the release of 40,000 hectares of community lands for sugar cane plantation. While the release of the community lands was clearly for business purposes, it was instead presented during the agreement meetings as a program for village empowerment (Siti Rakhma Marry 2012).

disappearing every minute (WWF 2013). The above figure 1 presents the rates of deforestation in Kalimantan, the biggest island in Indonesia.

Similar patterns are observable in other areas of development program. What is called 'natural resources development', for instance, is one of the favorite targets in economic programs. What takes place on the ground is little more than the issuance of exploration and exploitation licenses in an unregulated manner. According to researchers from the Australian National University, prior to 2000 there were only approximately 600 mining licenses in Indonesia. By 2010, more than 10,000 licenses had been issued. Many of these licenses were issued by local governments and overlap with other permits previously issued over the same area (cited in Ardiansyah 2013, 96).

In fairness, the government is not entirely lacking in development initiatives. Several attempts to re-launch development roadmaps along the Millennium Development Goals campaign (MDGs) have been cultivated, often by drafting specialists and cross-sectoral parties.[11] Nevertheless, the captive nature of development policies to the rent-seeking forces seems too strong, as that what is called 'development' is increasingly there only in name. It is within this context that criticisms have been directed against the market-based model of development since the nineteen-nineties. With the exit of the Soeharto regime in 1998, a stage was set for an outbreak of uncontrolled rent-seeking exploits which are made up of a marriage of convenience between an incompetent state bureaucracy and an unfettered pursuit for commercialization.

While this line of criticism has some bearings on the ground, it also runs the risk of discounting altogether the beneficial application of some market mechanism in managing development. This provision needs to be understood in the following context. As admitted by the government, "the government has very limited funds to finance development through its State Budget" (Coordinating Ministry of Economic Affairs 2011, 20). Unfortunately, proper mention is never made of the staggering amount of

---

11 For example, in mid-2013 the President's Office of the Delivery Unit for Development Monitoring and Oversight (UKP4) assembled more than 180 experts, scholars and activists from various sectors for a series of closed-door meetings in an attempt to gather cross-sectoral views on the state of development in Indonesia and their aspirations concerning its direction. All the views and aspirations were intended to be processed for the formulation of the country's Development Roadmap. There are also other documents on development roadmap produced by independent groups contending to be heard by the government. See, for example, Yayasan Indonesia Forum (2007).

budgetary losses incurred by the pervasive rent-seeking pursuits. In 2010, the total budgetary losses incurred by these practices were estimated to reach 150 trillion Indonesian rupiah or approximately 16.8 billion US Dollars (*Jakarta Post* 2011b; see also a special report on rent-seeking in *Kompas* 2011). A testimony by an economist-turned-parliamentarian, Dradjad H. Wibowo, revealed that "the real costs of government-funded development projects are actually only 30 to 40 percent of the total; the rest is for many parties to loot" (ibid., 35).

What is described here is necessarily parsimonious. Nevertheless one striking pattern is noticeable. It is the disappearance of the exercise of trusteeship. While the government has cultivated various avenues of reviving development agenda, it is increasingly clear that the exercise of trusteeship has lost its way. No doubt there are many underlying factors. Sometimes the problem concerns the flawed nature of the idea of development from the start. At other times, it concerns low commitment to sustained implementation. All this, however, seems to point to a converging deeper problem which is the fact that both the idea and conduct of development have been captive to the rampant nature of rent-seeking pursuit.

It is within the context of this parasitic character of development that its noble aim has gradually been obscured. Too much reliance on the market and the state makes the development process vulnerable not only to rent-seeking but also empties the purpose of development from the outset. Any meaningful attempts to revive the idea of development in the service of the common good are likely to encounter the question of how to bring the people-centered concern back into the idea and conduct of development. It is to this issue that we now turn.

3. Reviving Community Development as Development Approach

There is nothing new about the notion of community development as a genuine way of conducting development. It has a reputable pedigree, whose intellectual origins can be traced back to the nineteenth century (Gilchrist 2009, 24). But it was in the climate of the "development drive" after World War II that community development began to gain international currency. Community development (CD) was defined by the United

Nations "as process designed to create conditions of economic and social progress for the whole community with its active participation" (United Nations 1955).

It was recognized from the start that development trusteeship can be claimed to have been performed even while excluding the local communities as the *raison d'être* of development. This note of caution was prescient. With the shifting climate of politico-economic conditions, development trusteeship has always been vulnerable to capture both by the state and market forces. The way development degenerates into rent-seeking exploit, as exemplified by the Indonesian case, attests to the importance of this caution. Without taking into account the primacy of people-centered approach to development, the goal of development, instead of being intentionally pursued, will simply become an unintended consequence of the often rapacious character of the state-market nexus. Indeed, 'development' may remain a policy idiom, but as increasingly clear in the present character of globalization, governments are often more preoccupied with global ranking than with the exercise of development trusteeship. It is as if their constitutional mandate comes from the global ranking agencies rather than from their citizens.

The centrality of the people-centered approach and people participation in CD is not without its problems. It "has always been vulnerable to criticism" because it tends to be "both vague and pretentious—claiming too much". But "a more serious aspect of the problem lies in disagreements": whether it is "part of the tradition of social movements" or an "intervention, helping to ensure that local people have opportunities to participate as well as to be supported" (Henderson and Vercseg 2010, 29, 30). Disagreements notwithstanding, there is a common understanding with regard to the centrality of people participation and people-centered orientation as the hallmark of genuine development. It is the choice over methods which is the point of contention.

This contention over methods was reflected in the debate between the so-called 'advocacy approach' and the 'developmentalist approach' within the circle of civil society (CSOs) and non-governmental organizations (NGOs) in Indonesia in the nineteen-seventies and nineteen-eighties. What concerns us here is the way the semantic of CD was increasingly decayed by the evolving terms of the debate. Indeed, the story of how the idea of CD in Indonesia gradually became ill-reputed has its own background.

First, it was along the increasingly authoritarian character of the New Order regime that the notion of CD began to assume its derogatory meaning. In the nineteen-seventies and -eighties, the world of CSOs and NGOs in Indonesia was troubled by an ideological opposition between the so-called 'advocacy approach' and 'developmentalist approach' concerning the conduct of development. The point of contention lay not in the virtue of CD itself but, rather, in the way CD was abused by the regime for its parasitic purposes. That is why CD was closely associated with the conduct of the regime. With the regime assuming the name of "developmentalist regime", the way CD was conducted was then seen inextricably linked to the authoritarian character of the developmentalist regime; ergo, CD was called a "developmentalist approach".

As a young graduate participating in the CSOs and NGOs movements in Indonesia in the nineteen-eighties, I witnessed how criticisms were advanced in the language of Andre Gunder Frank's 'dependency theory'. Among several, one group revolved around human rights activists with their networks of independent legal-aid organizations. It was mainly from this group that the so-called "advocacy approach" was used in opposition to the "developmentalist approach". It was not unusual to hear jokes about the superiority of the advocacy approach over the developmentalist approach on the ground that "what the developmentalists do is planting cassavas like Soeharto's yes-men".

No doubt there were also many who saw the opposition between the two as flawed, for the question of human rights and that of community organization are inseparable in the process of conducting development. For this group, the main issue was community organization for self-reliance, in which both advocacy and development agenda should be pursued simultaneously within the process of organizing local communities. In the words of Bambang Ismawan, one of the group's principal pioneers:

"It was a tense situation. Community organizations (COs) were viewed as threats by the regime. The state of affairs was not without challenges and difficulties. I was often summoned by the military officers for questioning regarding my activities. To steer clear of military distrust, I offered to cooperate with state institutions on a variety of activities. We see our programs and the interaction between the people and our trainers simply as a social laboratory. For instance, Bina Swadaya worked with the National Family Planning Board (BKKBN) for six years on a campaign for women's participation in development. We helped the BKKBN to set up projects involving 13.5 million families. I also worked with the government to enlarge the funds available for financial aid for underdeveloped villages (IDT) across the nation. Bina Swadaya also collaborated with all forestry offices across Java, and with Bank Indonesia [the Indonesian Central Bank] on microfinance in 23 provinces. Our coverage is very extensive. But we don't highlight our name there. We are just like a virus—invisible, but it has its effects" (Ismawan 2013, 463f.).[12]

With the increasing authoritarian tendency of the New Order regime, clamors for democratization were also militantly waged in high-profile manners. So much so, that the routine and no-publicity nature of CO—even if conducted in opposition to the regime—was bound to be consigned to oblivion. It was against this backdrop that the real power of CD and CO as a genuine *modus procendi* of development was increasingly looked down. Still, there was another fatal twist.

Second, the meaning of CD/CO as genuine way of conducting development has been damaged further with its cooptation by the business sector through its corporate social responsibility programs (CSR). This certainly is not to belittle some CSR programs that are genuinely beneficial to local communities. Nevertheless, it is commonplace to find many CSR community-development programs that are little more than part of the business sector's public relations campaign. There is hardly any sizable company in Indonesia which does not have a community-development program for the locals in its CSR mission statement. Even a socially and environmentally damaging company would have one. It therefore comes as no surprise that business-driven community development program tends to be looked down, with a no less biting anecdote: "CSR community development is the business sector's way of giving one to the locals in the morning and taking ten at the end of the day".

Third, the idea of CD/CO in Indonesia can be traced back to some grassroots self-reliance movements in the nineteen-fifties (cf. ibid.). However, in the ensuing era it was perceived as not only having a close affinity with the parasitic conduct of the New Order regime but also with the ideological orientations of international development agencies, particularly the World Bank. It should be noted that there is nothing inherently unde-

---

12 Bambang Ismawan is one of the pioneers in sustainable development and community organization in Indonesia. He set off the movement over 40 years ago when he founded an economically sustainable rural development organization, Bina Swadaya (Self-Reliance Development Foundation). It has been organizing farmers into self-help groups (SHGs) and training community organization leaders. In an attempt to rebut critics who argued that CD/CO is not sufficiently informed by an entrepreneurial spirit, he led Bina Swadaya after 1998 to show that CO can be a way of simultaneously doing "sustainable development" and "social entrepreneurship" (Ismawan 2013, 464–48).

sirable about this affinity. However it needs to be admitted that in times of heated political debates, this affinity has easily been seen in an unfavorable light (cf. Törnquist 1990, 421). When the fiscal basis of the New Order regime was shattered by the collapse of oil prices in the first half of the nineteen-eighties, the period of the World Bank-driven 'structural adjustments' began in earnest in Indonesia. It was during this period that many types of community-driven development programs funded and guided by the World Bank were pursued more intensively (Eldridge 1990, 508).

The roles of the World Bank in development in Indonesia can be traced back to the second half of the nineteen-sixties, when the Soeharto regime was in ascendancy. Its involvement ranged from regional economic development projects to basic education programs, from export development projects to electrification projects.[13] One recent example is the Kecamatan (Sub-District) Development Program (KDP), launched in 1998 at the height of the East Asian financial crisis. It involved 1.6 billion US Dollars of grants and loans, covering more than 1,983 districts or 38,000 villages across Indonesia, "the largest social development project in Asia and one of the World Bank's flagship community-driven development (CDD) programs" (Barron et al. 2006, vii).

While these local community-driven development programs are not without their merit, the success rates of a program like KDP "remain rather thin". Indeed, "KDP does contribute in important ways toward making local democracy work", yet it often "inflames existing tensions and thereby becomes part of the problem" (ibid., vii, 165f.). It is not the World Bank-funded development programs that concern us here; they deserve more nuanced appreciation. What is relevant is that the notion of CD being closely associated with World Bank initiatives tends to be viewed with suspicion, in the way that the notion of CD was also tainted by its association with the parasitic exploits of the New Order regime. The two have been seen in an unfavorable light for different reasons: the latter for its autocratic affinity, the former for its perceived market-driven ideology. No doubt this perception remains unexamined, yet its impact is no less real.

Indeed, from all the foregoing accounts it seems clear that the notion of CD and CO has been tainted both by perceptions and malpractices. Add the pervasiveness of rent-seeking exploits to the equation, and what

---

13 The list of all World Bank projects in Indonesia since the nineteen-sixties can be found at the World Bank website: www.worldbank.org/en/country/indonesia/projects.

we get is the corrupted notion of CD and CO. It is unfortunate indeed to live in a climate of a corrupted semantic. There is, however, a need to remember a classical dictum, *abusus non tollit usum*—just because something is abused is no reason for putting an end to its legitimate use. The meaning of CD and CO needs be reinstated to its status as a genuine way of conducting development. While this imperative may sound old-fashioned, it is founded upon a robust ground. The remaining part of this section will be devoted to this point.

To begin with, if the quest for the common good involves the development of a whole person and his/her community's social and natural fabric, a sector-based approach may have a merit at some initial stages but it will eventually create the kinds of problem that development precisely intends to address. While the sectoral approach virtuously reflects the finite nature of human action, it also has a tendency of partitioning human life and its environment into disparate fragments, for example, economic development is sundered from political development as much as from environmental development. In the lives of local community members, however, there is hardly any separation between the political, the economic, the cultural, the social, the environmental, etc. All these spheres make up a seamless flow of both personal and community life.

In many respects, the separateness is simply a creation of the academic world—economics dealing with the affairs of human livelihood and exchanges, political science with the issue of power coordination, anthropology with values, law with formal rules and regulation, and so theology or environmental science with their respective objects of analysis. But, how did the phenomena of livelihood and exchanges, but not of religious faith, come to be understood as the domain of economics and be designated as the economy? There is nothing inherently "economic", "religious" or "political" about these phenomena. Indeed, they are designated as such by analytical partitions, in which each specialized mode of analysis focuses on a carved-out dimension of the phenomena with its own methodological approach (cf. Wolin 2004, 5ff.). In reality, the act of writing this study, for instance, involves a seamless entirety of the economic (for example, my computer was purchased at a certain price), the environmental (for example the release of carbon dioxide from my room's air-conditioner), the biological (for example, physical fatigue or hunger involved in the toils and troubles of researching/writing), etc.

The same can be said of development conduct. Each of these sectoral developments—political development, economic development, cultural development, environmental development, legal development, health development, etc.—is a way of approaching development from a particular point of view. But there is no development constituted only of economic development, as much as there is no development that is made up only of legal development. Even if some analytical distinction is necessarily at work, the order of development reality is never characterized by such partition. In the language familiar to most students of economics, the reality of development has no *ceteris paribus*.[14] At most, this sectoral partition is only the name for moments of analysis. Or, in the language of philosophical anthropology, there is nothing wrong to say that human person is *homo economicus* or *homo biologicus*, but it is patently false to claim that *homo biologicus* or *homo economicus* is the entirety of a human person.

This by no means is to say that these academically specialized approaches have no merit. Rather, in the absence of some well-planned and well-executed coordination, the sectoral approach to development runs the risk of serving many convenient purposes except people-centered development. This seems to be what happens in the conduct of development in Indonesia.

It is not unusual that every state ministry has its own development program, with its own name and projects. Often several of these state ministries/agencies come to the same communities with overlapping goals but no ministerial coordination. What arises is sheer confusion among community members. The following table 2 presents an example of each ministry's programs for rural development.

---

14 *Ceteris paribus* is a Latin expression for "other things being equal/constant/suspended". There is nothing distinctively "economic" about the expression. Economic science only borrowed it from an expression common in the classical rhetoric, referring to an act of suspending/bracketing other relevant factors during one single moment of analyzing a specific issue (cf. Marshall 1972, 304).

Table 2: Rural development programs by ministry/state agency (sample)

	State Ministry	Programme/Project	Scope of Activities
1	Home Affairs	• National Programme for Community Empowerment (PNPM) • Healthy & Bright Generation (PNPM *Generasi*) • Participatory Development System Programme (P2SPP)	• Rural infrastructure, micro credit, education, health, capacity building, development funds, expertise. • Health and education for women and children • Programme for integrating PNPM into participatory system
2	Public Works	• Rural Infrastructure Development (PPIP) • Regional Social-Economic Infrastructure Development (PISEW)	• Rural infrastructure, development funds, expertise. • Development funds, expertise, poverty reduction & regional disparities.
3	Agriculture	Rural Agribusiness Development (PUAP)	Development funds for farmers, expertise, mentoring.
4	Social Services	Hopeful Family Programme (PKH)	Protection for poor households, expertise & mentoring.
5	Health	Community-Based Water Supply Programme (PAMSIMAS)	Health infrastructure, development funds, expertise & mentoring
6	Development of Disadvantaged Regions	Acceleration of Poor & Disadvantaged Areas Development (P2DTK)	Poverty reduction & prevention, development funds, expertise & mentoring.
7	People Welfare	Strategic Alliance for Poverty Alleviation (SAPA)	Mobilisation of stakeholders for poverty alleviation programme
8	Central Bank	Micro-Credit for Small Businesses (KUR)	Development funds, micro-loans, start-up capital.
9	National Development Planning Agency	Masterplan for Poverty Prevention Programme	Quick Wins Projects: poverty reduction, prevention, alleviation; small-medium enterprises.
10	State Logistics Agency	Rice for the Poor (RASKIN)	Development funds & subsidy for foods security.

Source: The National Team for the Acceleration of Poverty Reduction

It is hard not to see that these disparate development programs serve as a convenient way to secure budgetary allocation from the development funds. If we put this within the context of pervasive rent-seeking pursuit, what we get is not unlike budgetary plunder in the name of development. In the words of a middle-ranking official from the Ministry of Home Affairs: "I've been into rural development for years. Observing these overlapping programs, often with no connection to each other, I can't help thinking that this is sheer looting of development budget; indeed, this is what has happened".[15]

It is against this prevailing tendency that an imperative to revive CD and CO needs to be understood. If development concerns a civilizing process for the betterment of life quality encompassing the overall spheres of personal and community life, which are analytically partitioned by academic specialization, CD and CO are precisely the locus of the real dynamics where such partition is transcended. That is why it is only within the dynamics of CD and CO that the currently perceived contradiction between the economy and the ecology, for instance, can possibly be overcome. In other words, only within CD and CO it is possible to cultivate an economy that is ecological, as well as an ecology that is economical. This is so because only within the dynamics of CD and CO, the economic, the political, the environmental, the cultural, the technological and even the gender issues within the fabric of community life are experienced as a totality that defies partition and separation. In the words of one of its practitioners: "Real process of development on the ground is like a stream or tapestry of sustained and interrelated community efforts to make income improvement, nutrition betterment, environmental stewardship, woman empowerment or even inter-religious dialogue being pursued in one breath of movement. Of course each effort can only be done once at a time, but separating community life into sectors simply won't work as a development".[16]

This last point is crucial. Again, in the words of its practitioner cited above: "In the real dynamics of CD, what is called success is neither sectoral nor partial, for any rise in income is less meaningful if it is done amidst or through environmental degradation or religious conflicts".[17] This also means that cost-benefit calculus in the dynamics of CD proceeds through a reciprocal equilibrium between all dimensions of both personal and community life and can hardly be conducted in the way a cost-benefit calculus is made on the score-sheet of a sectoral approach. It is through

---

15 Interview with a middle-ranking official at the Ministry of Home Affairs. He was a student activist in the early nineteen-nineties and is now retaining his critical stand and interest in rural development while working inside the government institution. He wishes to remain anonymous (Interview, 16 August 2013).

16 Interview with a female community leader-organizer who, for the past 10 years, has been involved with community organization in Central Java; she wishes to remain anonymous (Interview, 3 July 2013).

17 A female community leader-organizer, Central Java (ibid.).

this process of equilibrating all dimensions that the civilizing character of development is unfolding. No doubt this will take a long and arduous process, but it has an advantage of "naturalness", which seems to have been forgotten in the present conduct of development. Still, taking CD and CO into account does not entirely safeguard development process from being captured by rent-seekers. What seems clear is that genuine CD and CO makes rent-seeking more difficult to be perpetrated at the level of local communities.

A caveat is needed. All this is by no means to ignore the fact that many development programs require expertise and sophisticated technologies performed only by specialized agencies, such as toll-road construction, airports, power plants, laboratory for seeds cross-fertilization, etc. CD and CO may not be suited as the principal approach to these specialized projects. Nonetheless, for these projects not to be detrimental to the lives of local communities, strong CD and CO remain a prerequisite. Indeed, in most cases local communities are hardly consulted, which then results in the outbreak of conflicts between the contracting parties and the government in one side, and local communities in the other. The sources of conflict may vary, from the problems of land compensation to outright displacement of the locals, from communal tension arising from divide-and-rule tactic to water shortages due to environmental depletion. The case of land dispossession in the MIFEE project as described in the previous section is a case in point. As admitted by the National Land Authority (BPN), by June 2011 there were at least 14,337 cases of local conflict related to land disputes throughout Indonesia, most of which have to do in one way or another with "development projects" (*Kontan* 2011).

This also means that while CD/CO should not be seen as the only method, other methods are likely to have beneficial bearings on development if, and only if, they are supported by strong CD/CO. It can even be argued that in order for all development programs to have beneficial impacts on the ordinary people, CD/CO should be taken as the prerequisite. This imperative is pressing, in view of the fact that many aspects of development infrastructure have been increasingly deserted. Not only clinics or school buildings in remote areas are in depleted condition, but the provision of human resources for carrying out rural development is also in an alarming state. In 2000, for example, there were about 62,812 midwives providing medical services in remote villages across the country. By 2003, the number had declined sharply by 36 percent to 39,906. This means that

22,906 remote villages had been abandoned by midwives between 2000 and 2003. No wonder "maternal mortality in Indonesia remains stubbornly high at 229 maternal deaths per 100,000 live births", which is "among the highest in East Asia" (World Bank 2010, 1, 5).

In many respects, this is representative of the state of development infrastructure in Indonesia. The latest survey conducted by the 2012 PODES (Village Potential Census) also shows a wide gap between Java and other islands not only in public health but also in other development infrastructure like education, with Papua and Central Kalimantan showing the most severe conditions (PODES 2012, 50). Data on the deteriorating state of development infrastructure can be extended, all pointing not only to its depraved physical conditions but also to the symptom of its human resources abandonment. This may reflect the growing absence of CD/CO, which otherwise can serve as an organizational vehicle for posing demands of the local communities *vis-à-vis* the local governments.

It is necessary, however, to inject a sense of realism. One way of doing it is to compare the state of development in Indonesia with that in other countries in Southeast Asia with in the so-called Human Development Index (HDI). A sign of improvement may be noticeable, but Indonesia continues to fare poorly at the near bottom.

Even if the human development index is known for being a more reliable measure of development compared to other indices like GDP or GNP growth, we remain in the dark as to how the aggregate outcome comes to be "improved" year by year. In any case, no amount of claims can possibly prevent the appearance of improvement from being seen as merely an unintended consequence of irrelevant factors. Indeed, for the conduct of development to have any beneficial links to the common good, the intentional nature of trusteeship needs to be pursued vigorously. This point also needs to be understood against the backdrop of the predominant market-driven model of transformation, which tends to treat people-centered development as "positive externalities". It may be positive, but remains a side-effect that is never pursued intentionally.

While it is true that many development projects can be done only by specialized agencies, programs like women empowerment, eco-agriculture, community food security, nutrition improvement, literacy, education for environmental conservation/preservation, inter-religious dialogue, etc. can optimally be carried out through CD/CO. No doubt there are several programs that can be done optimally by way of a combination between the specialized approach and the CD/CO approach. But to dispense altogether with CD/CO is likely to make development programs more vulnerable to rent-seeking exploit.

If development is to be worthy of its name, the current practices of sectorally partitioning it by sector into the economic, the political, the environmental, the cultural, etc. may just work as a ploy to take the people-centered concern away from the notion of genuine development.

4. Epilogue

The need to revive CD and CO without doubt requires a set of preconditions. They range from bureaucratic reform to capacity building at the local community levels; from intensive anti-corruption campaign to steady efforts to re-engage CSOs and NGOs with grassroots organizing. Not so long ago social movements led by CSOs and NGOs were noted for their defense of the people-centered approaches to development *vis-à-vis* the parasitic exploits of the Soeharto regime. That era is now at risk of being a forgotten past. Like political parties that mushroomed after 1998, an increasing number of CSOs and NGOs seems content with going to local communities only if there is a chance to seize some slices of development budget.

To these myriad problems can be added others that are intellectual in nature, like the need to reassess the way development is being understood both by policy makers and the public, or how development has been misconceived as economic development, while the term 'economic' is being confused with 'the market' and 'business'. Still, another breed of problem has entered the scene since the departure of the New Order regime in 1998, which is growing religious fundamentalism and extremism.[18] The significance of this problem lies in the tendency in which many development-related conflicts are exacerbated by religious and other sectarian tensions.

---

18 The accelerating rise of religious fundamentalism and extremism since 1998 is attested by a growing number of field researches and surveys. See, for example, The Wahid Institute (2011); Hairus Salim et al. (2011); Hasani and Naipospos (2012); and annual surveys on the state of religious intolerance in Indonesia regularly conducted by the Jakarta-based Wahid Institute and Setara Institute.

Yet an irony is growing: the more development is absent, the more development is yearned. This yearning was reflected in the 2014 general elections, concluded at the end of July 2014, with the election of Joko Widodo as the new president. With his reputation for a people-centered leadership came a wave of high expectations. But it is sobering to keep in mind that politics in Indonesia has for some time been trapped in "a criminal democracy in which untamed oligarchs compete politically through elections" (Winters 2011, 180). That is why, after an idea to re-ally development with the common good is suggested, the odds of its realization remain precarious: the probability for genuine development to get lost in the twilight is as even as the chance for it to start enjoying a rare place in the sun.

Indeed, the plight of people-centered development is a story of being so near yet so far.

Works Cited

ACDP Indonesia (2013). "Education Corruption Suspected to Reach Rp600 Billion." https://acdpindonesia.wordpress.com/2013/08/29/education-corruption-suspected-to-reach-rp600-billion/ (15.09.2014).

Aspinall, Edward and Gerry van Klinken (2011). "The State and Illegality in Indonesia." In Edward Aspinall and Gerry van Klinken (eds.). *The State and Illegality in Indonesia*, 1–28. Leiden: KITLV Press.

Bambang Ismawan (2013). "Doing Well by Doing Good: Turning People's Enterprises Around—A Conversation with Bambang Ismawan of Indonesia's Bina Swadaya". *Asian Politics and Policy*, 5 (3), 461–468.

Barnes, Philip (1995). *Indonesia: The Political Economy of Energy*. Oxford: Oxford University Press.

Barron, Patrick et al. (2006). *Local Conflict and Community Development in Indonesia*. Jakarta: Decentralization Support Facility.

Bresnan, John (1993). *Managing Indonesia: The Modern Political Economy*. New York: Columbia University Press.

Buchanan, James M. (1980). "Rent-Seeking and Profit-Seeking." In James M. Buchanan et al. (eds.). *Towards a Theory of the Rent-Seeking Society*, 3–15. Texas: Texas A & M University Press.

Budiman, Arief (ed.) (1990). *State and Civil Society in Indonesia*. Clayton: Monash University Centre of Southeast Asian Studies.

Chalmers, Ian (1997). "Introduction." In Ian Chalmers and Vedi Hadiz (eds.). *The Politics of Economic Development in Indonesia: Contending Perspectives*, 1–35. London: Routledge.

Chalmers, Ian and Vedi R. Hadiz (eds.) (1997). *The Politics of Economic Development in Indonesia: Contending Perspectives*. London: Routledge.
Coordinating Ministry for Economic Affairs (2011). *Masterplan for Acceleration and Expansion of Indonesia Economic Development*. Jakarta: Coordinating Ministry for Economic Affairs, Republic of Indonesia.
Cowen, Michael P. and Robert W. Shenton (1996). *Doctrines of Development*. London: Routledge.
Crouch, Harold (1978). *The Army and Politics in Indonesia*. Ithaca: Cornell University Press.
Danang Widoyoko, J. (2011). "The Education Sector: The Fragmentation and Adaptability of Corruption". In Edward Aspinall and Gerry van Klinken (eds.). *The State and Illegality in Indonesia*, 165–187. Leiden: KITLV Press.
DEMOS Research Team (2011). *Masalah Perwujudan Hak Ekosob di Indonesia*. Jakarta: Demos.
Dick, Howard and Jeremy Mulholland (2011). "The State as Marketplace: Slush Funds and Intra-Elite Rivalry". In Edward Aspinall and Gerry van Klinken (eds.). *The State and Illegality in Indonesia*, 65–85. Leiden: KITLV Press.
Eldridge, Philip (1990). "NGOs and the State in Indonesia". In Arief Budiman (ed.). *State and Civil Society in Indonesia, Southeast Asia Studies No. 22*, 503–538. Clayton: Monash University Centre of Southeast Asian Studies.
Enggak Bahau'ddin (1974). "The Rulers Go into Business". In Ian Chalmers and Vedi Hadiz (eds.). *The Politics of Economic Development in Indonesia: Contending Perspectives*, 64–67. London: Routledge.
Feith, Herbert (1962). *The Decline of Constitutional Democracy*. Ithaca: Cornell University Press.
Ardiansyah, Fitrian (2013). Responsible Mining: Is It Possible? *Coal Asia*, June 11 – July 20, 96–97.
Gasper, Des (2004). *The Ethics of Development: From Economism to Human Development*. Edinburgh: Edinburgh University Press.
Geertz, Clifford (1973). *The Interpretation of Culture*. New York: Basic Books.
Gilchrist, Alison (2009). *The Well-Connected Community: A Networking Approach to Community Development*, second edition. Bristol: The University of Bristol Policy Press.
Green, Marshall (1990). *Indonesia: Crisis and Transformation 1965–1968*. Washington, D.C.: Compass Press.
Hairus Salim, H.S. et al. (2011). *Politik Ruang Publik Sekolah*. Yogyakarta: Center for Religious and Cross-Cultural Studies.
Hasani, Ismail and Bonar T. Naipospos (eds.). *Dari Radikalisme menuju Terorisme*. Jakarta: Pustaka Masyarakat Setara.
Henderson, Paul and Ilona Vercseg (2010). *Community Development and Civil Society*. Bristol: The University of Bristol Policy Press.
Higgins, Benjamin (1968). *Economic Development*. New York: W. W. Norton.

Hill, Hal (1994). "The Economy". In Hal Hill (ed.). *Indonesia's New Order: The Dynamics of Socio-economic Transformation*, 54–122. Sydney: Allen & Unwin.
Jakarta Post (2011a). "Stop the Rentseekers", 22 March 2011, 6.
— (2011b). "State Procurement a Hotbed of Corruption", 31 May 2011, 3.
Jones, Gavin W. and Terrence H. Hull (1994). "Demographic Perspectives". In Terence H. Hill (ed.). *Indonesia's New Order: the Dynamics of Socio-economic Transformation*, 123–178. Sydney: Allen & Unwin.
Kahin, George M. (1952). *Nationalism and Revolution in Indonesia*. Ithaca: Cornell University Press.
Khan, Mushtaq H. (2000a). "Rents, Efficiency and Growth". In Mushtaq Khan and Jomo K. Sundaram (eds.). *Rents, Rent-Seeking and Economic Development: Theory and Evidence in Asia*, 21–69. Cambridge: Cambridge University Press.
— (2000b). "Rent-Seeking as Process". In Mushtaq Khan and Jomo K. Sundaram (eds.). *Rents, Rent-Seeking and Economic Development: Theory and Evidence in Asia*, 70–144. Cambridge: Cambridge University Press.
Kompas (2011). "Fokus", 1 July 2011, 33–36.
Kontan (2011). "Konflikt Tanah Meningkat", 14 June 2011, 3.
Lev, Daniel S. (1990). "Intermediate Classes and Change in Indonesia: Some Initial Reflections". In Richard Tanter and Kenneth Young (eds.). *The Politics of Middle Class Indonesia*, 25–43. Clayton: Monash University Centre of Southeast Asian Studies.
Marshall, Alfred (1972 [1890, 1920]). *Principles of Economics*. London: Macmillan.
McVey, Ruth (1992). "The Materialization of the Southeast Asian Entrepreneur". In Ruth McVey (ed.). *Southeast Asian Capitalists*, 7–33. Ithaca: Cornell University Southeast Asia Program.
Moertopo, Ali (1997 [1972]). "National Development Strategy". In Ian Chalmers and Vedi Hadiz (eds.). *The Politics of Economic Development in Indonesia: Contending Perspectives*, 75–77. London: Routledge.
National Team for the Acceleration of Poverty Reduction (2014). "Acceleration Policies." http://www.tnp2k.go.id.19 (15.09.2014).
Palmer, Ingrid (1978). *The Indonesian Economy since 1965: A Case Study of Political Economy*. London: Frank Cass.
Peet, Richard and Elaine Hartwick (2009). *Theories of Development: Contentions, Arguments, Alternatives*, second edition. London: Guilford Press.
PODES Infrastructure Census (2012). *Report on Infrastructure Supply Readiness in Indonesia—Achievements and Remaining Gaps*. Jakarta: PODES.
Przeworski, Adam and Michael Wallerstein (1986). "Popular Sovereignty, State Autonomy, and Private Property." *European Journal of Sociology*, XXVII, 215–259.

---

19 The list is not exhaustive and serves only as an illustration of how various state ministries/agencies target rural development in an overlapping and uncoordinated way. The pattern was confirmed by a middle-ranking official at the Ministry of Home Affairs, Jakarta (ibid.).

Robison, Richard (1986). *Indonesia: The Rise of Capital*. Sydney: Allen & Unwin.
Sato, Yuri (1994). "The Development of Business Groups in Indonesia: 1967–1989". In T. Shiraishi (ed.). *Approaching Suharto's Indonesia from the Margins*, 101–153. Ithaca: Cornell University Southeast Asia Program.
Siti Rakhma Marry (2012). "MIFFE: Proyek Perampasan Tanah Orang Malind-Anim". Research paper presented at the National Seminar on The State and Rule of Law in Indonesia, 9–10 October, in Jakarta, Indonesia.
Soehoed, Abdul R. (1997) [1977]. "Commodities and Viable Economic Sectors—A Possible Basis for Development Planning". In Ian Chalmers and Vedi Hadiz (eds.). *The Politics of Economic Development in Indonesia: Contending Perspectives*, 85–90. London: Routledge.
Soeharto (1997 [1970]). "A Presidential Speech, 17 April 1970". In Ian Chalmers and Vedi Hadiz (eds.). *The Politics of Economic Development in Indonesia: Contending Perspectives*, 53–55. London: Routledge.
Sumawinata, Sarbini (1997 [1968]). "Repelita". In Ian Chalmers and Vedi Hadiz (eds.) *The Politics of Economic Development in Indonesia: Contending Perspectives*, 60–62. London: Routledge.
Sutter, John (1959). *Indonesianisasi: Politics in a Changing Economy 1940–1955*. Ithaca: Cornell University Press.
Tollison, Robert D. (1982). "Rent-Seeking: A Survey". *Kyklos*, 35 (4), 575–602.
Törnquist, Olle (1990). "Notes on the State and Rural Change in Java and India". In Arief Budiman (ed.). *State and Civil Society in Indonesia, Southeast Asian Studies No. 22*, 421–439. Clayton: Monash University Centre of Southeast Asian Studies.
United Nations (1955). *Social Progress through Community Development*. New York: United Nations.
United Nations Development Programme/UNDP (2012). *One Planet to Share: Sustaining Human Progress in a Changing Climate*. London: Routledge for UNDP.
— (various years). *Human Development Report*.
Van Klinken, Gerry and Edward Aspinal (2011). "Building Relations: Corruption, Competition and Cooperation in the Construction Industry". In Edward Aspinall and Gerry van Klinken (eds.). *The State and Illegality in Indonesia*, 139-163. Leiden: KITLV Press.
(The) Wahid Institute Research Team (2011). *Laporan Kebebasan Beragama dan Toleransi 2010*. Jakarta: The Wahid Institute.
Winters, Jeffrey A. (1996). *Power in Motion: Capital Mobility and the Indonesian State*. Ithaca: Cornell University Press.
Winters, Jeffrey A. (2011). *Oligarchy*. Cambridge: Cambridge University Press.
Wolin, Sheldon S. (2004). *Politics and Vision: Continuity and Innovation in Western Political Thought*, expanded edition. New Jersey: Princeton University Press.
World Bank (1966). *Annual Country Report: Indonesia*. Washington, D.C.: World Bank.

— (1981). "Annual Country Report: Indonesia". In Ian Chalmers and Vedi Hadiz (eds.) (1997). *The Politics of Economic Development in Indonesia: Contending Perspectives*, 96–98. London: Routledge.
— (1983). "Annual Country Report: Indonesia". In Ian Chalmers and Vedi Hadiz (eds.) (1997). *The Politics of Economic Development in Indonesia: Contending Perspectives*, 98–100. London: Routledge.
— (1985). "Annual Country Report: Indonesia". In Ian Chalmers and Vedi Hadiz (eds.) (1997). *The Politics of Economic Development in Indonesia: Contending Perspectives*, 100–103. London: Routledge.
— (2001). *Indonesia: Country Procurement Assessment Report—Reforming the Public Procurement System*. Jakarta: World Bank Jakarta Office.
— (2006). *Making the New Indonesia Work for the Poor*. Jakarta: World Bank Jakarta Office, November.
— (2010). "Indonesia Health Sector Review—Accelerating Improvement in Maternal Health: Why Reform is Needed." *Policy & Discussion Notes*, August 2010.
— (2012). "Gini Index Data". http://data.worldbank.org/SI.POV.GINI (02.07.2013).
— (2013). "List of All World Bank Projects in Indonesia". www.worldbank.org/en/contry/indonesia/projects/all (04.07.2013).
World Wide Fund/WWF (2013). "Data on Deforestation". http://wwf.org/about_our_earth/about_forests/deforestation (04.07.2013).
Yayasan Indonesia Forum (2007). *Visi Indonesia 2030*. Jakarta: Yayasan Indonesia Forum.

Common Good Arrangements in Germany—Ready for Global Challenges?

Katharina Hirschbrunn, Georg Stoll, and Verena Risse

In this paper, we outline the content and realization of the global common good in Germany and analyze existing discrepancies as well as potentials for transformation. We thereby focus on the following questions: What is the prevailing understanding of the global common good in Germany? Where are the corresponding values and norms that are already realized in social practices and institutions? Where do norms and institutions diverge, and how could a reorientation towards the global common good be implemented? To analyze these questions, we will rely on four core norms that constitute the basic understanding of the common good in Germany: Social justice, environmental sustainability, freedom and democracy. Major shortcomings in realizing these norms are, in particular, the shortcomings of the social market economy in the face of global challenges, the question of economic growth as well as the defectiveness of the democratic system. Finally, potential for transformation is outlined for each issue, with a particular emphasis on the concept of "commoning".

1. Four Core Norms and their Application in Germany

With regard to the common good, both a formal and a substantive approach can be distinguished. According to the formal approach, the common good is not pre-defined, but is determined in a democratic decision-making process. The substantive understanding, by contrast, considers that there is a material conception of what the common good is. In contemporary Germany, the common good is primarily a formal concept relying on democratic procedures and institutions. Democracy can thus be taken as a core norm in Germany. While there are some laws that refer to the common good in a formal way, there is no existing legislation that would give an explicit material definition of the common good. However, a closer look at recent history uncovers some core norms that have become vital for the perception of the common good in Germany, and that also became part of the German constitution. These are, in particular, social justice, freedom and environmental sustainability.

1.1. The Origins of the Four Core Norms in Germany

It was the capitalist industrialization in the 19th century, with its miserable working conditions and the impoverishment of large sections of society that initiated public debates about social justice and eventually led to the introduction of a basic public social security system. After World War II, the norm of social justice translated into the conception of Germany as a welfare state with the central concept of the social market economy. This economic system aims at unifying the two core norms of social justice and freedom. The norm of freedom can also be traced back to historical experiences in Germany: It was the oppression by authoritarian and totalitarian regimes that strengthened the sensibility not only of the value of democracy but also of individual freedom. As a consequence, the constitution of post-war Germany provided strong safeguards for freedom rights, especially in the sense of protection against interference from public power in the private sphere. While a whole range of rights to freedom and the definition of Germany as a democratic and social federal state have been part of the first 20 articles of the constitution from its beginnings, the core norm of environmental sustainability has just recently been added to the constitution—namely in form of the protection of the natural foundations of life and animals. Nevertheless, reference to nature has a longstanding tradition in German culture, as witnessed for example by the period of Romanticism in the 18th century.

Today, the four core norms of democracy, social justice, freedom and environmental sustainability are implemented in social practices and institutions alike. In the following pages, the content of these norms—as they are perceived in Germany—is outlined, and the institutions and social practices that realize the common good are elaborated upon.

1.2. Democracy

Democracy refers to the rule of people. To assure this, several aspects must be considered. First of all, democracy relies on the principles of generality and equality. The principle of generality claims that all those affected by a measure should be included in the process to decide on it. Equality, on the other hand, entails that each person's voice should have equal weight in the democratic process and everyone should have equal chances to state their views.

In Germany, elements of both procedural and substantive democracy are combined to determine the content of the legislation and—by extension—the common good. The advantage of a procedural approach is that it is, at least at first sight neutral and value-free. Yet, it also bears the risk of delegating all decision-making powers to the elected body. Substantive democracy, by contrast, denotes the fact that all societal groups are equally involved in the democratic process. In this, it must be distinguished from what could be termed "material democracy", which refers to the fact that democracy must encompass substantial norms as well. Material democracy, and this can for instance be seen by references to human rights or norms of justice, is also at place in Germany.

Democracy is institutionally realized in Germany through elections where the citizens vote for representatives to be sent to various parliamentary bodies. Germany practices a free, equal, universal, direct and secret ballot. Moreover, democracy in Germany is generally, organized according to the principle of subsidiarity. This is to say, following the idea of decentralization, the organizational entity that is best suited to deal with a matter, should be in charge of it.

Yet, democracy does not stop at the creation of institutions to which the responsibility can be delegated. Instead, it involves a constant engagement with this institutional system as well as with the society as a whole in order to align with the democratic ideal. A crucial element of this is the possibility to intervene in the work of the parliament for example by filing a petition for a referendum. In addition, it requires a vital public sphere in which the civil society can discuss political and social issues and in which minorities have an equal chance to express their views. This, however, depends on some (institutional) conditions such as a free press and the guarantee of certain political human rights like the freedom of assembly.

1.3. Social Justice

Social justice is a wide notion referring to social services and social politics generally. At the same time, it is inseparable from the social market economic system practiced in Germany, which relies on the idea of achieving social progress and redistribution on the basis of a market system. Overall, Germany spends a total of about 30 percent of the GDP on social services[1]—one of the highest figures worldwide. This fact indicates that social justice is considered an important value that is realized, for example, in a free school and university system and in a public health system. Nevertheless, the social inequality is growing faster in Germany than in all other OECD countries.

Besides the education and health system that have undergone major reformations during the last years, several other fields of social justice seem particularly pressing in the light of the question of the global common good. In particular, it can be debated whether Germany lives up to its principles of justice when it comes to question of justice with an international scope. So far, redistributive concerns *vis-à-vis* foreigners are usually dealt with in terms of development cooperation. Yet, the increasing economic, political and cultural interconnectedness as well as the fact that Germany benefits from trade relations also with emerging countries, might raise questions of global justice more specifically. Similarly, intergenerational justice, that is to say: justice between generations, is a pressing issue debated in Germany these days with regard to, for example, the use of resources or the financing of social systems and pensions. The issue is further exacerbated by the demographic change the German society is currently undergoing, involving a low birthrate and an expected increase in elderly people. In reaction to this development, the government has taken different steps to increase the birth rate, to facilitate the immigration of skilled laborers and to adapt infrastructure and housing to the needs of elderly persons.

---

1 The latest figure for 2011 is 29.9 percent (BMAS 2011, 6).

1.4. Freedom

The most important institutional protection of freedom is to be found in the codification of the basic rights and liberties in the articles 1 to 19 in the German Constitution, the so called Basic Law (*Grundgesetz*). The importance of these constitutional rights is not only visible in their prominent place in the constitution but also in the fact that a relevant violation not only occurs when the state passes a law that contradicts one person's right, but already through any form of action or inaction by an official body. In case a violation takes place, the right-holder may lodge a complaint directly with the German constitutional court.

These basic rights and liberties constitute on the one hand entitlements of the individual and conditions of the state's actions on the other. This is to say, in the sense of negative freedom, rights prescribe the realm of freedom that citizens have from interference of the state. In the sense of positive freedom, they prescribe duties of the state, in that the state must provide an environment which enables the realization of the rights. Besides being directed towards the state, rights to freedom also apply among individuals, but only in an indirect way. They constrain private persons insofar as the exercise of one person's freedom generally finds its limits in the exercise of another person's freedom. In addition, the different freedom rights stand in an ordered relationship to one another. For example, one person's freedom to action may not interfere with another person's right to bodily integrity.

Finally, what is referred to as positive freedom is also present in the German political practice. Positive freedom denotes the fact of disposing of the necessary resources to fulfill one's life plans or, more generally, to live a good life. This requires that everyone be given the possibility to realize her or his potentials. In this, positive liberty relates to several of the other values we are considering here. It is, for example, linked to issues of justice—in particular to the questions of equal opportunities and educational justice, for these are intended to level out unequal starting points. The provision of social welfare in Germany, by contrast, is generally not sufficient for full positive freedom as it provides the basic resources for a living, but does not cover special expenditures dedicated to self-fulfillment.

1.5. Environmental Sustainability

Since the environmental movements in the nineteen-seventies and -eighties which led to the creation of the Federal Ministry for the Environment in 1986, the environment was given ongoing attention by the government and society alike. Still, in order to reach sustainability it is not sufficient to simply set up institutions and norms. In addition, private and economic actors must be incentivized to act according to principles of sustainability. To this aim, several mechanisms have been developed both at the national and at the European level. Among these were the two solutions to either subsidize energy-friendly technology or to impose a higher tax on energy in the hope that it will be used more efficiently. Both solutions can be found in recent legislative moves in Germany. The strategy of taxation was chosen when the so called law on the "entrance into an ecological tax reform" ("Gesetz zum Einstieg in die ökologische Steuerreform") was passed in 1999. It involved a tax on electricity from conventional sources and a classification of the tax on mineral oil to ecological criteria. The effects of this tax were, however, rather limited (Steiner and Cludius 2010). That is, the strategy of subsidizing energy-friendly technology was also chosen by the German government. In 2000, the so called "law on renewable energy" was passed and keeps being updated since. The objective of the law regarding renewable energy is to increase its use and to extend the installation of renewable energy sources. The fact that the law is maintained and constantly renewed indicates that it does have an effect on the citizens' behavior. A third strategy was used at the European level, namely to achieve the sustainability of the public good of clean air by counteracting high CO2 emissions in the EU member states. With the European set-up of the European Union Emissions Trading Scheme (EU ETS) in 2005, a market was created, on which allocated certificates for CO2 pollution can be traded.

2. Central Conflicts and Discrepancies

The norms of democracy, social justice, environmental sustainability and freedom form the German understanding of the global common good are partly implemented in German institutions: Institutions are shaped by core norms, and institutions in turn influence norms. However, major discrepancies between norms and reality can be observed. These discrepancies are starting point and engines of societal change. Examples for discrepancies such as increasing inequality or the lack of environmental sustainability will be outlined in detail in sections three to five. Before, we shortly analyze three main causes for how these discrepancies come about.

2.1. Power Relations and Special Interests Challenging the Common Good

As outlined above, the norm of democracy necessitates an electoral process in which all citizens are equally represented. Yet, even if the electoral process itself takes place on an equal basis, groups with higher material resources or education can influence the political agenda more strongly than others. In Germany, special interest groups influence politics for example by providing lucrative jobs to politicians or by donating to parties (Lösche 2006, 66; Leif and Speth 2006a, 26). Furthermore, policy papers of lobbyists frequently leave their mark on draft laws or whole passages are adopted (Leif and Speth 2006a, 21). Thus, the political outcome does not necessarily mirror citizens' interpretation of the common good.

However, special interests do not only challenge the common good on the political layer. Also on the individual level, people do not act according to their norms—in their voting decisions, but also in their acts as employees, chief executives, consumers or citizens. Reasons may be lethargy, convenience, suppression or emotional distance to humans influenced by their actions. This inconsistent behavior may partially also be backed up by the decade-lasting influence of the paradigm that self-interest—channeled through the "invisible hand"—serves the prosperity of the whole society.

2.2. The Conflict between Different Core Norms

Furthermore, discrepancies between norms and existing institutions may be caused by the conflict between different norms. For example, redistribution measures, which are necessary to ensure social justice, may conflict with the right to property. Also, environmental sustainability may conflict with social justice, as eco-taxes may strongly affect those with lower incomes. Furthermore, different interpretations of data as well as diverging interpretations of the central norms may cause conflict. This is exemplified in the German discourse on ecological sustainability: While some defend "green growth" as being sustainable, others perceive this to be an oxymoron. Thus, while the compatibility of different norms may be over- or understated by the respective political currents, at some point trade-offs between different norms have to be addressed in a public discourse.

2.3. Globalization in the Context of Insufficient Global Institutions

In the course of globalization, various international institutions have been established, such as the United Nations or the International Criminal Court. However, during the past 60 years, institutions have been mainly designed to enable economic activities at the international scale, while environmental and social aims have not been fostered as strongly. Examples are the World Trade Organization (WTO) or the International Monetary Fund (IMF), which have been highly influenced by early industrialized countries. On the other hand, efforts like the ones to upgrade the United Nations Environment Program (UNEP) to an autonomous UN body failed so far because of entrenched resistance from some major political powers. International power relations thus influenced the shape of existing institutions as well as which institutions were being created at all. Certain norms may therefore lack enforcement due to the lack of institutions or due to the dominance of certain countries' influence within institutions. However, the current kind of globalization does not only imply a lack of consistency between norms and institutions on the global level, but— amongst others due to the high mobility of financial capital—also renders it hard to implement norms on the national level.

2.4. Discrepancies Informing the Potential for Transformation

The different causes outlined here condition norms to not being fully realized in existing institutions in Germany. Still, it is exactly these discrepancies that drive future transformation, and it is the analysis of these discrepancies that can give insights into how the current situation may be changed.

Therefore in the following sections, existing institutions and social practices will be assessed with regard to how the basic norms of democracy, social justice, environmental sustainability and freedom are being implemented. Three major narratives and their fields of practice—namely social market economy, economic growth, and democracy—will be considered with regard to divergences and discrepancies as well as to their respective potentials for transformation. With respect to the latter, the complementary perspective of commons and so called "commoning" will be introduced in addition to analyzing the roles of private and public actors.

3. Social Market Economy: Still the King's Road?

If there is a concept which could rightly claim to express a broad consensus about what a common good would look like for the majority of at least the West German population in the second half of the 20th century, it would be the concept of a social market economy embedded in a constitutional democracy. However, this model is facing severe challenges against the backdrop of environmental damage and increasing social inequality.

Ludwig Erhard, the first minister of economy in the post-war Federal Republic of Germany, gave a popular version of the ambition of a social market economy with the famous title of his 1957 book "Prosperity for All" ("Wohlstand für alle"). The concept itself was the result of debates in the late nineteen-forties about the fundamental economic orientation of the new state when ordoliberal approaches were combined with Christian social teaching (Müller-Armack 1947). Although disputed and ambiguous the concept became very successful and popular. It was also introduced in the reunification treaty in 1990 as the common economic order of the two German states. The basic idea behind the social market economy concept was and still is to found a welfare state on two pillars: a strong and competitive market economy on the one hand and high levels of social protection and economic prosperity for all citizens on the other hand.

3.1. Individual Freedom and Social Justice

With this double-pillar approach the social market economy contains the ambitious promise to reconcile freedom and social justice within a system of democratic governance. While market economy stands for the pursuit of individual freedom in the sphere of economic activity and for the production of material wealth by efficient resource allocation, the social orientation of the economic system is to grant legitimacy and social peace through the political containment of market forces. Individual liberties as expressed in strong guarantees for private property rights and in economic freedom (for example to choose one's profession, to conclude a contract, or to start an enterprise) are basic preconditions for a social market economy. The approach therefore has a clear priority for private against public economic activity spelled out in the principle of subsidiarity, which states that initiative and responsibility for economic activities be taken at the lowest possible agency level. But the founders of the concept were also aware of the possibility of market failures resulting in favoring particular interests at the cost of the common good. Hence, a social market economy needs a democratic state to set and maintain a framework for market activities (including limits where necessary) and to take compensatory action in favor of the economically weak parts of society, for example through a redistributive tax system and public social services.

Nevertheless, the concept has come under increasing pressure from at least two sides. After a period of economic liberalization from the nineteen-eighties to the early nineties, the financial crisis of 2007 marked a turning point. The economic reverberations of the crisis and the growing awareness that the liberalization agenda had not only provided for economic growth but also for increasing income and wealth inequality in Germany made the idea of a "social market economy" lose much of its former nimbus. According to the OECD (2011, 5) the income of the top decile of German households increased by 1.6 percent annually from the mid-nineteen-eighties to the late noughties while the income increase of the bottom decile did not exceed an average of 0.1 percent per annum in the same period. The situation is even more pronounced with regard to wealth inequality. A study of the Federal Bank of Germany revealed a Gini coefficient of net wealth distribution of 0.76 (compared to 0.63 for the entire Euro zone). The top decile owns more than 59 percent of the global net wealth of German households (Bundesbank 2013, 30).

In addition, the model is challenged by ecological problems it was not prepared for. With the externalization of environmental damage being a case of eminent market failure, supporters of free markets are struggling to adjust their model to build a "green" or "eco"-social market economy (if they don't deny the problems right away). Although there has been some considerable success in limiting, reducing, and avoiding environmental damage at the national level through legislation, the question to what extent this may also be possible at the transnational level (for example climate change, loss of biodiversity, pollution and acidification of the oceans) remains open: How would the position of Germany look like in an environmentally sustainable globalized economy? This question was part of the discussions of a special *ad hoc* parliamentary commission established for the period of 2011 to 2013 under the title of "Growth, Prosperity and Quality of Life". While the conflicting lines between more liberal, more social and more ecological approaches became rather clear in this commission, the political outcome remained modest: some complementary indicators for the measurement of prosperity, a surprising consensus on the limits of efficiency strategies, some declarations and appeals. As for now, there is no follow-up of the work of this commission in either the political debate or the political practice of the new government where the two biggest parties, the Christian Democrats and the Social Democrats, share power since 2013.

3.2. Challenges from a Global Perspective

The traditional social market economy, which enjoyed almost unanimous support for decades as a common good paradigm at national level, is now being questioned with regard to its capacity of coping with global challenges. Can transnational externalization of costs and risks—which has become common practice in international production and trade—be effectively contained within the market system? Can a free market economy work without inherent growth dependencies leading to an overstretching of the limits of the ecosystem? Is there a danger for the political system to be co-opted or even blackmailed by transnational financial and economic actors who can threaten governments with the loss of employment or with massive tax avoidance—and who are themselves invulnerable even in the case of failure because they are "too big to fail" and hence have to be saved with public money? Such fundamental questions are emerging in the debate, but the general attitude is to either neglect or minimize them. While there are punctual political interventions for example in the regulation of financial markets and institutions and even here the initial zeal has slowed down considerably, a general debate about the capacities and limits of the very concept of the social market economy is not only avoided but rejected. On the contrary, the concept is often heralded as having the potential of a new export product under the branding of a "global eco-social market economy"[2]. This attitude of turning a blind eye towards the deficits of the social market economy vis-à-vis global structural problems seems to be shared by the majority of the population. An opinion poll in 2012 revealed that on the one hand a majority was criticizing income inequality and stressed symptoms as effects of the economic system in Germany, but on the other hand only 13 percent could imagine a better alternative to the market economy (Institut für Demoskopie Allensbach 2012, table A5 and A8).

To conclude, the social market economy has proven its strengths as a model to support the common good in post-war Germany. Therefore, it deserves to be examined with regard to its potentials also in other national contexts, where more harmful concepts of running an economy prevail. On the other hand, the model has not yet passed the test of being able to cope with central global challenges and to be useful for pursuing also a "global common good". To make progress in this sense, questions like those mentioned above have to be given a chance to be seriously discussed publicly (with the participation of international partners) and to enter the agenda of political decision making.

4. Economic Growth and the Global Common Good: The Lost Link

A central issue being debated in Germany today is whether an "eco-social market economy" can grow further while at the same time, environmental impacts are reduced to sustainable levels. In other words, is so called

---

[2] This is for example the explicit program of the Global Marshall Plan Foundation (see: globalmarshallplan.org).

"green growth" possible or not? And is further economic growth even desirable? In this section, we outline the relation between growth and environmental sustainability, social justice and quality of life, as well as the potential for transformation.

4.1. Growth and Environmental Sustainability

Concerning the question of whether economic growth can be sustainable, the effect of efficiency is central. On the global level, emission efficiency did increase significantly during the last decades (Jackson 2011, 82ff.). Nevertheless, worldwide greenhouse gas (GHG) emissions even between 1990 and 2011 have *increased* by almost 40 percent (Jackson 2011, 85). Thus, efficiency gains were more than overcompensated by the increase in population and by the growth of GDP *per capita*. In order to stabilize the climate at a temperature increase of 2 degrees Celsius, global anthropogenic GHG emissions have to be reduced by 40 to 70 percent until 2050 compared to 2010 (IPCC 2014, 21). Thus, a dramatic turnaround of the trend has to be achieved. In the context of the expected rates of worldwide economic and population growth, emission intensity of worldwide production and consumption would have to increase by almost the tenfold speed on average than it does right now[3]. However, it seems improbable that even a massive progress in technology and its diffusion across the globe would lead to the increase of worldwide efficiency that is needed. Thus, efficiency gains in the past were and in the future most probably will be too low to reduce the sum of worldwide emissions sufficiently.

What about the European level? Peters et al. (2011) show that from 1990 to 2008, even Europe[4]—with its relatively high technological standards—did not reduce but *increase* its consumption-based emissions. It thus seems that no absolute decoupling of economic growth and GHG emissions did take place. This can partly be explained by the so-called rebound effect: Efficiency gains frequently bring about a decrease in costs of production and consumption and thereby cause an increase in consumption.

---

3 Population numbers are based on middle values of UN-estimations concerning population growth. Worldwide GDP/head growth is assumed to be of the same size as from 1990 to 2011 (Jackson 2011, 93f.).

4 "Europe represents the Annex B EU27 countries plus Croatia, Iceland, Liechtenstein, Norway, and Switzerland" (Peters et al. 2011, 8906).

Hence, a large part of efficiency gains is being offset by an increase in consumption. The size of this effect depends on various factors. Estimates of empirical studies range from 30 to 100 percent (Madlener and Alcott 2011, 3f.). While rebound effects are widely acknowledged today, for example by the above mentioned *ad hoc* parliamentary commission on growth, prosperity and quality of life (Deutscher Bundestag 2013, 435f.), they are currently not being taken into account in most efficiency policies (Hinterberger et al. 2011). What is more, if policies aim at further economic growth and thus set incentives for the increase of production and consumption, efficiency gains very likely are at least to some degree undone by the increase in total consumption.

The numbers at regional and global level suggest that a mere focusing on efficiency is not enough. As climate change is irreversible and causes immense damage to humans and the environment, a lot is at stake. This suggests that to decrease total emissions and other environmental pressures to sustainable levels, technological solutions and, for example, the transition towards renewable energy sources are necessary and urgent—but not sufficient. It seems that countries which at present emit multiple times the sustainable amount of CO_2 must rapidly reduce their emissions. On the national level, Germany's CO_2-equivalent emissions in 2011—even if measured conventionally—amounted to almost six times the sustainable level. Thus, if Germany takes its core norm of environmental sustainability seriously, it seems necessary to challenge the taboo of accepting a reduction in consumption and production. It has to be discussed whether the efficiency strategy has to be complemented by a sufficiency strategy in high-income countries.

4.2. Growth and Social Justice

The question of the environmental sustainability of growth is closely related to issues of social justice. First of all, a large part of humanity today as well as future generations are threatened by climate change, which was triggered by the economic growth in early industrialized countries. While it is high-income countries that mainly caused climate change, it is mostly people in low- or middle-income countries that will suffer most from it in coming decades. With regard to problems caused by climate change, there are two approaches to figure out who is responsible to take action: According to the concept of causal responsibility, it is those who caused the problem. The focus on growth in the past would thus have generated commitments in terms of global and intergenerational justice. The second approach: According to remedial responsibility, it is those actors best equipped to help that are responsible to do so. In both perspectives, it is clearly high income countries that are responsible to pay for and to remedy the adverse effects of climate change. Also with respect to current emissions, it is still the high-income countries that cause the highest emissions per head. Thus, early industrialized countries are obliged to take a leading role in curbing emission trends as fast as possible.

But also at the national level, the quest for economic growth is related to issues of social justice. The strong orientation towards economic growth may cause inequalities to increase: For example, if taxes on capital, high incomes and inheritances are avoided or reduced to relatively low levels on the grounds of not wanting to inhibit economic growth, this may have a negative effect on social equality in a country.

4.3. Growth and Quality of Life

It thus seems that economic growth in high-income countries hinders both environmental sustainability as well as social justice. Still, it is argued in the public debate in Germany that growth is needed to maintain and increase the quality of life of the population. Thus, how do citizens themselves perceive the influence of economic growth on quality of life? While in a recent poll, the majority perceives growth to be necessary for the quality of life *of society*, around 60 percent do not expect further economic growth to increase *their own* quality of life (Bertelsmann Stiftung 2010). Germans perceive quality of life to consist primarily of a good health, good family and social relations, of leading a self-determined life, living together peacefully, of civic engagement as well as of the protection of the environment (Bertelsmann Stiftung 2010). Increasing money and possessions, by contrast, is considered important for quality of life only by 12 percent of the respondents. While some of the elements of quality of life named above require financial underpinning, it seems that—perhaps apart from the health system—no constant *increase* in material wealth is necessary to enhance these goals. Instead it seems to be inequality of incomes that has a major impact on many social and health issues: For high-income countries, it is not average income that is most relevant for many health and social indicators, but the equality of incomes (Wilkinson and Pickett 2009). Thus, aiming at economic growth while at the same time accepting increasing inequalities may boost various social and health problems. A further discrepancy between economic growth and quality of life is displayed by research on subjectively perceived happiness. While in Germany, GDP has doubled since 1970, the subjectively perceived contentment did not increase (Helliwell et al. 2012). Likewise, in a broad range of high-income countries, the increase in a country's income did not increase happiness (Easterlin et al. 2010). An upper boundary for economic growth affecting subjectively perceived happiness seems to be an average income of around 10,000 Dollars per year (Wallacher 2012, 88). It therefore seems that focusing on economic growth serves the case of neither quality of life, nor environmental sustainability nor social justice.

4.4. Potential for Transformation

What could thus be a future orientation for politics? To reorient the economic and societal spheres towards the global common good, a public debate is necessary to figure out what the (global) common good and quality of life stand for in Germany today, and what the role of economic growth should be. One outcome of such a debate would be to define societal and economic goals anew and to reorient all policy measures and institutions to directly foster not economic growth but the common good. Furthermore, alternative indicators of welfare should be used (see Diefenbacher and Zieschank 2011, 85), that capture quality of life in Germany and that account for the norms of social and environmental justice, for freedom and democracy.

4.4.1. Reconciling Ecology and Social Justice

If in this debate, Germans perceive environmental sustainability—which is closely linked to intergenerational and international justice—as central, absolute environmental impacts would have to be substantially reduced until they reach sustainable levels. As a consequence, and to generate an efficient economic outcome, negative externalities of the production process would have to be internalized, for example in form of a tax or a cap-

and-trade scheme. The eventual revenues would have to be used for climate change mitigation as well as adaptation measures and compensation for loss and damage suffered by the poor. However, as the internalization of externalities increases the prices of many consumption goods, redistribution is essential to prevent further social imbalances from arising as well as to ensure social justice.

A further main issue in which environmental sustainability and social justice seem to conflict is employment. It is frequently argued that only by economic growth jobs can be saved or their number increased. However, there exist solutions to reconcile work and environmental sustainability. One example is to use productivity increases not to increase consumption but to reduce working time. Another option frequently proposed is the introduction of a basic income. These measures could at the same time further quality of life as they leave more time for social and democratic engagement, render the economy more sustainable and decrease social inequalities.

4.4.2. Independence from Economic Growth

It may well be the case that the transition towards sustainability, social justice and quality of life leads to a decrease in production and consumption: If by a democratic decision, true environmental costs would for example be priced and thus have to be internalized in all business calculations, various products would prove to be far less economical and consequently be consumed to a much lesser extent. Also if people individually or as a whole society chose to work less, consume less and free up time for social interaction, voluntary work, democratic participation or self-actualization, consumption and production may decrease. While this would be in accordance with societal aims, in the current system it would cause major problems: As many institutions in Germany were built up in times of constant economic growth after World War II, they now depend on growth and struggle even with the low growth rates of recent years. Amongst others, the social insurance systems, the health system, the system of deficit spending and the job market depend on growth (cf. Seidl and Zahrnt 2010b, 19ff.). This is particularly alarming as average relative growth rates in Germany have been declining since the nineteen-sixties (cf. Diefenbacher and Zieschank 2011, 18). Thus, to stabilize institutions against the background of decreasing growth rates at present, and against potentially decreasing consumption and production in the future, it seems necessary to thoroughly modify institutions and structures so that they can function independently of growth (cf. Seidl and Zahrnt 2010a, 34). This kind of resilience is also vital in times of recurring international financial or economic crises. Furthermore, an economic system that works independently from economic growth can render society the freedom to choose policy options that do not increase consumption and production.

4.4.3. Stability, Social Security and the Economic System

To render the economy independent from growth, a thorough transformation of the economic system as well as of society seems to be necessary. This would also include private business: In particular market-listed companies are currently forced to grow, while other types of economic actors have more freedom to focus on different goals (Seidl and Zahrnt 2010b, 21). Supporting cooperatives, non-profit organizations and foundations may lead to a change in company structures that could stabilize the economy in times of nonexistent, low or negative economic growth. Furthermore, many researchers perceive the interest-based credit system as well as the monetary system and the international financial market architecture as forcing enterprises and the whole economy to grow further (Seidl and Zahrnt 2010b, 21). Here, further research is needed. Various approaches to these problems are currently being tested and developed in Germany and Austria on the local scale, such as local currencies, depreciative money, a democratic bank, cooperatives or solidarity economy initiatives. It seems that it is only by adaptations like these that society can be free to choose the way in which it wants to interpret and implement its conception of the "common good".

4.4.4. Reorientation towards the Common Good

Furthermore, measures have to be figured out that directly serve the quality of life and the common good while not increasing environmental pressures and inequality. These could, amongst others, consist of giving citizens the prosperity of time and the freedom for self-actualization and for revitalizing the social and political sphere. A work time reduction could help to increase so called "time wealth" (Rinderspacher 2000). This is essential, as "liberated time" (Gorz 1994) as well as public spaces seem to be central for civic engagement as well as for health and social relations. Apart from this, as soon as growth in consumption would not be the major economic objective anymore, the whole concept of work as mere employment would have to be questioned: Other forms of work, such as the (re)production by nature, care or democratic work would have to be valued as well (Biesecker and Hofmeister 2010). Here, the concept of basic income could provide a way forward.

Further steps towards the common good would be to enhance redistributive measures in order to reduce poverty on the national and global level, and to reduce inequalities. This is not only essential to further social justice, but also to inhibit the concentration of economic power which threatens democracy.

Finally, forms of economic activity that directly foster the common good should be supported, such as public goods (like public transport), the shared usage of goods (like car sharing) and so-called "commoning" (see section five). Thereby, some sectors of the economy would grow and others would shrink. For example, more individual traffic might be replaced by public transportation and production and consumption could become more local. A lot of resources could be saved by diminishing transportation distances and by avoiding packaging. Again, experiences of towns or communities are essential for finding ways towards higher quality of life while lowering environmental impacts. Examples currently existing in Germany are eco-villages, the so-called transition town movement, solidarity economies, cooperatives, barter exchanges, local currencies, slow food initiatives, couch surfing, urban gardening or centers for do it yourself and subsistence work.

Transforming society towards the common good, rendering the economic and social system independent from economic growth and neutralizing growth drivers is a task that is not easy, cannot be achieved rapidly and needs stepwise political efforts, practical experiences as well as the strong participation of citizens. Research on how to transform society and economy towards independence from economic growth has currently been provided by the so called "degrowth" movement. While social sciences—in particular political economics—have to enhance research on ways to transform societies in this direction, the result of such efforts could be a model also for other countries: Finding a way to increase quality of life while at the same stabilizing the economic system and diminishing adverse impacts on environmental and social justice is essential in the light of the global crises the world is facing today.

5. The Management of Global Common Pool Resources

Environmental sustainability implies using resources in a sustainable manner and restricting the pollution of the environment. The question of how to manage "common pool resources" is essential for sustainability. Common pool resources are "natural or human made resources, where one person's use subtracts from another's use" (Ostrom 1990) and where excluding people from the use of the resources is difficult. While some regional common pool resources, such as forests or lakes have been managed quite successfully in Germany during the last decades, it is particularly global common pool resources that have been overused by Germany to a disastrous extent.

5.1. The Tragedy of the Unmanaged Global Common Pool Resources

Today, climate change is one of the most pressing environmental issues—among other things because the maximal possible extraction of fossil resources is more than 50 times bigger than the limited sink of the global atmosphere (cf. Edenhofer 2012a). In spite of ecological taxes and renewable energy legislation on national, the Emissions Trading System on the European level and the Kyoto Protocol on the international level, Germany will probably not even succeed in reaching the planned reduction by 40 percent of emissions compared to the level of 1990 until 2020. This renders it hard to achieve the reduction of greenhouse gases of 80 to 95 percent (compared to 1990) needed to reach the 2 degree Celsius goal until 2050. Thus, Germany currently fails to contribute adequately in protecting the global atmosphere. This is neither sustainable nor socially just. In the following we outline the causes for this discrepancy.

5.1.1. Power Relations and Vested Interests

A central cause for the discrepancy of norms and institutions is the influence of vested interests in the democratic system—this will also be outlined in detail in section six. As a result of the massive influence of vested interests, the total amount of emission certificates emitted in Germany between 2005 and 2007 exceeded actual emissions by far and even exceeded the amounts emitted in the time between 2000 and 2002.[5] In the first and up to now, the price of certificates has been inefficiently low and enterprises have had little to no incentive to reduce emissions (Altvater and Brunngräber 2008, 15). Furthermore, as various sectors such as agriculture and transportation induced politicians to exclude their sectors from the trading scheme (Böhringer and Lange 2012), reductions of GHG-emissions are not distributed amongst enterprises in a cost-efficient manner. The scheme thus does not treat different sectors equally, which increases the costs of avoidance measures, and thus inhibits the acceptance of climate protection. The handing out of admissions for no or far too low prices implies an implicit allocation of property rights to enterprises, thus to polluters, and not to humanity, environment or to those hurt by pollution. While in Germany it is also the special interests of residents and communities that hinder, for example, the construction of wind turbines in their municipality, it seems that it is mostly powerful economic interests that run counter to the norms of environmental sustainability, economic efficiency and environmental justice.

5.1.2. Norms in Conflict

The strong influence of enterprises on environmental legislation, however, is partly supported by citizens. It is frequently argued in the public debate that if national politics enforced strict rules regarding global common pool resources, enterprises would shift production to other countries. Thus the influence of enterprises on politics may in part be backed by the fear of unemployment, material losses or lower material growth. Basically, as environmental limits come to the fore, and growth is being contested, the question of distribution becomes essential. Thus, as with lower growth,

---

5 2 billion higher than the emissions that were actually emitted between 2000 and 2002 (FAZ No. 43, February 20th, 2013, 10); Brouns and Witt 2008, 83.

redistribution becomes harder to implement, the norms of environmental sustainability and social justice are perceived to contradict each other.

A further effect exemplifying the seeming conflict between environmental sustainability and social justice is that internalizing environmental externalities leads to increases in consumer prices. These price increases have a relatively stronger negative impact on the poor than on the rich. For example, in the so-called "energy transition" ("Energiewende") in Germany, all consumers have to pay higher prices for electricity to support the construction of renewable energy plants. But while this amounts to 1 percent of the income for poor households, rich households only have to spend 0.1 percent (Bardt et al. 2012). The distribution effects of ecological measures are determined by power relations. Some nevertheless object to climate protection with reference to its social impacts.

5.1.3. National Politics, Global Scale

A third cause for the discrepancy between norms and reality concerning environmental sustainability is the lack of environmentally binding and enforceable rules at the global level. While the early and thorough de-carbonization of the world economy could reduce the losses of world-GDP by climate protection to a few percent (Edenhofer 2012b, 474), finding a binding agreement proves to be hard in reality. The Kyoto-Protocol of 1997 fixed an upper limit for the emissions of greenhouse gases but reduction aims were not sustainable, various loopholes were included and the protocol did not comprise major players such as the USA (BUND et al. 2008, 459). In 2012, participants of the climate conference in Qatar could not agree on concrete reduction plans either. It seems that the free-riding option hinders an efficient outcome for all: With the costs of climate protection arising on the national level and benefits arising to a large degree outside of the protecting country, nations choose inefficiently low protection measures. If countries would agree on abatement measures, they could all be better off. One reason for this so called "tragedy of the unmanaged commons" (Hardin 2007) may be that norms such as sustainability and justice are still mainly applied at the national level—thus Germany does not adopt a "cosmopolitan welfare function" (Keohane [1984] 2005)—and that industrialized countries do not sufficiently take into account their historical responsibility. They seem to subordinate the catastrophic impacts of climate change on other nations to their own prosperity and social stability. Furthermore, the lack of solutions on the supranational level affects also the national policy: Germany hesitates to enforce national legislation concerning global common pool resources for fear of losing its competitiveness. The existence of international institutions that enable freedom of goods, capital and services on the one hand in the context of a lack of effective international institutions for environmental legislation on the other hand thus also diminishes the scope for political measures at the national level.

5.2. From Unmanaged Global Common Pool Resources towards Commoning

Generally, in order to eradicate the discrepancies between the norm of ecological sustainability and the institutional reality, the easiest thing to do would be to solve some of the problems that cause these discrepancies. On the following pages we furthermore focus on the concept of "commons" put forward mainly by Elinor Ostrom.

5.2.1. Reducing the Fundamental Causes for Discrepancies

First of all, the debate around the conflict between different norms such as environmental sustainability, freedom and social justice has in part been conducted in the recent parliamentary commission on growth, prosperity and quality of life, and must be continued and broadened: Through information and debate, the public has to discuss in depth the relation of material and immaterial needs and figure out how to reconcile different norms as well as the common good of humans in different times and countries. Furthermore, a discussion has to start on how personal and societal lifestyles can be altered and economic structures adapted in order to achieve sustainability and justice. Second, solutions have to be found that can soften the conflict of different norms. The adverse impacts of environmental taxes or emissions trading schemes on social justice could be offset for example by an increase in tax progressivity, a property tax or an energy allowance allocated to the poor. Furthermore, by reducing the privileges of vested interests in the EU ETS, as well as the market power of some actors, costs of climate protection could be reduced and thus the negative impact on poor households could be limited. The latter became particularly clear in the EU ETS, when electricity enterprises, which in the beginning received admissions for free, nevertheless used their market power to increase the price of electricity, which lead to billions in profits for suppliers at the cost of consumers (cf. Brouns and Witt 2008, Böhringer and Lange 2012). Finally, to reconcile environmental sustainability and employment, amongst others, taxes could be shifted from labor towards resources and emissions. While these measures could reconcile environmental sustainability with social justice, it is mainly the influence of vested interests that hinders their implementation.

Concerning the influence of vested interests on political processes, ambitious measures have to be enforced. Independent media and research should be guaranteed, and revolving-door-careers as well as party donations and sponsoring should be limited and regulated in a transparent way. While enterprises have the financial means to strongly influence the public discourse, social and environmental NGOs need financial support in order to guarantee a balanced debate as well as a balanced development of knowledge and research. Also financially or educationally weaker societal groups have to be given the capacity to participate in the public debate.

Finally, concerning the lack of effective legislation at the global level, existing institutions such as the WTO, World Bank and IMF have to adopt ecological—as well as social—criteria for trade, lending, investment etc. In addition, environmental institutions at the global level have to be built up and strengthened. While emissions on the global layer have to be limited, emission rights could be distributed according to the principle of "one person—one emissions right". Trading of certificates would lead to a global price for CO_2-emissions and stimulate low-carbon development. International and global solutions could limit the transfer of emission intensive production to otherwise non-participating countries. In order to regulate the trading with certificates, a CO_2 central bank has been proposed—for the time being at the European level (MCC 2014). As a means to gain political support from newly-industrialized countries, the mechanism could include exceptions for these countries' emissions in the initial period. Apart from supporting this solution, Germany can facilitate international binding climate agreements as a pioneer of change in the reduction of GHG emissions by providing environmental technology and cooperation in research and knowledge transfer to economically poorer countries to foster low-carbon development, and by supporting adaptation measures with regard to unavoidable climate change. This could partly be justified by Germany's advanced technological capacity to avoid emissions and to cope with climate change, but also by Germany's climate debt accrued not only in the past but also in the present due to its unsustainable level of consumption. In the meantime, it is essential to redress the malfunctioning European emissions trading system or to replace it by substantial taxes on emissions.

However, while several of the measures outlined here—caring for a higher compatibility of different norms, reducing the influence of vested interests, and strengthening international institutions—are necessary measures, experiences in the past decades have proved that it is hard for politicians to act against existing power constellations and social practices. One thus needs to break new ground. A new way to deal with adverse preconditions for managing common pool resources has been provided by Elinor Ostrom.

5.2.2. *From Common Pool Resources to Commons*

In 1968, Garrett Hardin saw only two ways to solve what he later termed the "tragedy of unmanaged commons" (Hardin 2007): Either property rights for environmental goods had to be enforced, such that the market would induce an efficient use of the resource, or the state had to impose regulation for the common pool resources top-down. Ostrom broke open this dominant "market or state" paradigm. Analyzing hundreds of case studies, she found that the two theoretical ways to handle problems of common pool resources—privatization and central state control—could in some cases avoid a dramatic destruction and overuse, but that efficient management of common pool resources was often organized in a third, previously neglected way (Cp. Helfrich and Stein 2011, 10): It was the users of the common pool resource themselves who frequently were able to manage long term sustainable resource use (Ostrom et al. 1999, 279) "Specific forms of social agreements for the collective, sustainable and fair utilization of common pool resources" were termed "commons" by Ostrom (Helfrich and Stein 2011, 9). According to Ostrom, commoning is easier if the users of a resource trust each other, are free to design the rules and sanctions themselves and if said sanctions are enforceable.

a) Implementing Multi-Layered Solutions: Ostrom found that common pool resources are more effectively managed when different formally independent but interrelated institutions existed on various additional levels

(Helfrich and Ostrom 2011, 43). This seems eminently suitable to the German federal state. Commons tie in with the principle of subsidiarity, whereby emphasizing that overlapping institutions need not be inefficient but may enhance stability and resilience.

As outlined above, the striving for more and more personal consumption in Germany seems to have given way to a quest for security and stability. Multi-layered solutions could meet these needs: Although various processes caused by an increase in emissions are irreversible, a mix of institutions could be more robust and may better "guard against low probability, high consequence possibilities and allow for change [that] may be suboptimal in the short run but prove wiser in long run" (Dietz et al. 2003, 1909). Multiple solutions may also balance out the ideological narrow-mindedness or faults in political or economic theories and could reduce the ability of enterprises to sidestep regulations by lobbying or deception. What is more, experimenting with different institutional arrangements on various layers could bring valuable empirical data on which systems work best under which conditions.

To some degree, multi-layered solutions already form part of German politics' strategy to cope with climate change. Parallel to the EU ETS there exist national regulations such as eco-taxes or the energy transition. Regional or local institutions such as "Local agenda 21-projects"[6] or cooperative projects for renewable energy find great support in the population and serve as a kind of small safeguard mechanisms. These institutions also take into account some environmental problems as well as sectors that are not covered by the EU ETS. To facilitate multi-layered solutions, the state has to provide autonomy and resources to lower layers. Furthermore, commons need a vital democratic environment and engagement, whereby material as well as immaterial conditions (like education) for just participation of all societal groups have to be guaranteed. Also with respect to global institutions, additional layers could facilitate commoning: Additional negotiations among groups of states like the 20 mayor emitting nations might increase efficiency in climate protection (Edenhofer 2013b).

b) Strengthening Local Institutions: To complement the idea of multi-layered solutions, according to Ostrom, local institutions must be strengthened. Benefits are that the usage of the commons can better be observed and

---

6 In these projects, communes and regions consult their citizens to find ways towards sustainability.

might less easily be captured by vested interests. While the social dilemma on the global scale might still exist, citizens on the regional level may well be motivated to care for the environment and to reduce their use of the resource if they do not act as individuals but as a group (Scherhorn 2011, 21). This particularly holds true if the reduction of emissions has direct positive effects in the region—such as increasing autonomy or reducing air pollution. Trust can be fostered if people know each other and institutions can be adapted to local and cultural[7] circumstances. Furthermore, if the state intends to regulate every single environmental externality, the dominance of external authoritative power and a huge bureaucracy might lead to a strong increase in control costs and to outrage from citizens who feel patronized. Creating thousands of "bottom-up" systems (cp. Helfrich and Stein 2011, 12) is also central for practicing cooperative behavior (Stollorz, 2011), which is of increasing importance: "With increased specialization, people have become more interdependent. Thus, we all share one another's common interests, but in more complex ways than the users of a forest or grassland" (Ostrom et al. 1999, 281). Finally, the process of "commoning" enhances participation in political and economic processes and thus promotes democracy. The lack of a democratic agreement of how to manage global commons could thereby be mediated.

In Germany, various examples for local processes of institutionalization for the protection of common goods already exist. Energy cooperatives are especially relevant for the energy transition: More than 80,000 Germans participate in those cooperatives and invested 800 Million Euro in wind parks, solar energy plants and the like (cp. Helfrich and Stein 2011, 12, 14). Furthermore some towns got paired with towns abroad in order to exchange experiences concerning sustainability and climate change. Further cooperative projects include sustainable apartment houses or ecological banking, which provides credit for ecological projects. The relatively young "transition towns" movement, with 1000 initiatives worldwide and around 40 in Germany, aims at developing a post-fossil fuel style of urban life. This includes urban gardening and organizing resilient, sustainable local and/or solidarity economies.

---

7 While cultural diversity may be a hindrance to finding a global solution to climate change—especially in the context of dramatic economic differences—it may as well be an opportunity. Through the currently observed re-culturalization, regional and local communities have better preconditions to save and use their cultural knowledge on how to best handle common pool resources (cp. Ostrom et al. 1999, 281).

In order to enable the changes necessary to stabilize the climate, these bottom-up initiatives need strong political support. National or state governments should facilitate the creation of commons. This means to encourage the association of users and to provide necessary information. While higher layers should help by enforcing sanctions, users should be given the autonomy to create and control the rules and sanctions for the usage of resources themselves (Cp. Scherhorn 2011, 21; Ostrom et al. 1999). Stronger involvement of citizens could also facilitate the acceptance of solar or wind energy plants, power supply lines, storage power stations or public infrastructure projects.

However, while these measures may be helpful, commoning is especially difficult in the case of climate change: here, the number of users of the resource is immense, trust nearly impossible, change occurs fast and interrelations are complex. Furthermore, there is only one chance and no place to migrate in case of failure (Ostrom et al. 1999, 282). Thus, building powerful institutions on the national, regional and global layer are is essential as well as complementary initiatives by pioneers of change at individual, group, country and regional level.

c) Calling into Account Private Property and Supporting Forms of Common Property: An interesting suggestion is given by Gerhard Scherhorn, who proposes to introduce the commons-idea into German and international law. According to the basic principle "Property entails obligations" ("Eigentum verpflichtet"), the competition law should be changed: Price reductions caused by damaging the environment should not be treated in the same way as "real" increases in the efficiency of production but as a violation of the competition law. He suggests that competitors or clients themselves, who have more information on production processes, can care for the implementation of laws—which implies an element of commoning.

However it seems also necessary to pose the fundamental question of freedom and property anew. While private property once signified economic and political freedom, the increasing destruction of environmental, social and cultural common pool resources hints at its shortcomings. Thus, "an understanding of freedom that destroys commons and perceives co-operation as restraint undermines the condition for the possibility of freedom" (Edenhofer 2013a). Commons may serve human's needs more directly, as all those affected by the usage of the common pool resource can decide on how to handle it. Thus, the trend towards privatization in Germany should be corrected: state and market are not the only alternatives. Forms of common property—such as cooperatives and collectives—could orient economic activity stronger towards needs of people, towards social and environmental concerns than towards the pure maximization of profits.

6. Democracy: Conflicts and Potentials for Transformation

The norm of democracy faces different challenges which hinder its full achievement. These challenges target two claims of democracy. First, its claim to represent all those concerned and secondly, its claim to legitimize the decisions taken. In order to meet both claims, it seems crucial that as many constituents as possible take part in the democratic process. This, however, is undermined as soon as certain persons are excluded from or drop out of the democratic voting procedure or if the voices of some persons gain unequally more weight. These problems will be discussed with regard to the question of partial interests in the first section, before democracy in its global dimension is assessed in the second section.

6.1. Partial Interests

Democracy risks undermining by partial interests in different ways. The perhaps best-known case for how interest groups try to influence the democratic procedure is by way of lobbying. Here, some interests are over-represented. Conversely, the interests of some groups may not be given sufficient attention in a democratic law-making process, although the resulting legislation does have an impact on them. Both cases imply a tense relation between interests and democracy and will be considered in depth in the following paragraphs.

6.1.1. Lobbying

There are different ways in which the interests of some groups can be over-represented in a political decision-making process. Due to specific abilities or positions some people are more likely to intervene in the demo-

There are several reasons why lobbying works relatively smoothly in Germany. One is that the lines between political consulting, journalism, public relations and politics on the one hand and lobbying on the other are blurred. This problem is increased by the fact that people change jobs between the fields so that someone who has worked in the government goes to work for an interest group later or *vice versa*. A second and somewhat related point is that the techniques of communication in either of the fields resemble one another. This means that journalism is no longer practiced only by external and objective journalists, but rather that press releases, journals or magazines are also provided by lobbying groups. Similarly, when it comes to promoting their views and ideas, politicians use the same spectrum of PR and marketing techniques as private companies or organizations.

In Brussels, where most EU legislative and executive institutions are located, lobbying plays an even greater role. Especially the open character of the EU system facilitates lobbying activities. This openness is particularly due to two factors. The first is the heterogeneity of the institutional apparatus; the second is the small size of the Commission as the organ possessing the dominant legislative power. There are only about 140,000 public servants and other 8,500 staff members. This number of employees is smaller than that of some national ministries (Schendelen 2006, 135f.). For this reason, the Commission relies on external expertise which is delivered by different organizations and representations of states, interest groups or large companies. These also send experts to specific committees. Therefore, the institutional system of the EU prepares the ground for lobbying activities of different kinds. Not all of these are negative, but it is not always easy to draw the line. The risks of this practice became visible when the website lobbyplag.eu published legal texts that were taken word-by-word from a proposal that a lobbying organization had submitted (LobbyPlag 2013).

What can be done about these problems? First, it seems important to stress that democracy cannot function without lobbying. Interest groups must find a way to make their voice heard. Still, the dominance of some groups like the pharmaceutic industry pressure group and the fact that many of the lobbying activities are unknown to the public must be objected. Therefore, it seems necessary to create publicity and awareness for lobbying activities. This involves conducting more research in lobbying both at the domestic and the European level, because the actual scientific and public knowledge is still relatively limited. Furthermore, it seems necessary to correct the way in which lobbying is presented in the media. While so far scandalous cases dominate, this picture must be complemented and amended. On the other hand, this also requires that lobby groups in Brussels respect the demand to sign up with the Transparency Register, so that it is known which companies, agencies and organizations try to influence the legislative process (Alter EU 2014). To further back up the call for transparency, lobbying groups could also be asked to submit an annual report on their activities (Leif and Speth 2006b, 354). Finally, one might think about the introduction of a code of conduct for lobbying groups.

6.1.2. Neglected Interests

Secondly, it seems necessary to investigate the problem of personal interests neglected throughout the democratic process. Although the case of non-voters which risks undermining the legitimacy of the democratic procedure is equally problematic, we will focus on the case of those who cannot take part in the democratic process, even though although the decisions taken according to the institutionalized democratic process do have an impact on them. Two minority groups seem to be particularly pertinent in this respect. The first are future generations, the second the interests of foreigners.

The problem of neglected interests concerns foreigners living both in- and outside Germany. Although we are primarily concerned with foreigners living in other countries, it should be stressed that foreigners living inside Germany are affected by democratic decisions without being given a voice in the democratic process. That is, although they live in the country, they do not possess any voting rights due to their immigrant status.[9] Yet, since our focus here is not on migration policies, we will concentrate on the question of whether the interests of foreigners living abroad as well as the interests of future generations are given sufficient attention. The interests of people living in foreign countries happen to be concerned by any legislation whose effects are global in scope or at least do not stop at the country's borders. Obvious examples for this are environmental laws and

---

[9] Given the limited amount of space, we can unfortunately not discuss this problem in detail.

(non-)regulations, but also subsidies on certain products or economic sectors.

The neglect of the interests of future generations is equally problematic. Legislation in the field of ecology, infrastructure or on the public debt are likely to affect the interests and the living environment of future generations. Hence, there is a gap between being affected by a law and participating in its formation. Indeed, it is impossible that someone who is not yet born or who is very young age at the moment of the decision be elected a member of parliament. Still, there seem to be alternatives.

In general terms, what this problem demands is a decision-making practice that is guided by something like Rawls's "veil of ignorance" (Rawls 1999, 11). This means that legislative decisions should be made by acknowledging that one could also be in the position of those suffering (most) from the consequences of the law to be passed. This would help see and incorporate foreigners' or future generations' interests at the present stage. An institutional possibility could be to give voting rights to babies and children, too. Till a certain age, however, these would have to be exercised by their parents (Serikawa 2013, 10). Alternatively, one could designate a representative of future generations to be part of the government. It would be her duty to point out where interests of future generations are touched by legislative decisions. Likewise, one could designate at least one representative from another country to be present in the national government.[10] These representatives would not be democratically elected either, at least not by the constituents whom they are supposed to represent. Still, it seems justifiable to correct the democratic deficit in this equally 'undemocratic' way. In the case of foreigners, it would also help to accelerate the development of shifting decision-making competences to international institutions. Yet this requires that these are organized in a democratic fashion, too. We will turn to this issue in the next paragraph.

6.2. The Local-Global Divide

Further discrepancies appear when one considers democracy in the context of a globalized world and an ever-growing network of international institu-

---

[10] An interesting example is the Franco-German parliament exchange whose aim is rather cooperation than correction, but which takes into account the narrow relationship between the two countries.

tions endowed with more and more executive and legislative competences. We have seen above that due to the world's institutional and economic connectedness, decisions that are taken in one country may also have consequences for people in other countries. In this paragraph, however, we will focus on a different problem, namely the democratic deficits in the decision-making process of international institutions. The central concern is that while legislative consequences are shifted to the international level, this is not accompanied by a shift of democratic procedures to the same degree. To make this point we will consider the case of the European Union, since this is particularly pertinent for the German context as well, as the case of the WTO as one of the most potent international organizations.

The EU arguably constitutes one of the most successful endeavors in terms of integration and peace-building during the last centuries. In legal terms, it constitutes an international organization in that it originally relies on an intergovernmental treaty. Ever since its creation[11], it has been constantly expanded both in terms of the number of member states and in terms of policy fields to be decided at the European level. Its focus still lies on the economic integration, which was crowned by the introduction of the Euro as the single currency in 1999[12]. This integration has reached a degree that constrains and demands political actions. This was, for instance, visible during the economic crisis where the bankruptcy of states like Greece or Cyprus accompanied by rating agencies downgrading the state's credit rating demanded *ad hoc* reactions and commitments from the European governments which became known as the "rescue packages". The democratic problem that these measures pose, however, is that they mobilize large amounts of money without being submitted to a thorough democratic procedure (Habermas 2012, 337).

Similar concerns arise with regard to international organizations like the WTO. The WTO provides a framework, regulation and a dispute settlement system for the trade relations between its member states. As such, it constitutes one of the most advanced and comprehensive international organizations (Bogdandy and Venzke 2012, 37). While this comprehensiveness has advantages in terms of clarity and prospectiveness, it also

---

[11] The fundament was laid in 1951 with the European Coal and Steal Community, followed by the European Economic Community in 1961 and the European Community, before the EU was founded on the basis of the Maastricht Treaty in 1993.

[12] In 1999, the Euro was introduced as the accounting currency, while actual coins and banknotes entered circulation in 2002.

implies that the WTO may impact rather strongly on the lives of individuals. In the state, citizens are on the one hand submitted to the state measures, but also decide upon and control them on the other hand. It is the second element that is largely missing in the international arena. That is, the WTO is still governed by its member states and so citizens only have a mediated say in the decisions. At the same time, the shift of competences to the WTO and the steadily-growing corpus of trade rules increase the potential influence on individuals' lives. For this reason, one may assume that an imbalance has emerged.

In both the European and the international case, the way out of this democratic deficit problem seems to be to improve the democratic procedure so that individuals have a say in the legislation and can control the actions of the organization's executive. In the case of the WTO, this need not imply a full-blown democratic electoral procedure, but could demand appointing citizen representatives to the organization's decision-making body like it is practiced in the International Labor Organization, for instance.

7. Summary

Our examinations have shown that there is often a fine line between the problems and the solutions. That is, what seems to be a solution to one challenge can be problematic in another respect. Hence there is not one single policy recommendation that one could derive from the findings above, although we have indicated some ways out. Still, one may detect some general lines that could guide a transformational process.

First, it seems important to encourage active citizenship on a broad basis, in a way that encompasses as many members of society as possible. This might demand that civil engagement is assisted at first and also that various different organizational forms of involvement are valued and accepted. On the other hand, nontransparent influence of lobby groups which are shortcutting democratic procedures and oversight need to be curtailed. These are basic preconditions to prepare the ground for an open public debate on controversial issues (like employment, economic growth, social security, consumption, global sustainability etc.) with regard to how the common good can be pursued in a globalized world.

Secondly, we consider that our democratic system must better accommodate the interests of groups that are excluded from but affected by contemporary democratic decisions and economic activities at the national level. In this context, the case of future generations as well as of foreigners has been discussed. In addition to institutional changes, it seems important to sensitize the German citizens for this problem. This seems to be crucial, since it is not a one-sided process, for Germans (today and in future) are also affected by, for example, the US-American or Chinese legislation and economy. One important step into this direction could be to take up the discussions of the parliamentary commission working on "Growth, Prosperity and Quality of Life" from 2011 to 2013 to initiate a broad-based public debate on priorities with regard to how our society wants to live up to its basic values of freedom, social justice, democracy and environmental sustainability—including the perspectives of future generations and the global community.

Thirdly and relatedly, it must be stressed that regional institutions like the EU and international institutions like the WTO should incorporate more democratic elements in order to become fully legitimate. This does not mean that there ought to be a democratic voting procedure for every international organization, yet first steps could be the election of citizen representatives or a better awareness on the part of the national governments. Equally, the issue of externalization of social and environmental costs should be addressed and duly regulated by these institutions.

Fourthly, discrepancies, conflicts and obstacles that foster the global common good, need to be identified and addressed. Besides the analysis of deficits in the private and public spheres, the perspective of global commons may open new ways for overcoming existing obstacles and deadlocks.

Overall, we do consider that it is only possible to achieve the global common good by way of dialogue and cooperation on an equal basis. These are both intrinsically democratic values—including a strong option for plurality which will necessarily leave its traces in the search of what "global common good" might consist in. So far, human rights play an important role to shape and guide this planetary dialogue and as such form something like the common basis. Still, it might be necessary to move beyond this catalog of rights towards other material and institutional concepts like the ones we have identified as the core elements of the common good, namely freedom, democracy, justice and sustainability.

Works Cited

Alter EU (2014). *Greater Lobbying Transparency.* http://www.alter-eu.org/ taxonomy/term/23 (17.12.2014).
Altvater, Elmar and Achim Brunngräber (2008). "Mit dem Markt gegen die Klimakatastrophe?" In Elmar Altvater and Achim Brunnengräber (eds.). *Ablasshandel gegen Klimawandel?*, 9–20. Hamburg: VSA-Verlag.
Bardt, Hubertus, Judith Niehues, and Holger Techert (2012). *Das Erneuerbare-Energien-Gesetz—Erfahrungen und Ausblick.* Köln: Institut der deutschen Wirtschaft.
Bertelsmann Stiftung (2010). *Bürger wollen kein Wachstum um jeden Preis.* www.bertelsmann-stiftung.de/bst/de/media/xcms_bst_dms_ 32005_32006_2.pdf (20.10.2014).
Biesecker, Adelheid, and Sabine Hofmeister (2010). "Focus: (Re)productivity: Sustainable relations both between society and nature and between the genders." *Ecological Economics,* 69 (8), 1703–1711.
Bogdandy, Armin von, and Ingo Venzke (2012). "In Whose Name? An Investigation of International Courts' Public Authority and Its Democratic Justification." *The European Journal of International Law,* 23, 7–41.
Böhringer, Christoph, and Andreas Lange (2012). "Der europäische Emissionszertifikatehandel: Bestandsaufnahme und Perspektiven." *Wirtschaftsdienst,* 92, 12–16.
Brouns, Bernd, and Uwe Witt (2008). "Klimaschutz als Gelddruckmaschine." In Elmar Altvater and Achim Brunnengräber (eds.). *Ablasshandel gegen Klimawandel?*, 67–87. Hamburg: VSA-Verlag.
BUND (Bund für Umwelt und Naturschutz Deutschland), Brot für die Welt and Evangelischer Entwicklungsdienst (eds.) (2008). *Zukunftsfähiges Deutschland in einer globalisierten Welt. Ein Anstoß zur gesellschaftlichen Debatte.* Frankfurt am Main: Fischer.
Bundesbank (2013). "Vermögen und Finanzen privater Haushalte in Deutschland. Ergebnisse der Bundesbankstudie." *Deutsche Bundesbank Monatsbericht,* 65, 25–51.
BMAS (Bundesministerium für Arbeit und Soziales) (2011). *Sozialbudget 2011.* Bonn: BMAS.
Deutscher Bundestag (2013). *Enquete-Kommission Wachstum, Wohlstand, Lebensqualität. Schlussbericht.* Drucksache 17/13300. Berlin: Deutscher Bundestag.
Diefenbacher, Hans, and Roland Zieschank (2011). "Woran sich Wohlstand wirklich messen lässt." *Alternativen zum Bruttoinlandsprodukt.* München: Oekom.
Dietz, Thomas, Elinor Ostrom, and Paul C. Stern (2003). "The Struggle to Govern the Commons." *Science,* 302 (5652), 1907–1912.
Easterlin, Richard A., Laura Angelescu McVey, Malgorzata Switek, Onnicha Sawangfa, and Jacqueline Smith Zweig (2010). "The Happiness–Income Para-

dox Revisited." *Proceedings of the National Academy of Sciences,* 107 (52), 22463-22468.

Edenhofer, Ottmar (2012a). *Beyond Green Growth: Challenges of Rio+20.* Launch Event Climate Change, Justice and Sustainability, Potsdam, June 5th, 2013.

Edenhofer, Ottmar (2012b). "Die Atmosphäre als globales Gemeingut." In Silke Helfrich (ed.). *Commons. Für eine neue Politik jenseits von Markt und Staat,* 473–478. Bielefeld: Transcript.

Edenhofer, Ottmar (2013a). "Mit Kant gegen den Klimawandel." *Philosophie Magazin,* 2, 20–21.

Edenhofer, Ottmar (2013b). "Kohle und Öl sind die Energieträger des 21. Jahrhunderts schlechthin." *FAZ,* November 26th, 2012. http://www.faz.net/aktuell/wirtschaft/klimaforschung-kohle-und-oel-sind-die-energietraeger-des-21-jahrhunderts-schlechthin-11972540.html (19.12.2014).

Erhard, Ludwig (1957). *Wohlstand für Alle.* Düsseldorf: Econ.

Gorz, André (1994). *Capitalism, Socialism, Ecology.* London/New York: Verso.

Habermas, Jürgen (2012). "The Crisis of the European Union in the Light of International Law." *The European Journal of International Law,* 23, 353–348.

Hardin, Garrett (2007). "The Tragedy of the Unmanaged Commons." *Evolutionary perspectives on environmental problems,* 105–107.

Helfrich, Silke and Felix Stein (2011). "Was sind Gemeingüter?" In Johannes Piepenbrink (ed.). *Gemeingüter,* APuZ, 61 (28-30), 9–15.

Helliwell, John, Richard Layard and Jeffrey Sachs (2012). *World Happiness Report.*

Hinterberger, Friedrich, Elke Pirgmaier, Elisabeth Freytag and Martina Schuster (2011). *Growth in Transition.* London: Earthscan.

Institut für Demoskopie Allensbach (2012). *Das Unbehagen am Kapitalismus: Eine Dokumentation des Beitrags von Prof. Dr. Renate Köcher in der Frankfurter Allgemeinen Zeitung Nr. 45 vom 22. Februar 2012.* Allensbach: IfD Allensbach.

IPCC (Intergovernmental Panel on Climate Change) (2014). *Climate Change 2014 Synthesis Report.* Geneva: IPCC.

Keohane, Robert O. ([1984] 2005). After hegemony: Cooperation and Discord in The World Political Economy. Princeton: Princeton University Press.

Leif, Thomas, and Rudolf Speth (2006a). "Die fünfte Gewalt—Anatomie des Lobbyismus in Deutschland." In Thomas Leif and Rudolf Speth (eds.). *Die fünfte Gewalt: Lobbyismus in Deutschland,* 10–36. Bonn: Bundeszentrale für politische Bildung.

Leif, Thomas, and Rudolf Speth (2006b). "Zehn zusammenfassende Thesen." In Thomas Leif and Rudolf Speth (eds.). *Die fünfte Gewalt: Lobbyismus in Deutschland,* 351–354. Bonn: Bundeszentrale für politische Bildung.

LobbyPlag (2013). "Transparency for the EU." http://lobbyplag.eu/lp (03.07.2013).

Lösche, Peter (2006). "Demokratie braucht Lobbying." In Thomas Leif and Rudolf Speth (eds.). *Die fünfte Gewalt: Lobbyismus in Deutschland,* 53–68. Bonn: Bundeszentrale für politische Bildung.

Madlener, Reinhard, and Blake Alcott (2011). *Herausforderung für eine technisch-ökonomische Entkoppelung von Naturverbrauch und Wirtschaftswachstum unter besonderer Berücksichtigung der Systematisierung von Rebound-Effekten und Problemverschiebungen.* Kommissionsmaterialie M-17(26)13, Berlin: Deutscher Bundestag.

MCC (Mercator Research Institute on Global Commons and Climate Change) (2014). "MCC für Klima-Zentralbank." http://www.mcc-berlin.net/media/in-den-medien/in-den-medien-detail/article/mcc-fuer-klima-zentralbank.html (9.1.2015).

Müller-Armack, Alfred (1947). *Wirtschaftslenkung und Marktwirtschaft.* Hamburg: Verlag für Wirtschaft und Sozialpolitik.

OECD (2011). *Growing Income Inequality in OECD Countries: What drives it and how can Policy tackle it?* Paris: OECD Publishing.

Ostrom, Elinor (1990). *Governing the Commons: The Evolution of Institutions for Collective Action.* Cambridge: Cambridge University Press.

Ostrom, Elinor, and Silke Helfrich (2011*).* Was mehr wird, wenn wir teilen: Vom gesellschaftlichen Wert der Gemeingüter.* München: Oekom.

Ostrom, Elinor, Johanna Burger, Christopher Field, Richard Norgaard, and David Policansky (1999). "Revisiting the Commons: Local Lessons, Global Challenges." *Science,* 284 (5412), 278–282.

Peters, Glen P., Jan C. Minx, Christopher L. Weber, and Ottmar Edenhofer (2011). "Growth in Emission Transfers via International Trade from 1990 to 2008." *Proceedings of the National Academy of Sciences,* 108 (21), 8903–8908.

Rawls, John (1999). *A Theory of Justice,* revised edition. Cambridge, MA: Harvard University Press.

Rinderspacher, Jürgen P. (2000). "Zeitwohlstand in der Dreizeitgesellschaft." In Hartmut Seifert (ed.). *Flexible Zeiten in der Arbeitswelt,* 398-449. Frankfurt am Main: Campus.

Schendelen, Rinus van (2006). "Brüssel: Die Champions League des Lobbying." In Thomas Leif and Rudolf Speth (eds.). *Die fünfte Gewalt: Lobbyismus in Deutschland,* 132–162. Bonn: Bundeszentrale für politische Bildung.

Scherhorn, Gerhard (2011). "Die Welt als Allmende: Marktwirtschaftlicher Wettbewerb und Gemeingüterschutz." In Johannes Piepenbrink (ed.). *Gemeingüter,* APuZ, 61 (28-30), 21–27.

Seidl, Irmi, and Angelika Zahrnt (2010a). "Argumente für einen Abschied vom Paradigma des Wirtschaftswachstums." In Irmi Seidl and Angelika Zahrnt (eds.). *Postwachstumsgesellschaft. Konzepte für die Zukunft.* Marburg: Metropolis, 23–36.

Seidl, Irmi, and Angelika Zahrnt (2010b). "Anliegen des Buches und Übersicht." In Irmi Seidl and Angelika Zahrnt (eds.). *Postwachstumsgesellschaft. Konzepte für die Zukunft.* Marburg: Metropolis, 23–36.

Serikawa, Yoichi (2013). "Wahlrecht für Japans Babys." *FAZ,* July 16th, 2013, 10.

Steiner, Viktor, and Johanna Cludius (2010). "Ökosteuer hat zu geringerer Umweltbelastung des Verkehrs beigetragen." *DIW Berlin Wochenbericht* 77 (13-14), 3–7.

Stollorz, Volker (2011). „Elinor Ostrom und die Wiederentdeckung der Allmende." In Johannes Piepenbrink (ed.). *Gemeingüter*, ApuZ. 28-30, 3–8.

Wallacher, Johannes (2012). *Mehrwert Glück: Plädoyer für menschengerechtes Wirtschaften*. München: Herbig.

Wilkinson, Richard, and Kate Pickett (2009). *The Spirit Level—Why Equality is better for Everyone*. London: Penguin.

III. Critical Perspectives on the Intercultural Dialogue Process

Development for the Global Common Good: A Comment[1]

Clara Brandi

The studies of the individual countries offer a very rich basis for the project "Development for the Global Common Good". With a view to the success of the project, it would be useful to discuss potential (1) synergies and (2) tensions in the context of the country-specific case studies, (3) consider potentially missing elements, and (4) ponder additional questions, including those with regards to methodology.

1. Opportunities and Synergies

It would be helpful to reflect on opportunities and synergies in the context of the prepared country case studies. With a view to the various norms being discussed in the individual country case studies, there seem to be a number of important opportunities for synergies. There is room for synergies, for instance, with respect to the notions of human dignity, human welfare/improving the quality of life, environmental sustainability, democracy, social justice/equality, and human rights.

---

1 The contributions by Clara Brandi and Jan Aart Scholte represent reactions to the national studies intended to enrich the intercultural workshop and ongoing project work. As such they have informed the article on "Intercultural Reflections" as well as the case studies in the respective versions published in this book.

2. Potential Tensions and Contradictions

It would also be useful to consider potential tensions and contradictions among the various case studies. First, there is a potential tension with a view to the concept of development that is being referred to. While some country case studies appear to accept conventional approaches to development, others argue in favor of post-development or other alternatives to the more traditional understanding of development. This raises the question of which concept of development the researchers can agree on—or whether it is fine to work with a number of different approaches in parallel. Second, there is room for disagreement regarding the role of economic growth. While most studies indicate that the mere focus on economic growth is too limited, others do not include a critical discussion of the concept of growth and its role. This poses the question as to whether or not all researchers agree that an exclusive focus on growth is too limited. Finally, while some studies focus on the community, there might also be a need to reflect on rules to reconcile individual and community interests.

3. Missing Elements

A reflection of the missing elements in the individual case studies would also be useful. First, there should be a detailed discussion of the relevant methodologies: Which methods have been used in order to prepare the studies? The transparent discussion of the methods used and the authors' disciplinary background and values could be more elaborate in some studies.

Furthermore, where possible, multi-level approaches should be taken into account—and, in light of the project focus on the "Global Common Good", the emphasis should be at the global level. It would be desirable to discuss norms and entry points for change at different levels and differentiate among them (global, regional, national, local level). For example, which global rules and institutions would be conducive to development for the global common good? Finally, entry points for change should also be addressed. In the context of some papers, it might be useful to reflect more on transformation potential and the role of various actors, including civil society and the media.

4. Additional Questions for Reflection

In order to safeguard the successful conclusion of the project, a number of additional points should be pondered. First, the choice of the country cases should be convincingly justified. Which countries are included for which reasons? To what extent would the researchers consider their studies to be representative not only of their country but also their region?

Second, considerations as to which additional methods could be used in order to work towards the success of the project could have been reflected upon. For instance, how can it be ensured that the views in the paper are representative of the views in the countries they originate from? For example, could elements of discourse analysis—such as discourses in the media—be added?

Third, the focus should be on the common ground of all researchers involved in the project. Which norms and visions should be in the focus of the joint publication and thus be addressed by all authors in order to try and find a common ground regarding these norms and visions? How much room is there for plurality? And last but not least, the question of disagreement among the views of the different researchers who are part of the project should be tackled. For instance, how can it be made sure that apparent agreement among researchers in this workshop on certain norms and concepts does not hide underlying disagreement? Where can we find true agreement and differentiate between agreement and disagreement? If there is seeming disagreement, can it be resolved by improving the mutual understanding of the concepts used or the empirical facts in that context or is there a deeper normative disagreement? And how could disagreement about relevant norms and practices within countries be dealt with?

Development for the Global Common Good: Discussion Points[1]

Jan Aart Scholte

The project 'Development for the Global Common Good' raises large and vital questions that touch on no less than the future of humanity. The distinctive approach is to bring into deep conversation contributors from diverse world regions. The resulting reflections are probing and critical, and the intercultural dynamic potentially generates new insights. My own ponderings on the project have revolved around the following points.

These considerations start with the project title and a question whether 'development' and 'global common good' necessarily go together, or at least whether 'development' on mainstream understandings of the term is the most promising path to 'global common good'. Seven decades since the early spread of development discourse in the 1940s, much of humanity is still denied elementary dignities. The United Nations has pursued four so-called 'development decades' between the 1960s and the 1990s, followed by the Millennium Development Goals (MDGs) and now the Sustainable Development Goals (SDGs). Yet the outcomes are each time disappointing. At some point does one need to ask whether the 'development industry' deserves more 'investment', or whether it is time for alternative discourses?

This question may be especially pressing in regard to ecological conditions. Discourses of 'development' are deeply anthropocentric and extractivist. That is, they presume a separation of humanity from the wider web of life and a subordination of 'nature' to human ends. With unprecedented numbers of human beings pursuing unprecedented levels of resource extraction from the planet, 'development' could prove to be the ruin rather than the salvation of the species. An incipient recognition of this unviable

---

1 The contributions by Clara Brandi and Jan Aart Scholte represent reactions to the national studies intended to enrich the intercultural workshop and ongoing project work. As such they have informed the article on "Intercultural Reflections" as well as the case studies in the respective versions published in this book.

situation may be evidenced in the increasing turn to narratives of 'sustainable development', but this phraseology still cannot let go of 'development'.

The project title also begs some questions around the notion of 'common good'. What exactly does this concept cover, beyond broad ideas of shared human dignity? Common Good might encompass values of, for example, cultural vibrancy, democracy, distributive justice, ecological integrity, individual liberty, material security, moral propriety, peace, and solidarity. Different visions of the 'common good' might cover these (and/or other) core values in different combinations and with different relative priorities. Difficult issues also arise when certain core values might in certain contexts clash, at which point trade-offs are necessary and one must decide which vital values to sacrifice in favor of others. In short, specifying the 'common good' is not so straightforward.

There is moreover another key political question of who defines 'common good', for whose benefit, and for what purpose? In this regard it could be relevant to consider not only the diversity of views that have been present in this project, but also who has not participated in the academic part of the project, including non-professionals, indigenous peoples, and other world religions besides Christianity. How might absent voices have understood 'common good' differently?

Indeed, could it be important also to guard against hegemonic uses of 'common good' language? All too often appealing vocabulary can be used to legitimize unjust and disabling situations. Consider the number of times that dominant powers have invoked notions of 'the international community', 'democracy' and 'human rights' to justify self-interested interventions? One must be careful that ideas of 'common good' are not used to 'cover up' and sustain violations of human dignity.

Then there is the 'global' part of the project title. Does 'global' refer to countries and localities spread across the planet; or does 'global' refer to planetary domains as a spatial scale in its own right? This is a vital distinction with far-reaching implications. In the first understanding, 'global common good' would be achieved when national populations and local communities all over the planet attain certain conditions of human dignity. In the second understanding, living well would be achieved on a planetary scale itself. For example, there is a difference between having distributive justice within every country across the planet and having distributive justice on a planetary scale. It is possible to realize the first and still be very far from the second.

Another key issue around globality is its relationship to universality and diversity. Sometimes narratives of the global presume that everyone on the planet would have the same views, needs and interests. In this perspective there would be a single 'global common good' which applied equally to all of humanity. In contrast, others emphasize that people across the planet have highly diverse views, needs and interests. In this latter perspective there would be many and often conflicting ideas and practices of what constitutes 'global common good'.

If—as actual experiences seem to bear out—global arenas are often marked by diversity and difference rather than uniformity, then ethical and political questions arise about how to handle this situation. Is it best to strive for a consensus on 'the global common good'? Or is it best to minimize contacts between conflicting visions of 'global common good', since too much interaction is bound to generate fear and violence? Or is it best to encourage mutual engagement and learning among diversities, while accepting that significant divergences will persist? Intercultural projects such as 'Development for the Global Common Good' need to discuss quite carefully the terms on which they handle difference.

A further question relates to practice. Arguably notions of 'global common good' need to be continually related to actually prevailing conditions and the concrete institutions and policies. Philosophical speculations that are not explicitly linked to the real possibilities of lived history may do little to advance human flourishing, or indeed could be counterproductive by offering false hopes. Hence, if arguments around 'Development for the Global Common Good' are to contribute to actual human betterment, they need to include concrete proposals and realizable strategies. This is not to counsel moderation of ambition: on the contrary, the realizable strategy could be deeply transformational. However, it is important to pursue philosophy and action as two sides of a same coin.

In considering institutional channels for the concrete promotion of 'global common good', proposals would do well to think beyond the territorial nation-state. Modern government certainly remains an important site of public policy; however, contemporary 'polycentric' governance also offers many other places to build social arrangements for living well. In addition to nation-states there are local governments, regional arrangements (both micro-regions within countries and macro-regions among countries), and global governance. In addition to public authorities current governance includes many private regulatory mechanisms (through market and/or civil society actors) and public-private hybrid institutions. Thus today's pursuit of 'global common good' demands a broader institutional approach than yesterday's concentration on capturing the state alone.

Finally there is the obvious comment that realizing 'global common good' needs more than appealing visions and clever strategies, but also sustained political mobilization. Deep reflection of the kind undertaken in the 'Development for the Global Common Good' project is indispensable, but its impact on actually lived lives will be minimal if the ideas are not embodied in action. Unfortunately practice-research engagement is all too often wanting around questions of global ethics, as academic reflections and change activism operate with minimal interplay—and to the impoverishment of both. It is encouraging in this regard that a number of participants in this dialogue have extensive experience of political mobilization, and hopefully the results of the conversation can be widely spread to transformational movements.

IV. Intercultural Reflections on the Global Common Good

Reflections on the Global Common Good: Systematization of an Intercultural Dialogical Research Process

Olga Lucía Castillo, Leonard Chiti, Cândido Grzybowski et al. [1]

The world faces a number of serious political, economic and ecological challenges that demand concerted efforts to be properly analyzed and to implement the necessary changes. It is, however, unclear whether the concept of development is still adequate to guide these transformational efforts. This is because development, in the way it has been propagated for decades, may well be too closely linked to an economic model of expansive market fundamentalism, which itself is at the core of the global problems calling for in-depth transformations.

Therefore, one might turn to the notion of a "global common good" as an alternative guiding concept. This paper provides the conceptual reflections of scholars from Brazil, Colombia, Zambia, the Democratic Republic of Congo, Indonesia and Germany who engaged in an intercultural reflection process on these matters. This process took place in three steps. First, all participant prepared in-depth studies to reflect on the conceptual dimensions, institutionalization and shortcomings with respect to the common good in their region. Secondly, a discussion was initiated during a face-to-face meeting in autumn 2013 where reflections on a transformation towards the global common good were discussed. Third, the different versions of this paper were revised in a written dialogue.

This paper will be structured as follows. It starts by clarifying why the concept of development is defective and should be scrutinized if not given up altogether. In a next step, an alternative concept of the global common good could consist in is laid out. Afterward, three important dimensions in which the common good plays out are considered in more detail: economy, democracy and communities.

---

1 This paper is co-authored by Olga-Lucía Castillo, Leonard Chiti, Cândido Grzybowski, Katharina Hirschbrunn, B. Herry-Priyono, Ferdinand Muhigirwa Rusembuka, Michael Reder, Verena Risse, and Georg Stoll.

1. Development: A Problematic Notion to Be Abandoned?

The notion of development has known a long tradition of theoretical investigation and practical application. Yet not all programs or actions operated in the name of development have led to their desired aims. And what may be even more crucial: Development aims themselves are often questionable as they mirror ideological presumptions which are imposed on the alleged beneficiaries regardless of harmful downsides or lacking consent of the latter. It therefore seems important to analyze the concept of development both with regard to why it is problematic and with regard to what aspects are valuable and ought to be safeguarded—or whether the notion should be dropped altogether.

There are several worries with regard to the traditional concept of development which can be situated at different conceptual levels. First of all, it may be considered that the notion of development has hegemonic traits. This refers to the fact that development and development policies have been traditionally defined and carried out by Western states. In this, they are considered to be marked by Western concepts and values like, for instance, individualism, competition, economic growth, and consumerism. This worry is even reinforced in those cases where it is former colonial powers that conduct development programs, thereby risking to continue the older practice under new labels. In Latin America, for instance, processes such as the acquisition of formerly local, national or regional banks by the Spanish financial sector are popularly considered a case of neocolonialism. Another way in which these values are conveyed is through the conditionalities that accompany the transfer of development aid. This is not meant to say that conditionalities are necessarily problematic. They also can help assure the accountability of the governments involved.

Furthermore, the economic focus of development can be regarded as problematic. While in the Global North, the radical economic liberalism of recent decades was regarded as a new shift in order to reinforce its economies, in the Global South the same move, known as "neoliberalism", has always been promoted (some scholars would say imposed) as a "development model".

This focus not only influences the economic sphere as such, but also determines the way in which human society relates to nature. This is the risk of reducing nature and its resources to goods that can be extracted and commodified without taking into account the consequences this might have for the stability of the ecosystem or the needs of future generations. Such a commodification of nature's tangibles seems even more problematic when it leads to the accumulation of wealth of just few people (for instance of those who own the license to extract resources in one region) whereas nature belongs truly to humankind as a whole.

Within this framework it follows as a logical consequence that development is measured by growth in GDP with growth regarded as an indicator for a prosperous economy. This is problematic, since growth is intrinsically linked with capital accumulation. The hegemonic development, today globalized, has generated wealth concentration, social exclusion, inequality, domination and environmental degradation in many places.

With regard to the problems arising at the level of implementation, it appears that the governments involved in the process of development cooperation are not only the ones from the Global North, but also those from the Global South. Both are to be held accountable for the outcome of the process. This means that while the donor countries from the West risk imposing their economic or legal-institutional visions, it must also be stressed that the receiving countries from the Global South are responsible to not embezzle the funds received and to diminish internal problems such as corruption.

This pertains to the assumption that development cooperation is part of a power relationship which is marked by inequality. Yet, this power relationship is not one between the Global North on the one end and the Global South on the other. Rather, power can be unequally distributed in the other way around as well and in particular within high, low and middle income countries.

Still, even if the concept of development cannot be maintained because of its ideological and practical downsides, it must be stressed that many countries (including those from the Global North) and the world as a whole are facing serious social and ecological problems, which must be addressed at all relevant levels. This hypothesis supposes the need for change, transition or progress—along with a specific kind of ideology or hope—to overcome those problems which also lie at the heart of the notion of development, if neutrally understood. Thus, if one agrees to the fact that the world presents us with problems and conflicts that need to be resolved, this implies the concerted formulation and addressing different issues both at the national and international level. Among these are questions of how to deal with the market economy, with political, ecological and social challenges, with community and state organization and administration.

One might therefore conclude that it could help to abandon the notion of development altogether in order to open the way for alternative terms that denote concepts which are not as ideologically marked, yet still reflect the idea of moving from the present to a new and hopefully better state. Candidates for such alternative notions are the terms of transition, social and ecological change, transformation, holistic transformation or paradigm shift. Moreover, turning to the notion of the (global) common good could be another alternative. It is this notion of the common good that will be explored in the following paragraphs.

2. Global Common Good: Aspects of a New Approach

The notion of the common good is a multifaceted one involving different considerations and aspects. Most generally, one might consider that it refers to the idea of pursuing a communal or social good that is more than just an aggregation of particular interests. This implies that common good is common insofar as it is available for all and shared by all. The notion appears as a helpful starting point for future reflections on cooperative and sustainable forms of living together that avoid the selfish or ideological connotations that are associated with, for instance, the term of development. Furthermore, given the interconnectedness of the world, it seems advisable to broaden the notion at least in spatial terms so that it covers what could be called a global common good. In addition, it might be questioned whether it should be extended beyond human beings to all living species more generally.

In a next step, a more specific and more substantive understanding of what the global common good encompasses will be outlined. As a starting point, one may consider the global common good as the central basis of what can be called "fullness of life", (the French) *"promotion humaine"*, or "humanity". In this, the concept shares common ground with approaches such as *buen vivir*, well-being and life quality. All these have as their object the human being[2] and acknowledge the human dignity of the person. Yet,

---

2 "Fullness of life" and *buen vivir* also include non-human species.

one should not see the person as a mere interest-driven market participant or holder of individualistic interests, but rather as a social and interrelated individual that stands in close connection with other living beings, including the non-human environment. Acknowledging the dependency on nature and the fact of being rooted in nature can lead to adopting a non-anthropocentric standpoint. Yet, it is not clear to what degree such a non-anthropocentrism can be maintained under the notion of the common good. What seems indubitable, however, is that the global common good demands to give up the focus on mere human needs by acknowledging that these can stand in stark contrast to the natural conditions.

This already indicates the social and ecological dimension as well as the global scope of the concept. The social dimension encompasses the values of inclusion, participation and solidarity. Inclusion refers to the idea that everyone carries fundamental unalienable rights and is given the possibility to be a full member of a (global) community on an equal and respectful basis with shared responsibilities. This leads to the idea of participation, which refers to the fact of taking part in social activities and having the opportunity and capability to shape it politically, economically or culturally. Solidarity, finally, pertains to the idea of adopting responsibility for others even if this commits oneself to giving up some of one's own interests or benefits. If one considers common good to be global in scope, these derivative values too must be of global scope. In addition, it is important to stress that a conception of the common good ought to overcome the sectoral boundaries between, in particular, the economy, the environment, politics and society. Instead, the lead idea of a global common good maintains a holistic picture of human life and flourishing where the different spheres are seen as mutually interrelated.

Moreover, conceptualizing the common good must take into account the fact that environmental resources are a fundamental part of the common good. There is no life without natural resources and there is constant exchange with nature. And yet the resource distribution on the planet is not homogeneous, and the environmental resources are limited. This dependency is of such crucial importance that it sets the framework for all considerations, even if the conception is not meant to be a specifically environmental one.

With regard to the institutional conditions broadly understood, some elements seem crucial when it comes to realizing the common good. These are rights, democracy, the requirements of the rule of law and a fair process of distribution. Both first and second generation human rights, that is civil and political as well as economic, social and cultural rights are considered relevant and can also be linked to an understanding of the common good in the international or global dimension. With regard to democracy, it seems especially important to stress that the open, equal and inclusive character the democratic procedure of legitimizing and controlling political power ought to maintain, no matter what kind of actual democratic system is set up. Realizing the common good in material terms also involves elements of distribution which ought to be organized in a fair and respectful way. In addition, the role of the economy can only be a serviceable one. This implies that the economy or any economic activity cannot constitute an end in itself. Instead, it must be considered a means to be employed and framed so that it can serve the common good of all. This will be explained in the following paragraph.

3. Economy: An Embedded and Ecologically Conscious Economy Serving the Common Good

As mentioned above, economy should play an instrumental role for the common good. However, while quality of life is multi-dimensional, there is a danger that various societal aims are deformed by economic aims. To curb this tendency and to achieve a transformation towards the common good, people-centeredness is central as a starting point: people have to be given primacy over business interests. If the direction of transformation is defined, as nowadays frequently happens, not by citizens themselves or by congruent institutions but by business and by business-led politics, an economy-driven "development" may well benefit a few market actors at the cost of the most vulnerable (today and in future) instead of enabling all to lead a flourishing life.

Central problems of the current economic system are the shortcomings with regard to social justice and ecological sustainability. In many countries of the Global South, a kind of "development paradox" is rampant: although the country is rich in natural resources, the majority of the population stays poor and suffers from human rights violations; poor and indigenous people are displaced in search for natural elements considered resources. By contrast, foreign companies earn immense profits from the irresponsible and abusive exploitation of nature and it is consumers in foreign countries that reap their benefits. Furthermore, by the rapid exploitation of natural resources, not only present generations are deprived, but the environment is damaged to an extent that human life on planet earth is threatened. As a consequence, future generations will not be able to be provided with the same environmental quality that we benefit from today. Today as in the future, it is particularly the poor and vulnerable who suffer from polluted air and water, from erosion of forests and soil as well as from toxic and nuclear deposits. Even within an anthropocentric world view, societies have to carefully assess whether they want to exploit some resources at all. In case natural goods are extracted, it must be secured that health, social and political conditions of the population as well as environmental quality are not diminished. Furthermore, there exist different views on how to distribute possible revenues: to the extracting enterprises, to those affected by exploitation within the country or throughout the world, to the most vulnerable, or to future generations. An alternative view is that all nature—including the atmosphere—is the common heritage of humankind. From a non-anthropocentric view, as the one proposed by the already mentioned *buen vivir* approach, nature has the inherent right to exist and therefore ought not to be exploited at all.

But there are further problems with respect to the present relationship between economy and development. Wealth inequality is increasing especially in high and middle income countries. Furthermore, high income countries as a whole live at the ecological cost of other nations and of future generations. Economic activity by far exceeds the basic needs and wants of most people in these countries, as the huge budgets spent for advertising to create further wishes and cravings may indicate. While advertising creates new wishes, which may not be satisfied, this may, among other factors, explain why in spite of economic growth during the last decades, according to commonly accepted indicators, neither happiness nor quality of life increased in most high income countries. Ways have to be found to guarantee a fair and sustainable distribution among current and also future generations. To achieve a fair distribution and just economic rules, distorted relations between state and business, corruption, lack of transparency and rent-seeking have to be overcome. It is crucial that the transformation towards the common good is inclusive and brings benefits to all. In addition, the consumerist lifestyle of the upper and middle classes in high income countries but also increasingly in middle income countries hinders the transformation towards the common good and cannot be maintained. It is in open contradiction to ecologic sustainability and social justice. Redistribution measures are of central importance to reconcile economic sustainability with social justice and poverty reduction.

A structural problem lies at the core of these shortcomings: the current economic system reduces the "economy" to activities performed in the market (market fundamentalism). Various societal spheres which are vital to the common good are either neglected and thus eroded, or colonized by reducing them to commercial contributions at market-value. Examples are the natural environment, cultural and spiritual domains, care work done frequently by women as well as the economies of indigenous communities. Cultural traditions of minorities often fall victim to commercial land acquisitions which completely ignore any cultural value that a territory may have beyond its market price as an investor's asset. These traditions only 'count' in such a reductionist economic view if they themselves can make market actors pay for them like a folklorist consumer good for tourists. An example for the consequences of this limited concept of economy is climate change: While ecological sustainability is a basic precondition for all dimensions of quality of life, the environment is heavily devastated by the current capitalist system.

What are possible alternatives? Basically, the market as an arena for exchange of products and goods is useful for economic activities under certain conditions and within certain limits. However, the market frequently furthers competition instead of cooperation and solidarity. It does not provide the basis for a responsible relationship with nature. Neither can it deal with future shortages or, on the other hand, with boundlessness. "Free market", unregulated trade and investment leads to the exploitation of nature (understood only as resource) and to land grabbing, which endanger the sovereignty of countries, the food sovereignty of the local people and—in a further step—of humankind, among other negative effects. "Development" dominated by those free market forces does not lead to diversified and thus stable income sources, nor does it respect natural boundaries, leading to the destruction of the integrity of nature as a part of the global common good. Thus, the market has to be re-embedded in social and political structures (Polanyi 1944, 57), also at the global level. Examples for first steps in this direction at the national and local level are the social market economy in Germany and local community organizations in Brazil or Colombia. However, this transformation towards fair economic rules serving the people and, at the same time, adjusting themselves to the limits of natural resources is only possible if the pervasive influence of business on governments, as well as the dominance of few powerful enterprises over several markets is broken. In order to prevent the further commercialization and unlimited market integration into cultural, social and environmental spheres, beyond the necessity to have competent governmental institutions, the creation of alternative economic systems from the bottom up is necessary. Examples are the peasant reserve zones in Colombia and transition town movements in Europe, which do not focus on competition but on cooperation and sharing. At the local level, sectoral borders between ecologic, social and economic aims can be overcome more easily, and ecological costs from long transport can be avoided. A vibrant civil society and alternative economic systems are central as they inspire the re-democratizing of the economy and contribute to working out comprehensive concepts of transformation which may later be applied also on national or global levels. Among these alternative forms of living together, old and new forms of how to manage the so called "commons" gain importance: Through the implementation of cooperative, participatory regimes, a fundamental alternative to the organization of societal life through market or state is achieved. Another important aspect is the transfer of power to local layers and the sovereignty of local communities. Still it is necessary to change rules additionally at the global level in order to allow for free spaces for alternative economic models to emerge.

A further central issue is ecologically sustainable and socially fair consumption. This could be a fruitful option for middle and upper classes in countries of the Global South and North. However, financial inequalities within countries render it difficult for relatively poor people to choose such forms of consumption. In order to make a difference, the externalization of social and ecological costs cannot be addressed at the level of the individual consumer only; production patterns leading to unsustainable and unfair consumption must also be dealt with. Furthermore, to focus solely on more ecological ways of consumption while constantly increasing consumption will not solve the problem of climate change, but make it deeper.

A central question concerning the connection between sustainability and economy is the question of growth. This issue is discussed especially in the Global North. Available knowledge (Jackson 2011, Fournier 2008, Latouche 2009, Mishan 1967 among others) suggests that worldwide economic growth and environmental damage cannot be decoupled to an extent that makes further growth ecologically sustainable. Industrialized countries, which are already emitting a highly unsustainable amount of emissions per head, have to restrict environmental impacts to sustainable levels, thereby not only focusing on efficiency measures and on ethical consumption but also taking sufficiency into account. Instead of aiming at a further increase in material consumption, these countries have to focus on the various dimensions of quality of life and on the common good. Furthermore, in order to stabilize the economy in times of economic downturn and to render political decisions independent of the pressure to grow, it is vital for all countries to render social and economic institutions independent of growth of GDP. Examples are social security systems, the monetary system and the social organization of labor.

For a reorientation of the economy towards ecological sustainability and social justice, the global level is of utmost importance. How can a redirection of economic spheres be implemented at the global level? Between countries there exist multiple economic interdependencies. Examples are international trade, investment and resource extraction. While the power of transnational companies and of international financial capital is growing, political regulation remains largely limited to the national level—and by these very forces is eroded even there. And even where international political institutions do exist, they often support the business cases of the private sector as can be observed with the mainstream policy of international institutions like WTO, IMF and OECD. On the other hand, some institutions support the protection of basic rights and facilitate the balancing of interests at the global level. Examples for this are ILO with its rules for "decent work" as well as national and international labor unions. Another positive example are the OECD Guidelines for Multinational Enterprises.

To ensure that the economy is embedded in society, democratic political rule setting and enforcing has to be made effective at all levels, from local to global. A democratic approach demands to overcome the traditional unilateral dependencies of the South on the North and to move towards acknowledging mutual interdependencies. This may help overcome a one direction flow of ideas on "development" from North to South and promote a global ethic that treats every nation as equal, regardless of its economic power. Currently, nations in the North and the West that are highly industrialized dominate debates on economics, politics etc.

A good example of this is the World Economic Forum that takes place every year in Davos, Switzerland. This is an exclusive club of representatives of highly industrialized countries where few representatives from the South are invited to participate. Another example is the IMF, which is managed as a plutocracy and in which countries have voting rights in proportion to the contributions they pay. Thus, the 34 OECD countries control more than two-thirds of the votes in the IMF while most of the world has no real decision power (Mondragon 2007). To achieve a reorientation of global institutions towards the common good, vibrant and competent NGOs and civil society are necessary. A worldwide political engagement and networking of civil society is needed to urge nation states and global institutions to be responsible towards all citizens and not mainly towards capital. While one approach is to reform institutions such as WTO, IMF or OECD, an alternative approach is to democratize and rebuild new institutions from the bottom up.

4. Democracy: Expressing and Administering the Global Common Good in Societies

Democratic procedures and institutions play a significant role in implementing the common good in societies. Democracy is a form of government based on the rule of the people and the equality of all citizens. The aim of democracy is to represent all citizens in procedures and institutions, to grant space for free public debate and to provide the basic conditions that enable citizens to make use of their political rights and act according to their shared responsibilities.

Three different aspects should be reflected in the specific global debate about democracy: the cultural differentiation of democracy, the relation between economy and democracy, and the global dimension of democracy itself. Fair and transparent procedures and institutions are essential to reflect and to realize the different contents of the common good on the social and political level. Strengthening democratic procedures and institutions is therefore important. On the other hand, institutions alone cannot make up for the lack of an open democratic society. It also requires the active participation of citizens which is best expressed in social movements that take up concerns of the common good and bring them to the fore.

Yet it remains an open question as to how much attention should be paid to institutions and how much to social movements when it comes to developing strategies for a democratic eco-social transformation. Moreover, those basic conditions which are required to exercise democracy (such as education, free press, freedom of expression, among others) need to be strengthened.

As was stated above, democracy is based on the idea of the rule of the people and on fair and transparent participation of all people who are concerned by the decisions of a political system. Democracy is instantiated in a variety of ways in different cultures, which means that democracy can only exist in plural cultural forms. These cultural differences of democracy are an essential part of the concept of democracy itself. In what way the participation of the people is realized and which institutions are built to secure this participation differs between different cultural contexts and social histories. Just as a transformation towards the global common good needs a socio-cultural foundation, also the concept of democracy needs to be related to the different cultural traditions. Furthermore, democracy is insofar an open concept as democratic procedures and institutions have to be developed and reformed continuously in the face of new social, political and economic challenges. In these processes of adapting the concept of democracy to different cultural contexts and of reforming democracy over time, experience plays an important role. Democracy should therefore be developed by learning from experience and not adopting a given theoretical concept.

In this cultural and temporal perspective, different understandings of the concept of democracy have emerged. For example, in some societies democracy is understood as a process of consensus and in other societies as a struggle or even a fight. This plurality of concepts of democracy is an expression of cultural and historical diversity. Therefore, world politics should refer to these different traditions to find convincing answers to the planetary challenges. The aim is to integrate the different cultural traditions of democracy with their potentials to deal with these challenges in a comprehensive way.

Modern societies are differentiated into a number of distinct sub-systems. Looking at the last three decades of the so-called globalization, especially the social power of the economic system has grown. In some sense, the economy has become an independent social system which tries to colonize other systems and also the political system itself. From the perspective of the common good, this process is problematic, because democracy needs to set the rules of the economy. This is a problem today in many countries all over the world. Democracy has been captured by business, as can be seen in practices like corruption or lobbyism. Therefore, economy has to be embedded in society again and should be ruled by democratic procedures and institutions. This is an important issue of further concepts for transformation towards the (global) common good. Deepening and strengthening democratic procedures is essential to curb the power of multinationals and to re-locate political power in society.

In order to enforce the process of making democratic societies more equal, not only do fair and transparent institutions play an important role, but also the citizens. Democracy can only be brought to life if people as citizens take part in social and political processes. Civic education and voter training is to be promoted to empower citizens to play their role in democratic procedures and institutions. The power of the people should be strengthened, for example to better counter multinationals. The resistance of social movements as associations of citizens could contribute to making democracy more equal. This, too, demands processes of political education. Global citizen movements could play an important role given the interconnectedness of different political communities.

Finally, in the face of planetary problems, new forms of democratic procedures and institutions (global governance) should be developed. Traditionally, democracy is linked to the concept of the nation state, which is not sufficient to tackle challenges with a global scope. But even the current forms of global governance like the UN conferences in the nineteen-nineties were often not effective enough. Therefore new forms of democratic global procedures and institutions should be developed in order to foster the global common good. A positive example of the direction this development could take is the International Labor Organization (ILO) with its more inclusive and democratic character. Ideally, however, these institutions of democratic global governance should be based on the participation of all people and should be founded in plural cultural traditions and practices.

5. Communities: Where the Common Good is Embodied

Both in the process of fostering democracy and of embedding economy in society, local communities play an important role, because here people take part directly in political processes by different forms of local participation. In this perspective a clear distinction between local and global is not convincing because global processes always influence the communities on the ground and communities can take part in shaping global processes. Decision makers at the 'global' level (for instance at the UN) are equally forming 'local' communities (the UN staff works in an office building in New York). This implies that actions with a global impact often manifest themselves in a local environment and that it is hard to draw a line between actions that are purely local and those whose consequences are at least global to a certain degree. Communities that act locally but think globally can thus constitute an example for what is referred to as "glocalization". In a similar vein, it seems that when it is referred to the distinction between "global" and "local", often this alludes to a difference in power rather than in geographical extension (Scholte 2008, 1486). Still, it must be stressed that institutional structures can increase or alter the scope of community action. This is to say, by means of institutions, old and new media as well as through networks, the consequences of individual actions can be transmitted and therefore impact at the international or global level.

This institutional aspect leads to another question, which is not restricted to communities only. This is the question of the relation between institutions and civil society proper. The question is not precisely tied to communities since these are not necessarily to be seen as in opposition to legal and political institutions, but can also form within these. Therefore, one might spell out the question as one of the relation between social movements and legal and political institutions. Several occurrences of the relation are conceivable. First, social movements could control institutions, for example by questioning their activities and keeping them in check. Alternatively, one could draw a more complementary picture of the relationship between institutions and social movements. This would imply that institutions can serve social movements and help implement their goals. In the end, these two understandings are more compatible than it would seem at first sight. Thus, whether the two complement one another or whether civil society must control the institutionalized political structures very much depends on the set-up of the political system itself and on the distribution of power. Here, democratic procedures can help to articulate the different views.

One way of founding the concept of community-based democratic procedures is the tradition of liberation theology. Community as a (local or in other ways territorially based and/or virtually linked) political unit is a basic dimension of democracy because political and economic issues could be decided at the level of the people directly concerned. The enhancement of community approaches is part of a political strategy which tries to strengthen and implement the principle of subsidiarity.

Although communities are important in the context of eco-social transformations oriented towards a global common good, they are also in some sense ambivalent. On the one hand, communities are located in a certain place, where people find their identity hosted and promoted. In this perspective diverse territories are a basis of community and livelihood; they are seen as citizens' territories. Elements of community can be shared interests, communication and moral commitment. On the other hand, communities are always culturally heterogeneous and people often belong to different (primary and secondary) communities which are not automatically rooted in a concrete place. Additionally, communities always have the tendency to exclude others and in general do not adopt a cross-border, let alone global perspective.

In summary, communities are important if we want to explore (and, if successful, to implement) a bottom-up approach to new democratic procedures in order to sustain the global common good. They are also important to relate these concepts to the variety of cultural traditions and to embed economy in concrete socio-cultural contexts. But the enhancement of communities should always be aware of the global backgrounds of social challenges. In addition, a community approach should always reflect on people who are excluded and in what way those people could be integrated in fair and sustainable social procedures.

6. Conclusion

This paper has outlined elements of a conception of the global common good as a result of a discussion among participants from different parts of the world. It opened with an assessment of the notion of development.

This notion turned out to be problematic in particular due to its strong focus on market fundamentalism which itself is responsible for global problems such as persisting poverty, and climate change.

The notion of the global common good could serve as an alternative model to go beyond the notion of development in that it relies on a holistic understanding of the human being, This involves viewing the person not only as a member of the social, political and economic sphere, but also as a part of and dependent upon nature. Within the limits set by the environment, three core aspects to which the global common good pertains, namely the economy, democracy, and communities, were considered. As for the economic system, it seems crucial that it serves the common good instead of commodifying aspects of life and nature. Democracy is necessary in order to articulate different views on the global common good and to ensure the power and rule of the people in contrast to the dominance of governments or economic actors. Communities form an important counterweight to established political structures in that they constitute a forum where people form and promote their shared interests.

However, the academic discussion has also stressed that some conflicting views cannot be conciliated. First, this regards the question of whether a holistic understanding of human beings as part of nature requires a non-anthropocentric viewpoint. A strong non-anthropocentrism would hold that all living species possess equal rights and may therefore not be mistreated or exploited. A more anthropocentric view, on the other hand, would still accommodate the fact of being dependent on and rooted in nature, yet without granting a similar legal status to other species.

Secondly, the issue of the limits of the market has not been settled. This involves the question to what degree the market ought to be regulated or whether some societal and private spheres ought to be excluded from being organized by markets at all.

A third question that remains open is whether transformation towards the global common good would be prompted rather by national or international political institutions, or by community action at the local or international level. In either case, both options are confronted with resistance from powerful financial and business actors who dominate world markets and influence politics. How to balance the roles of civil society and institutionalized political structures will therefore be left for further debate.

Finally, a fourth issue that participants felt would deserve more in-depth discussion is—despite the planetary approach of the concept of the global common good—to what degree a differential approach towards high income, middle income and low income countries is needed. This pertains to the question of how the common good should be defined for example with regard to resource extraction in different country groups and at the global level—and how one ought to deal with resulting trade-offs between conflicting views of the common good.

Notwithstanding these open discussion points, the notion of the common good as outlined in this paper provides a framework for further reflections and debate on issues of worldwide concern.

Works Cited

Fournier, Valérie (2008). Escaping from the economy: politics of degrowth. *International Journal of Sociology and Social Policy*, 28, 528–545.
Jackson, Tim (2011). *Prosperity without growth: Economics for a finite planet.* London: Routledge.
Latouche, Serge (2009). *Decrecimiento y posdesarrollo: el piensamento creativo contra la economía del absurdo.* Barcelona: El Viejo Topo.
Mishan, Ezra (1967). *The Costs of Economic Growth.* London: Staples Press.
Mondragón, Héctor (2007). *La Estrategia del Imperio—Todo para el Capital Transnacional.* Bogotá: Ed. Plantaforma Interamericana de Derechos Humanos.
Polanyi, Karl (1944). *The Great Transformation: the Political and Economic Origins of Our Time.* New York: Farrar & Rinehart.
Scholte, Jan Aart (2008). Defining Globalisation. *The World Economy*, 31, 1471–1402.

Views from Civil Society Practitioners

Georg Stoll

In addition to the academic analyses and reflections collected from experts from Asia, Africa, Latin America and Europe, the issue of a "global common good" was also discussed in six regional dialogue forums, each of which had 15 to 20 participants from civil society organizations and movements.[1] These dialogues on the one hand confirmed some of the general discussion lines already explored in the previous academic dialogue. On the other hand they also provided complementary aspects, views and questions missing so far. Notwithstanding the diversity of participants' regional backgrounds and their specific perspectives stemming from this diversity there were also some common concerns which emerged in the contributions of the dialogue forums.

1. With regard to the Academic Dialogue: General Confirmation—and Some Remarkable Differences

The above chapter on the "Intercultural Reflections"—a systematic summary of the main discussion lines of the academic dialogue—highlights five issues as focal points: Development, Global Common Good, Economy, Democracy, and Communities. All of these also reappeared in the dialogues with civil society discussants.[2] While the dialogue forums in gen-

---

1 The dialogue forums took place from March 2014 to May 2015 in the following regions (chronological order): Andean countries (Peru, March 2014), Anglophone African countries (South Africa, August 2014), South Asian countries (India, September 2014), Southeast Asian countries (Philippines, October 2014), Cono Sur countries (Uruguay, November 2014), Francophone African countries (Ivory Coast, May 2014).

2 An earlier version of the "Intercultural Reflections" was part of the preparation packs that were sent to the participants of the dialogue forums in advance. Yet, it was made clear from the beginning (explicitly and also in the structure of the programs) that the

eral confirmed the analysis of the academic contributors, there were some differences in how the discussion points were weighted and interpreted.

Development: There was a strong and unanimous agreement in the fundamental criticism of the present development model, although dialogue participants would not go as far as some of the academic contributors to ask for abandoning the concept altogether. Civil society practitioners who are engaged with social and environmental concerns have a very critical stance towards the official development agenda as it is propagated by governments and international institutions. This agenda is seen as being fundamentally flawed in several respects. First, this agenda does not include the local communities concerned. Development, as one participant from South Africa had it, is a means of channeling public money for the benefit of some "elites" but not of the population. The issue of corruption was much more discussed in the civil society dialogues than it was in the academic dialogue. A second point is linked to the first: Development not only almost completely ignores the situation but also the traditional knowledge of indigenous people. Since official development is following a reduced economic agenda—this constitutes another fundamental flaw—individuals and groups are only of interest in as far as they enter the economic equation, as, for instance, consumers, occupants of land, cheap workforce etc. Those who have nothing to offer on the market just do not exist in this concept of development and consequently are often denied their basic rights in the name of development. Numerous cases of land being taken from native tribes, small scale farmers or fishing communities for the sake of big projects of large-scale monoculture farming, real estate development and the construction of dams were cited as evidence for this destructive development in all dialogue forums. Instead of empowering the poor, mainstream development was perceived as being an integral part of an economic system which exploits and reproduces massive power imbalances. The Anglophone African forum summarized its critique in the following way: "Development" which destroys human relationships (interhuman as well as to nature) cannot be good development.

---

civil society dialogues were undertakings in their own right and not just to discuss and comment the outcomes of the academic dialogue. Hence, the dialogue forums took note of the academic dialogue (and of those dialogue forums that already had taken place) but every one developed and followed its own process.

Global Common Good: There was general consent among the discussants in the dialogue forums that a "common good" with global scope is a helpful concept to address both local and international challenges of globalization. Participants also agreed amongst one another and with the academic dialogue partners in stressing that such global common good cannot be a uniform model but needs to be defined in continuous participatory and plural processes by those concerned. As discussions in the civil society dialogue forums tended to be more practice-oriented, the focus was less on conceptual distinctions than in the academic dialogue. Thus, the participants sometimes had difficulty distinguishing between the concept of the "global common good" and that of global "commons". Yet, while these two concepts are different, the task of managing global commons in a democratic and sustainable way was identified as one of the major challenges for obtaining a global common good. Another issue that was more intensively discussed in the civil society dialogues than in the academic dialogue was the relationship between local and global common good. Without attaining final results, there was broad consensus that efforts should first focus on the local common good and then extend to broader and even global concerns and possible trade-offs and conflicts. But it was obvious that this question needs further exploration.

Economy: While discussants underlined the need for supporting entrepreneurship among the poor in communities, they felt at unease with impacts of big business on the poor and on the environment and with the complicity of governments with business. By and large, civil society activists in the dialogue forums didn't trust what they repeatedly called "big business". On the one hand, they see harmful impacts on communities and nature with almost no way for affected groups to claim their rights. This situation is aggravated by clandestine negotiations between representatives of transnational companies and governments. On the other hand, civil society practitioners on the ground don't see the bright promises of companies and governments with regard to job creation and local development materialize. Discussants in India and South Africa were very clear on this point: Government and the private sector will not be able to provide jobs in any sufficient quantity; other ways have to be explored to build resilience in communities and especially among the youth. In this context, the issue of informal labor was addressed but not deepened. In fact, large sectors—if not the majority—of the workforce in the home countries of dialogue participants are not in the formal economy. Here again, the limits of a development model focusing on economic parameters like GNP growth, which cannot even account for vast parts of the population, were obvious in the dialogues.

Democracy and Communities: Dialogue forum participants upheld the principles of participation, transparency and accountability. But when it came to existing political structures and institutions it seemed more difficult to reach a consensus on concrete propositions. Indeed, dictatorship as it is still experienced in many countries was unanimously rejected. But what is to say about leftist governments who are continuing the extractivist policies of their predecessors in Latin America, or about the only formally democratic arrangements in many Asian countries? How to valuate the structural difficulties of democratic governance with integrating long-term transnational concerns like climate change? With elections being close in some of the participating countries (India, Indonesia, Brazil, Uruguay, South Africa), it became clear that the process of not only defining but also implementing key aspects of a common good may be a cumbersome task already at the national level. Many participants felt discouraged from engaging in serious dialogue with state representatives given their negative previous experience. On the other hand, most participants were also aware of the limits of civil society which cannot substitute a democratically elected government. As for the question of how to make national governments integrate global concerns into their policy in a democratic way, this question was only dealt with on the margins of the discussions. The clear focus was on the task of making local communities participate and thus benefit from and contribute to a true democratization of their society. Participants in the dialogues very much stressed the importance of the community level for an integral development that cares for the needs and rights of the poor. This didn't come by surprise as most of the discussants had their professional occupation in some sort of participatory community assistance. Nevertheless, the experiences of these practitioners came in strong support for the positions made in the academic dialogue before.

2. Beyond the Academic Dialogue: Complementing the Picture

In addition to these issues, which had also been part of the academic dialogue, the civil society dialogue forums raised a number of questions that were largely absent so far: violence and conflict, traditions versus modernity, mentality and spirituality. Finally, discussants were interested in ways of better linking existing work and initiatives to the challenge of jointly promoting the perspective of a global common good.

Violence and Conflict: Many of the dialogue participants and the communities they are working with have experience with violence either linked to open conflict or just as a day-to-day practice. These experiences of violence are understood as consequences of unbalanced and uncontrolled power relations which in turn are rooted in and supported by specific political and economic conditions. There are groups possessing the economic and political power to resort to force and violence for imposing their rules and pursuing their interests, while at the other side there are victims who do not count politically and/or economically. Therefore it was clear in all discussions that human rights and democratic rule must be at the center of any effort to give space for the common good, from local to global. It was also clear that challenging existing power imbalances will not *per se* stop the use of force and violence. On the contrary, beneficiaries of the current status quo in general will try to fight any change that might threaten their privileges. As a result, any development concept and practice which does not address the crucial question of power relations (including its own power position) ought to be rejected.

Tradition versus Modernity: In all dialogue forums the issue of traditions came up. This generic term covered traditional knowledge and wisdom as well as traditional habits and institutions for example with regard to governance, to conflict resolution, or to the relation with nature. It was often discussed in the context of indigenous minorities, but also as a broader phenomenon touching complete societies in all continents experiencing the impact of integration into a global economic system, which is strongly informed by European and North American culture. It is clear that not only local but also regional traditions are under enormous pressure from the fast change that many societies are experiencing, often under the headline of "development". Labor migration, accelerated urbanization, shifting power relations in families and communities, mass media, reorientation of education systems towards technical know-how, conversion of complete economic sectors, all often accompanied by the loss of livelihood for hundreds of thousands of people, are contributing to changing cultural patterns and life styles. Conflicting traditional and modern values and concepts are creating tensions which are at the root of much suffering. But ironically, as it was observed in the dialogues, at the same time when "modern" values and behavioral patterns are winning over, the confidence in this modernity is shrinking. Hence, it is not only the loss of one's past—which may be stored with a mix of regret and nostalgia in records and museums now—that is felt but also the fear of losing precious resources which may be needed soon in a situation where the still dominant concept of "modern" economic development comes under scrutiny itself. While the stocktaking of the situation was clear so far in the discussions among dialogue participants, the question of what to do about it left the groups rather helpless. Two main positions could be distinguished. Some discussants especially from Latin America wanted to challenge and delegitimize Western cultural concepts of anthropocentrism, individualism and the dichotomy of subject and object all held responsible for the expansive and exploitative patterns of the dominant technology-based economic system. Others, mainly from Africa and Asia, would rather like to see their traditional ways of life (with core values like relationship or harmony) being transformed in a fertile manner as a critical force for defining and building a good life in modern societies. But how the two positions could reach their objectives was left open in the discussions.

Mentality and Spirituality: This subject was raised in all dialogue forums but again rather as a task which still needs more orientation and clarification. Still, three references were made to guide this orientation, one negative and two positive. The negative reference comes with the critique of the reduced and distorted anthropology that stands behind a limitless and disembedded economy, whose rules and values tend to be extended on any area of life, human and non-human. Global competition, efficiency, growth dependency, liberalization and privatization of all economic activities, the *homo economicus*, and the valuation of everything through market prices (market fundamentalism) are not only key elements of a certain way of organizing the economy, but have also become features of a mind-set and by this way are strongly influencing individual and social behavior far beyond the economic sphere. To question this mentality and search for a "spirituality" capable of freeing human minds from such captivity makes clear that the reintegrating of the economy in society (and hence its subordination under some "common good") is a task that goes beyond politics. It also touches the very basics of our self-understanding and our fundamental values.

The second, now positive, reference hints at the already mentioned traditional wisdom as a resource for founding alternative concepts and practices. Indeed, to fulfill this role, traditional knowledge, practices and wisdom need to be given the space to interact with the central threats of modern life. Only then can the potential of traditions be examined and eventually adapted and used. A third reference, also positive, was given by some participants with religious backgrounds. They demanded more efforts of reflecting on the spiritual sources of religions to make their basic hopes and beliefs a force for discernment of dominant structures and behavioral patterns in present times. But participants also warned against the danger of partisan abuse of the potentials of religions. Therefore, self-critique and inter-religious dialogue as well as dialogue between religious and secular worldviews would have to constitute integral elements of these efforts to tap into religious resources in the search of spiritualities that may help to achieving shared visions of a common good at local as well as global scale.

3. Linking Existing Work and Initiatives for the Promotion of a Global Common Good

In the dialogue forums it became clear that much of the work being done by civil society organizations and social movements is already contributing to a greater awareness of and support for a common good, including global concerns. The manifold efforts towards human rights already making a difference in the life of poor and marginalized groups can be mentioned in this regard. On the other hand, much more needs to be done to be at the height of present global and globalization challenges. While in practice for most civil society organizations there still will be a priority given to promoting the common good at local and community level, sufficient time and effort should be spent to examine external and global structural causes for local problems and to look for allies beyond the limits of the own local community to address these causes. With regard to specific global problems like climate change or the deficits of the global economic system, participants felt the need and the potential for a deeper mutual exchange and understanding of different contexts and challenges in order to be able to develop joint strategies. This will be necessary for example to present convincing alternative approaches to address the existing dependency on economic growth at regional levels, which can be as different as those of high-income resource-importing industrialized countries on the one hand and resource exporting low income countries with high poverty rates on the other hand. While there are already expertise and structures for international civil society networking and cooperation on specific lobby issues (like world trade, corporate social responsibility, tax justice etc.), which ought to be maintained, more dialogue will be needed to address themes like mentality, traditional knowledge, values or power relations. These subjects may be more difficult to grasp in intercultural dialogues, but they play an important role when it comes to questioning existing destructive patterns and searching for alternatives in a peaceful and democratic way. Paving some ground in this direction could be a valuable contribution of civil society on the way of orienting public and economic life towards a "global common good".

Contributors

BRANDI, CLARA: Senior researcher, German Development Institute/Deutsches Institut für Entwicklungspolitik (DIE), Bonn, Germany.

CASTILLO, OLGA-LUCÍA: Full Professor, Department of Rural and Regional Development and member of the Conflict, Region and Rural Societies research group, both part of the School of Environmental and Rural Studies, Pontificia Universidad Javeriana, Bogotá, Colombia.

CHITI SJ, LEONARD: Director, Jesuit Center for Theological Reflection, Lusaka, Zambia.

GRZYBOWSKI, CÂNDIDO: Director, Ibase, Rio de Janeiro, Brazil.

B. HERRY-PRIYONO: Lecturer in social sciences and philosophy at the Driyarkara School of Philosophy, Jakarta, Indonesia.

HIRSCHBRUNN, KATHARINA: Research associate, Institute for Social and Development Studies at the Munich School of Philosophy, Munich, Germany.

MUHIGIRWA RUSEMBUKA SJ, FERDINAND: Managing Director, Arrupe Research and Training Center (CARF), Lubumbashi, DR Congo.

REDER, MICHAEL: Chair in Practical Philosophy, Munich School of Philosophy, Munich, Germany.

RISSE, VERENA: Research associate, Institute for Social and Development Studies at the Munich School of Philosophy, Munich, Germany.

SCHOLTE, JAN AART: Faculty Professor of Peace and Development, School of Global Studies, University of Gothenburg, Sweden, and Professor of Politics and International Studies, University of Warwick, United Kingdom.

STOLL, GEORG: Senior advisor, Department of Policy and Global Challenges, German Catholic Bishops' Organization for Development Cooperation Misereor, Aachen, Germany.

Index

agriculture 78–80, 123, 125, 132, 184, 211
anthropocentrism 53, 55, 62, 237, 247, 249, 259, 266
bottom-up approach 142, 218, 258
buen vivir 54, 57, 60, 62, 144, 246, 249
Catholic social teaching 96, 101–3, 140
citizens 27, 48, 67–69, 76, 81, 83–87, 91, 108, 110, 130, 217, 225, 254, 255
civil society 68, 83, 93, 109, 130, 193, 235, 240, 251, 253, 257, 259, 261, 264
   civil society organization 133, 261, 268
climate change 24, 52, 136, 205, 210, 216, 250
colonialism 20, 35, 48, 74, 153, 244
commons 58–60, 213–19
communities 13, 256–58, 264
   local communities 129, 133, 142, 166, 171, 174, 177, 183, 238, 251, 256, 262, 264
   peasant communities 13, 33, 54
constitution 79, 91–93, 98, 104–14, 130, 192, 195
corruption 126, 132, 156, 162–68, 245, 255, 262
crisis
   East Asian financial crisis 156, 160, 178

   financial crisis 12, 139, 141, 145, 200, 225
   political crisis 34, 49
degrowth 210
democracy 66–69, 83–86, 123, 178, 193, 197, 217, 219–25, 238, 253–56
development
   alternative development 19, 21–25, 42
   economic development 21–24, 85, 97, 139, 152, 170, 178–80, 185, 266
   human development 22, 39, 97, 102, 108, 123, 139–41
   neo-development 80
   post-development 19f., 24–27, 32, 234
   sustainable development 23, 25, 97–99, 128, 132f., 176, 238
development paradox 13, 95–97, 249
diversity 64–66, 68, 239, 255
economic growth 19–23, 25, 32, 74, 81, 127, 139, 155, 161, 200, 203–10, 234, 244, 252, 268
economy 20, 24, 32, 36, 39, 56, 68, 74, 76, 78, 82, 85, 93, 114, 124, 151, 157, 159, 182, 199–202, 208, 212, 248–53, 256, 258, 263
   political economy 153, 155
education 81, 84, 105, 147, 158, 164–67, 178, 194, 197, 254f.

environmental concerns 60–62, 133, 136, 146, 172, 198, 207, 247
happiness 27, 29–32, 58, 162, 206, 250
human dignity 12, 28, 90–92, 98, 99–102, 107, 144, 238, 247
human rights 11, 62–64, 90–92, 100, 102, 104–8, 117–20, 142, 167, 176, 193, 227, 233, 238, 248, 265, 268
indigenous people 13, 33, 54, 75, 238, 249, 262
individualism 66, 116, 244, 266
industrialization 20, 38, 53, 60, 134, 159, 192
inequality 9, 21, 49–51, 60, 116, 145, 194, 200, 205, 209, 245, 252
justice
  ecological justice 64
  economic justice 133
  global justice 194, 207
  social justice 9, 29, 36, 49, 60, 71, 192, 194, 197, 200, 205, 207, 213, 250
lobbying 220–22, 255, 268

middle classes 13, 153, 250
Millennium Development Goals 9, 11, 173, 237
minorities 193, 222, 250, 266
natural resources 73, 123, 128–30, 133, 141, 148, 163, 172, 247, 249
nature 20, 38, 40, 50, 53–55, 58–62, 66, 192, 237, 244, 247, 249, 251, 263, 266
neoliberalism 49, 94f., 115, 120, 244
oil 76, 125, 154, 177, 196
privatization 48, 56–60, 94, 115, 156, 215, 219, 267
quality of life 110, 129, 203, 205–10, 248, 250
rule of law 13, 248
social market economy 192, 199–202, 251
trickle-down theory 20, 21, 116
ubuntu 95, 119
urbanization 86, 95, 153, 218, 266
violence 32–36, 67, 156, 171, 239, 265
well-being 12, 26, 49, 107, 133, 142